Sir Gawain and the Green Knight
Pearl
Cleanness
Patience

Edited with an introduction by A.C. Cawley
Emeritus Professor of English Language and Medieval English Literature in the University of Leeds
and
J.J. Anderson
Senior Lecturer in English Language in the University of Manchester

J. M. Dent & Sons Ltd
London
Charles E. Tuttle Co., Inc.
Rutland, Vermont
EVERYMAN'S LIBRARY

Prefatory matter, notes and editing
© David Campbell Publishers Ltd, 1962, 1976
All rights reserved

Made in Great Britain by
The Guernsey Press Co. Ltd, Guernsey, C.I.
for J.M. Dent & Sons Ltd
91 Clapham High Street, London SW4 7TA
and
Charles E. Tuttle Co., Inc
28, South Main Street,
Rutland, Vermont 05701, U.S.A.

Pearl and *Sir Gawain and the Green Knight*
first published in Everyman's Library in 1962
New edition, including *Cleanness* and *Patience,* published 1976
Reprinted with minor corrections 1978
Reprinted with minor corrections 1983
Reissued 1991

This book if bound as a paperback is
subject to the condition that it may
not be issued on loan or otherwise
except in its original binding

ISBN 0 460 871013

Everyman's Library
Reg. U.S. Patent Office

A. C. CAWLEY worked for the British Council in Romania, Yugoslavia, Egypt and Iceland from February 1939 until 1946. He was Darnell Professor of English in the University of Queensland from 1959 to 1965 and Professor of English Language and Medieval English Literature in the University of Leeds from 1965 to 1979. His papers in academic journals include several on medieval English drama, the latest of which is to be published in *Leeds Studies in English*. His editions of *Everyman* and *The Wakefield Pageants in the Towneley Cycle* were both published by Manchester University Press, and he contributed a section on the staging of medieval drama to the first volume of *The Revels History of Drama in English* in 1983. Together with Professor Martin Stevens of the City University of New York, he is at present preparing a new edition of the Towneley cycle for the Early English Text Society.

J. J. ANDERSON is Senior Lecturer in English Language in the University of Manchester. He is a graduate of the University of Otago and has taught in the University of Adelaide and the University of Sydney. His interests and publications are chiefly in the fields of medieval literature and early English drama. His scholarly editions of *Patience* and *Cleanness* were published by Manchester University Press in 1969 and 1977, respectively.

CONTENTS

PREFACE

THIS Everyman edition of *Pearl, Cleanness, Patience* and *Sir Gawain and the Green Knight* attempts to present the texts accurately, but with some modernization of spelling. The texts have been transcribed from photographs of British Library MS. Cotton Nero A.x, and one or two new readings and emendations have resulted. Full use has also been made of emendations of the texts suggested in earlier editions and in periodical articles, with the editorial aim that is so well expressed by Henry Charteris in his Preface to the 1568 edition of Lindsay's *Works*—'to reduce and bring thame to the native integrite and first mening of the wryter'.

The modernization of spelling is limited to the differentiation of *i* and *j*, and *u* and *v*, as vowel and consonant; to the transcription of *þ* as *th*, of *3* (Old English *g*) as *y*, *gh* or *w* according to the context, and of final (*t*)*3* (French *z*) as *s*. Other peculiarities of spelling are preserved, either because they are of infrequent occurrence or because they are unlikely to cause serious difficulty. These are noted in Appendix I.

The marginal glosses and footnote paraphrases are intended as a prosaic aid to the reader, not as a substitute for the poet's own language. Judiciously used, they should considerably reduce the labour of reading these poems, of any one of which we could say (as Kittredge has said of *Sir Gawain and the Green Knight*) that 'it would be a credit to any literature'.

This augmented edition replaces the edition of *Pearl* and *Sir Gawain and the Green Knight* by Professor Cawley which was first published in Everyman's Library in 1962. The texts of *Pearl* and *Sir Gawain* are unchanged from those of the original edition, and Professor Cawley's Introductions and Appendices remain substantially unchanged. Dr Anderson has added texts of *Cleanness* and *Patience* to the original edition, together with introductory matter on these two poems, and has compiled a new Bibliography.

The editors wish to express their appreciation of the help given them in the preparation of this edition by Miss Gale Owen.

A. C. C. J. J. A.

INTRODUCTION

Pearl, *Cleanness* (or *Purity*), *Patience* and *Sir Gawain and the Green Knight* are contained in a small and undistinguished manuscript (British Library MS. Cotton Nero A.x) of the end of the fourteenth century. The four poems are illustrated by crudely drawn pictures in colours. Like the *Pearl*-poet's 'Fenyx of Arraby' this manuscript is unique, and phoenix-like it survived the fire that consumed so many of the Cotton manuscripts in 1731. Otherwise English literature would have lost its 'best boke of romaunce' and three of its finest religious poems.

All four poems are written in the same dialect, which has been localized in the north-west midland area, where the counties of Cheshire, Staffordshire, and Derbyshire adjoin. All four have stylistic and metrical features in common, and it is evident that they must be by the same author or by authors who have influenced each other. In spite of various guesses, learned and not so learned, the identity of the author (or authors) remains unknown.

Pearl and its companions are not isolated phenomena but are members of a considerable body of alliterative poems which were composed in the north and west of England during the fourteenth century. These poems comprise romances, chronicles, satires and allegories, and they draw their subject-matter from the stories of Troy and Alexander as well as from the legends of Arthur's Britain.[1] All belong to the native alliterative tradition which ultimately goes back to Old English poetry (see *Sir Gawain*, lines 34–6).

No one knows why there was a flowering of alliterative poetry in the remoter districts of England during the fourteenth century. The theory has been advanced that the poems in this volume were products of provincial baronial courts which vied in splendour with the royal court in London.

[1] The main varieties of fourteenth-century alliterative poems are described by J. P. Oakden, *Alliterative Poetry in Middle English* (Manchester, 1935), pp. 24 ff.

It is certainly important to realize that the *Gawain*-poet, though living far from London, was 'not . . . a backwoodsman, a gifted but secluded provincial . . . isolated from the European intellectual or literary currents of his times'.[1]

PEARL

A brief summary of the twenty sections of the poem is given below as an aid to understanding the interpretation that follows.

(I) The poet tells how he has lost his pearl in a garden. Grief-stricken he falls asleep on the mound where the pearl has vanished from his sight. (II–IV) He is transported in spirit to a land of radiant loveliness where, on the other side of a stream, he sees a beautiful maiden dressed in white and adorned with pearls. He recognizes her as his lost pearl. (V) She tells him that he is wrong to grieve for her or think of her as lost. (VI) She rebukes him for not believing the Lord's promise to raise us to life, although the flesh must die. (VII) In spite of her tender age when she departed this life, she has become a bride of the Lamb, who has crowned her as His queen in heaven. (VIII) The dreamer doubts the truth of her statement, and wonders how she can possibly have usurped the queenship of the Blessed Virgin. The maiden answers that all in God's kingdom are kings and queens living together in perfect charity. (IX–X) He still finds it hard to believe that God could be so unjust as to treat a child less than two years old as generously as a person who has suffered long in the world for His sake. She then tells him the parable of the vineyard in order to convince him that God's grace is not constrained by human limitations. (XI) In reply to further protests she assures him that all enjoy the same reward in God's kingdom. To herself has been given the reward of innocence—that innocence forfeited long ago by Adam, but restored to her by the Christ-given sacrament of baptism. (XII) The contrite sinner and the righteous person alike are saved by God's mercy; the innocent child is justified in baptism. (XIII) For

[1] Denton Fox, *Twentieth-Century Interpretations of Sir Gawain and the Green Knight*, p. 5, who suggests that the poet's 'audience was presumably drawn from the wealthy and cosmopolitan Lancastrian nobility'.

those who come to the kingdom of heaven with the innocence of a child the gate is quickly opened. The pearl of great price for which the jeweller sold all he owned is like the radiant kingdom of heaven. This is the pearl, the maiden tells him, that she wears on her breast. The dreamer then asks who has given her such beauty of form and raiment, and she answers that her benefactor is the peerless Lamb, who has chosen her for His bride. Still incredulous, the dreamer asks her about this Lamb who has exalted her above all other women. (XIV) The maiden replies that she is but one of the 144,000 brides of the Lamb who died for us in Jerusalem. (XV) All His brides live in perfect harmony, their life of eternal happiness made possible by the death in this world of God's Lamb. And again she refers to John's vision in the Apocalypse of the 144,000 maidens standing beside the Lamb on Mount Zion. (XVI) The dreamer then asks her where the city is in which she and the rest of these maidens live. (XVII) She tells him to follow the river upstream to a hill near its source. He does so, and from this hill he sees the New Jerusalem, even as John the Apostle saw and described it in the Apocalypse. (XVIII) Each of its twelve gates is a perfect pearl that never fades. This radiant city takes its light, not from the sun or moon, but from the Lamb. (XIX) Suddenly he sees a procession of maidens, each of whom, like his own pearl-maiden, wears a crown and is arrayed in pearls and white robes. With the Lamb at their head they make their way to the throne, where the elders and the legions of angels are waiting to laud Him. (XX) The dreamer is so moved by longing for his pearl-maiden that he tries to cross the stream and join her. But before he can do so he wakes up in the garden, his head resting on the mound where he has lost his pearl. Despite his longing for her, he is reconciled to his dungeon of sorrow now that he knows she is pleasing to the heavenly Prince.

Pearl is the record of a spiritual crisis brought about by the loss of a beloved child and resolved by the assurance, reached after prolonged mental debate, that the child's soul is safe in heaven. Expressed in these general terms the theme of the poem seems desperately commonplace. But in the poet's own language his theme becomes intensely personal: the Christian creed is subjected to the severest possible trial and emerges triumphant.

Recording this experience after it is all over, the poet contrives to recapture the turbulence of mind and body through which he has had to pass before he succeeds in finding peace. His faith is seriously disturbed by the first shock of grief at losing one who is nearer to him than aunt or niece (233) and who has died before the age of two (483). In the beginning he can think of her resurrection in physical terms only: she lives on in the flowers on her grave, like the dead child in Hardy's 'Voices from Things Growing in a Churchyard'. He first has to be persuaded by the maiden in his vision—his lost pearl—that while the rose of her body has faded, the pearl of her soul is more radiant than ever. Next he has to be persuaded, very much against his will, that the child is not only saved but, by virtue of her innocence, has been granted a high place in the hierarchy of heaven. The maiden is hard put to it to convince him that she is indeed a bride of the Lamb, and her heavenly reward as great as any given to those righteous folk who have suffered long in this world for Christ's sake. After all her persuasive arguments he is intellectually rather than emotionally won over. The old longing to be with her remains, and his vision of the maiden is abruptly shattered by his vain attempt to cross the stream that parts him from the New Jerusalem.

It will be difficult for most readers to have any sympathy with the tiresome controversy once carried on by scholars as to whether *Pearl* is a personal elegy or a lesson in theology expressed in allegorical terms.[1] Clearly it is both, and just as clearly there would have been no poem, and so no allegory, if the poet had not suffered the loss of a child who was dear to him.[2] The task the poet sets himself in a little more than twelve hundred lines is to journey from earth to heaven, from a grave-mound in a garden through the Earthly Paradise to a sight of the Celestial City. The transfigured maiden, like Dante's Beatrice, helps him to learn the humility and largeness of soul which will allow him to understand some of God's mysteries. Completely earthbound at first in his thinking, obsessed with death and decay, with the social distinctions of his own day, and with material considerations of more and less, he is made to

[1] For a useful summary of earlier commentaries on *Pearl* see R. Wellek, '*The Pearl:* An Interpretation of the Middle English Poem', *Studies in English*, iv, Charles University (Prague, 1933).

[2] See N. Davis, 'A Note on *Pearl* [l. 1208]', *Review of English Studies*, n.s., xvii (1966), 403–5.

utter heresy after heresy before the child is able to convince him that the orthodox Catholic creed is the only one which gives meaning to life.

The symbol unifying the whole poem is the pearl, standing for the dead child, as the poet remembers her in all her loveliness, for the beatified maiden, for the grace of God conferred on her because of her innocence, and for the kingdom of heaven in which she enjoys the reward of eternal felicity. The poet's lost pearl is also a symbol of his own lost innocence, which he sees his way to recovering through meditation on the pearl-maiden's death and salvation. The loss of the pearl typifies the death of the child; he recovers his pearl when the conviction grows on him that her soul is safe and that she is the recipient of God's grace through the Christ-given sacrament of baptism. He becomes convinced that he too may receive God's grace through sacramental penance—the adult's way of recovering that baptismal innocence which has been sullied by life in this world.

The doctrine and symbolism of *Pearl* are only a part of what makes this poem interesting to the modern reader. Its setting—the device of the dream and vision—is no less essential to the meaning of the poem as a whole. Made popular by the thirteenth-century *Roman de la Rose*, this device is also used as the framework of an elegy in Chaucer's *Book of the Duchess* (*c.* 1369) and in a *planctus* like that beginning 'My feerfull dreme nevyr forgete can I'.[1] Related to these is the *Olympia* Eclogue (*c.* 1361) of Boccaccio, in which the poet has a vision of his daughter Violante, who died at the age of five and a half. However, the combination of vision and elegy is rare enough in medieval literature, and it is tempting to believe that the *Pearl*-poet, although influenced by the literary convention of the dream-vision, was recording an actual vision he had experienced. Certainly his vision of the dead maiden has a striking parallel in real life in De Quincey's vision of Wordsworth's daughter Catherine, who 'was not above three years old when she died' (in June 1812).[2]

While allowing for this possibility of a real-life vision, we have to recognize that the *Pearl*-poet drew freely on his reading

[1] R. L. Greene, ed., *The Early English Carols* (Oxford, 1935), No. 165.
[2] D. Masson, ed., *De Quincey's Works*, vol. ii (London, 1896), pp. 440 ff.

of medieval literature to give expression to his vision. Few students of *Pearl* since Osgood[1] have thought it worth pointing out that the poet's vision of the Earthly Paradise and of the stream separating it from the Heavenly Paradise has very probably been influenced by Dante's *Purgatorio*, Canto xxviii. Some of the features common to *Pearl* and this canto of the *Purgatorio*—the forest, the flowers, the fragrance, the bird song and the stream—are properties to be found in any medieval Earthly Paradise, and are indeed an established rhetorical device in medieval nature description.[2] But the function of the stream in both the *Purgatorio* and *Pearl* is not to separate the Earthly Paradise from the inhabited world, as in most medieval descriptions of the *locus amoenus*, but the Earthly from the Heavenly Paradise. Again, in both works the poet sees a maiden on the other side of the stream; Matilda and the pearl-maiden each acts as a mentor in reply to the poet's questions; each instructs the poet to follow her on the opposite bank towards the source of the stream, and each shows the poet a vision of the New Jerusalem taken from the Apocalypse.

In addition to these external details in common, it seems likely that the central idea of *Pearl* has been influenced by the *Purgatorio*. The following comment on the *Purgatorio* can be applied equally well to *Pearl*: 'When man fell he forfeited immediately the perfect earthly life, and ultimately the perfect heavenly life. His first task, then, must be to recover the life of the Earthly Paradise; and as purgation, or recovery from the fall, consists primarily in regaining Eden . . . the Garden of Eden becomes by a necessity of symbolic logic the scene of purgation.'[3] The *Pearl*-poet also, in his journey from earth to heaven, must through penance recover that innocence the pearl-maiden has never lost before he can join her across the sundering stream.

Of all the other influences which have moulded *Pearl* an important place must be given to the Passion lyrics, and in particular to the Marian laments (*planctus Mariae*). If the *Purgatorio* has influenced the thought-content and setting of

[1] C. G. Osgood, ed., *The Pearl* (Boston, 1906), p. xxvi. The influence of Dante on the *Pearl*-poet has since been thoroughly explored (see Bishop and Kean in Select Bibliography).

[2] *See* E. R. Curtius, *European Literature and the Latin Middle Ages* (London, 1953), pp, 195 ff.

[3] *Dante's Purgatorio* (London, Dent, 1941), p.433. Cf. *Dante: The Divine Comedy: II. Purgatory*, trans. Dorothy Sayers (Penguin Books, 1955), p. 293.

Pearl, the *planctus* may well have strengthened the emotion of *Pearl*, and perhaps even provided some of the words in which this emotion is expressed. The parallelism between the *planctus* and *Pearl* is closest when the *planctus* takes the form of an *estrif* or *debat* between Christ and His Mother, in which Christ tries to console her sorrow as a mother. One of the best known of such dialogues is the Harley lyric beginning 'Stond wel, moder, under rode'.[1] In *Pearl* the Virgin's 'moder kare' (mother's sorrow) is replaced by the poet's 'fader kare', but the expression of human sorrow for the loss of a beloved child, as well as the attempt to console this sorrow, are common to both *planctus* and *Pearl*.

When doctrine and elegy, analogues and influences have all been duly noted, we are still left with the poet's language, imagery and rhythmical ordering of words, which do more than anything else to make *Pearl* a distinguished poem. The *Pearl*-poet's language changes, chameleon-like, with the context: clear and direct in argument, forthright and idiomatic in conversation, richly wrought and alliterated in description, with a studied use of words like 'schene', 'clere', 'clene' and 'bryght'. Words steeped in courtly associations are used in unusual and arresting contexts. The earthly poet identifies his love for his lost maiden with the 'luf-daungere' (power of love) which holds the courtly lover in thrall. The heavenly maiden plays variations on the word 'cortaysye' (courtesy), elevating its meaning to the level of Christian charity and divine grace.[2] The use of the word 'luf-longyng' (love-longing), with all its courtly aura of meaning, is aptly used to describe the mad impulse which brings the poet's vision to an abrupt end. His vision ended, he returns to earthly ways of thinking and quite naturally imagines this world, in which he has to live in separation from his pearl, as a 'doel-doungoun' (dungeon of sorrow).

Some of the images are commonplace enough; others show a lively imagination and an observant eye for details of the world of nature and the world of man (e.g. lines 1115, 1093–4). Apart

[1] G. L. Brook, ed., *The Harley Lyrics* (Manchester University Press, 1948), No. 20.

[2] See pp. xxxii–xxxiii of the Introduction to E. V. Gordon's edition of *Pearl*, noted below in the Select Bibliography.

from the dominant symbol of the pearl there are images which recur throughout the poem and help to give it unity. This is particularly true of the water images, suggesting on a human level the irrepressible upsurge of grief, and on a religious level the river of life, the cleansing water of baptism and the outpouring of God's grace. The 'floty vales' of the poet's own country, where the streams cry aloud, are never far from his thoughts. Again, the radiance of the poet's vision, growing in intensity until it dazzles us with a sight of the Heavenly City, is often expressed by the image of light shining through glass (e.g. lines 114, 990, 1018, 1025, 1106).[1]

From the point of view of its metrical form *Pearl* is probably the most complex poem written in English. Its 101 twelve-line stanzas are grouped into twenty sections, and within each section the last line of every stanza is repeated with variations in the manner of a refrain. Moreover, stanza is linked to stanza and section to section by the repetition of a key-word or phrase.[2] Metrical complexity could not go much further. And yet, far from petrifying the poet's sorrow, his exacting metre actually helps him to bring it under control, and serves as a formal counterpart of the strenuous mental debate which enables him to escape from his first blind paroxysm of grief.

The final result is a poem intensely personal and passionate, 'gostly' (spiritual) in purpose, and so brilliantly coloured that

. . . wern never webbes that wyyes weven
Of half so dere adubbement. (71–2)

CLEANNESS

At the end of the poem, the narrator refers to the 'three ways' in which he has dealt with his theme, and these 'three ways' must refer to the three main stories which the poem contains, those of the Flood, Sodom and Gomorrah, and Belshazzar's Feast.[3] But the poem begins with a general dis-

[1] Light shining through glass is a familiar figure in medieval poetry for the conception of Christ.

[2] For a note on the metre of *Pearl* see Appendix II.

[3] The main biblical sources for these narratives are: the Flood, Gen. vi. 1–ix. 2; Sodom and Gomorrah, Gen. xviii. 1–xix. 29; Belshazzar's Feast, Jer. lii. 1–27, conflated with 2 Chron. xxxvi. 11–20 (for the siege and destruction of Jerusalem), and Dan. iv. 25–v. 31 (for the feast).

cussion of the virtue of cleanness, with reference to the sixth beatitude: 'Blessed are the pure in heart, for they shall see God' (Matt. v. 8), and to the parable of the wedding feast (Matt. xxii. 1–14 and Luke xiv. 16–24), which is given an extended retelling. Then come brief accounts of the Fall of the Angels and the Fall of Man, leading into the first major narrative, that of the Flood. In between the three main stories are two passages of comment, each of which looks backward to the preceding story and forward to the next. It is difficult to pinpoint exactly where one story or section ends and another begins; the poet refuses to allow us to chop the poem up into neat compartments.

The structure is handled fluidly and so is the theme. To summarize what the poet means by cleanness is difficult as the whole poem is a working out of the concept. From the outset, the poet insists on the negative side of his subject. We are told that God rewards cleanness (line 12), but there is rather more emphasis on the fact that He is angry with uncleanness (lines 4–5, 16, 21), and the positive statement of the beatitude, with its promise of the beatific vision, is immediately recast in negative terms:

> As so says, to that syght seche schal he never
> That any unclannesse has on, auwhere abowte. (29–30)

The main argument of the poem is that cleanness is an essential virtue because God cannot tolerate uncleanness. Fundamental to this argument is a distinction between a more general and a more specific kind of uncleanness. The former kind alienates man from God, depriving him of the heavenly reward for the pure in heart, but it is redeemable through penance. Uncleanness in this sense is part of all sin, or, we may say, it is sin itself in one of its aspects; hence the long miscellaneous list of sins in lines 177–92. But the more specific kind of uncleanness is irredeemable, producing a violent reaction in God so that He is moved to take drastic vengeance, like a man in the grip of a passion he cannot control. The poet goes to great lengths to make the distinction when he contrasts God's 'moderate' punishment of Lucifer and Adam with the violent destruction of the whole world in the Flood. God's violence here, as in the destruction of Sodom and Gomorrah, is occasioned by man's 'filth of the flesh', his indulgence in perverted sexual practices. In the story of Belshazzar's Feast, the occasions are Zedekiah's idolatry and Belshazzar's profanation of the sacred vessels of the Temple. The poet seems to be saying that it is the uncleanness of sin which God finds hardest to tolerate, to the extent that, when a sin is unclean in an extreme way, He forgets His own nature. Cleanness is part of God's very being, as the poet insists constantly (e.g. lines 17–22), but, more than this, God's cleanness, as 'cortaysye', is that aspect of the divine nature which is of most benefit to man, the channel of God's grace; Christ, the ultimate expression of God's charity to man, is presented in the poem as the epitome of cleanness and courtesy. What God cannot abide is the wilful rejection of His best gifts, the refusal of men to respect Him in His charity. Thus sodomy is a perversion of God's greatest physical gift to man, which enables him to experience on earth something of the bliss of Paradise (line 704). Zedekiah and Belshazzar indulge in a kind of spiritual sodomy,[1] abusing the gift of worship whereby God has established channels of spiritual communication with man; so Zedekiah turns his back on the Covenant in which God bestows His grace on the Jewish people, and Belshazzar perverts the instruments of God's worship to the use of Satan (line 1449), in spite of the example of his father before him. We are warned that to accept the gift of the sacrament of penance, and then to turn to sin again, is an act of disrespect which will rouse God to the anger He reserves for extreme uncleanness (lines 1133–44). Such wanton refusal of God's grace is profoundly unnatural; hence the Dead Sea, which 'overturns all of the laws of nature' (line 1024), turning everything to corruption, is an image of the sin of Sodom and Gomorrah. It is set against the ministry of Christ, 'king of nature', whose cleanness makes all corruption whole. It is appropriate that such unnatural sin evokes an 'unnatural' response from God, driving Him out of His divine reasonableness. In hindsight, one can see some of these matters adumbrated in the wedding feast parable. As the poet explains, the feast is an allegory of

[1] Or sodomy may be regarded as physical sacrilege; cf. Margaret Williams, *The Pearl-Poet* (New York, 1967), p. 43: 'The defilement of the sacred vessels is a sacrilege; impurity in a member of Christ is also a sacrilege, in the light of St Paul's words: "If any man defile the temple of God, him shall God destroy, for the temple of God is holy, which temple you are." (1 Cor. iii. 17).'

the kingdom of Heaven, to which, by God's grace, all Christians are invited. In His charity, God accepts people of all kinds at His feast, the worse as well as the better, so long as they are prepared to make the effort to come and to present themselves decently. But twice He is made angry, first by those who make excuses not to come, secondly by the man who comes in foul clothes. In both instances, it is the flouting not only of God, but of God's grace, which gives intolerable offence.

Though the emphasis in the three main stories is on uncleanness and its punishment, there is a positive side to each, embodied chiefly in Noah, Abraham and Nebuchadnezzar. The cleanness of all three is seen to consist in the respect they show to God, manifested for instance in Noah's sacrifice to the Lord after the departure from the Ark, Abraham's hospitality under the oaks of Mamre, and Nebuchadnezzar's respectful treatment of the Temple vessels. And if God reacts to extreme uncleanness with violent hostility, cleanness in man is seen to move him in an opposite way, activating His mercy; so God establishes His covenant with Noah 'In comly comfort ful clos and cortays wordes' (512). God responds both to Abraham's hospitality and to his plea that He should show mercy to Sodom and Gomorrah; the point of the poet's retention of the long biblical dialogue in which Abraham makes his plea is to show the extent of God's response, and, to sharpen the point, the poet greatly develops the biblical hint (Gen. xix. 29) that Lot's salvation later is to be ascribed to Abraham's intervention with God on his behalf. Nebuchadnezzar's cleanness carries more weight with God than does his pagan background, and it is on this that his great power is shown to depend.

Although the poem has a main theme and a main line of development, it is by no means entirely linear in either theme or structure. The main theme generates others which are related to it in various ways, for instance, the theme of external beauty and inner uncleanness, and the theme of the fall of pride which is prominent in the last section of the poem. From a structural point of view, the poem's meaning depends to a considerable extent on implied parallels and contrasts between one passage and another, the passages often being widely separated. Thus the fall of Lucifer functions chiefly as an example of sin punished in moderation, in contrast to 'filth of the flesh', and the main relation is a contrastive one with the episode of the Flood. But Lucifer is also an example of the sin of pride, and here there is a parallel, made obvious by parallelisms of language, with Nebuchadnezzar's fall later; this relation is also contrastive, however, in that whereas Nebuchadnezzar repents and regains his former position, Lucifer does not. Again, Lucifer's sin is like Adam's in that it does not attract God's anger, but unlike Adam's in that it is never expiated. Adam sins through disobedience, failure in 'trawthe', and he therefore relates not only to the Flood and to Lucifer but also to Lot's wife, whose sin is likewise 'mistrauthe', though the relation is contrastive in that the 'mistrauthe' of Lot's wife involves contempt for God as well as disobedience, while Adam's does not. One may go on to compare and contrast Lot's wife with Sarah and with the good wife of Belshazzar. One relation leads to another, and the number of possible relations is very large, indeed hardly definable. Such thematic and structural fluidity makes for a rich texture, enabling the poet to impose complex meaning on pre-existing material in an economical fashion.

The complexity of the poem's theme and structure is matched by a wide range of poetic effect. There is the cheerful freshness of Abraham's open-air meal with God, the splendour of the decorations of the Temple vessels, the superlative celebration of the birth of Jesus, tender but with an intellectual content which gives the passage strength. But the poem is dominated by images of violence and horror, such as the panic-stricken flight of men and animals as they try to escape the rising flood-waters, moving to us, but, horrifyingly, not to God; the cataclysmic destruction of Sodom and Gomorrah; the savage treatment of the Jews by Nebuchadnezzar and Nebuzaridan; the ruthlessly efficient killing of Belshazzar. The detail is explicit to the point of disgust—flesh rotting in the mud after the Flood, the stomachs of the women of Jerusalem ripped open so that their bowels burst out over the ditches, Belshazzar's brains a bloody mess on the bedclothes. Poetry and argument together insist on God's abhorrence of the most loathsome of sins.

PATIENCE

Most of *Patience* is taken up with a retelling of the story of Jonah as it is found in the Book of Jonah in the Bible. The poet holds Jonah up to us as an example of impatience, to be contrasted unfavourably with the patience of God—a view of the Jonah story which appears to be very much the poet's own, standing apart from the traditional interpretations. There is a preface to the story in which the poet speaks in his own voice, offering a pragmatic argument in favour of patience; it may be a displeasing virtue, but if one does not have it in times of trouble, one's troubles will only become worse. He refers to the Beatitudes, taking the eighth as embodying the virtue of patience; Matt. v. 10 has 'Blessed are they which are persecuted for righteousness' sake', which the poet interprets as 'Thay ar happen also that con her hert stere' (27). The poet quotes all eight of the Beatitudes, mainly to establish a connection between poverty and patience; poverty is first in the series of Beatitudes, patience last, and they receive the same reward. Moreover, we are told, they are of the same kind, as the only valid response to poverty is patience. Poverty does not feature in the story of Jonah (unless we are to take it that Jonah, deprived of his comforts in the belly of the whale and on the plain outside Nineveh, endures a kind of poverty), and it seems likely, particularly in view of the slightly rueful, whimsical tone of the prologue, that poverty is introduced because it is something the poet knows about in his own life; it is an example of a 'destyné due' requiring patience which is of immediate concern to him. The connection between his 'destyné due' and Jonah's is rather elaborately made in lines 49–60.

Jonah in the poem is a splendid example of one who cannot 'steer his heart', as he is unable to accept either good or bad fortune with equanimity—he reacts impulsively both to God's command that he should go to Nineveh and to God's gift of the woodbine. The whale teaches Jonah the need for obedience to God's will, but the lesson is not properly learned, for when God changes His mind about destroying Nineveh Jonah cannot accept the situation, seeing only that God has made him a liar. God uses the woodbine to demonstrate to Jonah his new error

—his selfish insistence on justice—and to show that true patience involves not only acceptance of compelling circumstance, but active charity. The poet convinces us that patience is indeed a highly desirable virtue, and we are made aware of possible serious consequences of impatience. But the story is managed with a light touch and an awareness of its comic possibilities. Jonah is a prophet of God and he is capable of an appropriate dignity, as in his prayer from the whale's belly, but he is also a wilful old man ludicrously pitting himself against the power of God, and being constantly slapped down for his pains. He is so human in his failings, and the cards are so heavily stacked against him, that he wins some sympathy from the reader. We at least see what he means when he accuses God: 'With alle meschef that thou may, never thou me spares' (484). At the same time we recognize that Jonah is in the wrong in putting his own honour before the salvation of a city. Amusement, sympathy and criticism are kept nicely in balance. God too is attractive, dignified but approachable, though we are not allowed to forget the terrible possibilities of His absolute power. In this poem, however, the power is always tempered by patience, so that God teaches by example as well as by correction. God has a real relationship with Nineveh, and still more with Jonah, whom He treats like an erring child. The pervading tone of the poem, established already in the prologue, is one of light irony, appropriate for exposing the absurdity of Jonah's conduct.

It is natural to consider *Cleanness* and *Patience* together. Each poem takes as its subject one of the virtues of the Beatitudes, which is then applied to stories from the Bible. The stories as the poet tells them are based firmly on the biblical text, in its Latin Vulgate version, which the poet must have had before him as he composed. The poet uses a variety of means to adapt his original to his own purposes, the most obvious of these being imaginative elaboration, as with the storm and the whale in *Patience*, the Temple vessels and the flight from the Flood in *Cleanness*. In both poems the major elaborations are showpieces of an outstanding poetic talent. But, in spite of such basic similarities, the two poems read very differently. *Cleanness* has an epic sweep, a formidable complexity, and an uncompromising morality; in the passage on the birth of Christ it rises to sublimity. By comparison *Patience* is small-scale in every sense, not only much shorter but more accessible and personal. We enter into Jonah's thoughts and feelings in a way that we cannot with any of the characters in *Cleanness*, and the message of *Patience* is softened by a play of irony and humour which is absent in the longer poem. Singly and together the poems amount to an impressive achievement, contributing to the status of MS. Cotton Nero A.x as the most important collection of Middle English poems outside the work of Chaucer.

SIR GAWAIN AND THE GREEN KNIGHT

Kittredge and others have shown that the plot of *Sir Gawain* is made up of two originally independent stories—the Beheading Test and the Temptation—the first of which can be traced back to the eighth-century Irish saga of *Bricriu's Feast*. It is certain that neither Beheading nor Temptation had anything to do with the Arthurian legends originally, and possible that both stories go back to ancient Irish and Welsh sources.[1]

The Beheading Test in *Bricriu's Feast* has been interpreted mythologically as the annual struggle between the old sun-god (Curoi) and the new sun-god (Cuchulainn).[2] This seasonal myth may also underlie the Beheading Test in *Sir Gawain*, but it is a matter for dispute how far it informs and gives vitality to a courtly romance of the late fourteenth century.

The poet, whether French or English, who was the first to contrive the plot of *Sir Gawain* must be credited with architectonic skill of a high order in fusing together such diverse elements. As Kittredge says: 'The poem as we have it is a skilful combination of two entirely independent adventures so managed as to produce a harmonious unit. No reader who was ignorant of the parallels which we have been discussing would think of taking it apart, or would suspect that it had

[1] For a discussion of what the Temptation owes to Welsh sources see R. S Loomis, *Wales and the Arthurian Legend* (Cardiff, 1956), p. 79.
[2] R. S. Loomis, *Celtic Myth and Arthurian Romance* (Columbia University Press, 1927), p. 60.

been put together out of elements that originally had nothing to do with each other.'[1]

In the manuscript the poem is divided by large capital letters into four sections which are, in effect, the main stages in the development of the story. The first section gives the setting in time and place: the time is New Year's Day, the place is Arthur's court. The Green Knight makes his challenge, is beheaded by Gawain, and Gawain agrees to meet him at the Green Chapel a year later to receive the return blow. The second section describes Gawain's winter journey in search of the Green Chapel and his arrival on Christmas Eve at a castle where he is warmly welcomed by the lord and lady. The lord persuades him to stay as his guest until New Year's Day, when he promises to have him escorted to the Green Chapel. Further, Gawain accepts the lord's merry proposal that the last three days of the old year shall be enlivened by a covenant to exchange anything they happen to win on each of these three days. In the third section Gawain's quest for the Green Chapel is not forgotten, but it is subordinated for the time being to three temptations and three hunting scenes. On the first two days Gawain faithfully exchanges the lady's kisses for the spoils of the lord's hunting expeditions; on the third day, however, he conceals from the lord the green belt that the lady has given him. The fourth section describes how Gawain is conducted to the Green Chapel, how the Green Knight aims three blows at him and slightly wounds him with the third blow. He explains to Gawain the significance of the two pretended blows and of the slight wound he has inflicted with his third blow. The mortified Gawain then returns to Arthur's court.

Accomplished storyteller that he is, the poet gives his story a considerable element of suspense. The link-stanzas between the first and second sections bridge the gap between New Year's Day and All Saints' Day (1st Nov.), when Gawain sets out on his quest for the Green Chapel; but they are also tinged

[1] G. L. Kittredge, *A Study of Gawain and the Green Knight* (Harvard University Press, 1916), p. 107. For a brief survey of the French parallels to the Beheading Test, some of which may have influenced the form and even the wording of this episode in *Sir Gawain*, see Dr Mabel Day's Introduction to Gollancz's edition of the poem, pp. xxii–xxiv, and also pp. xv–xvii of the edition by J. R. R. Tolkien, E. V. Gordon and N. Davis (both these editions are noted below in the Select Bibliography).

with melancholy and foreboding, and help to create suspense by putting a gloomy question mark after future events. During the whole of the third section we are kept guessing about the relationship between the Beheading and the Temptation. It is not until the fourth section, when the Green Knight reveals himself as the lord of the castle, that we are in a position to understand the significance of some of the details of the third section—why, for instance, the lady knew about Gawain's dangerous mission, and why she chose to represent the green belt as a charm against violent death in order to persuade Gawain to accept it.

It is impossible to read the poem without realizing the almost geometrical patterning of persons and events, in which a grouping into threes is the dominant motif. For example, there are three leading personages at Arthur's court, three at Bertilak's court; there are three court scenes, three journeys, three hunts and three temptations on three successive days, and three blows aimed at Gawain by the Green Knight. But while this patterning gives the poem an external order, in which parallelism and contrast have an important part to play, its internal unity springs from its central theme of the testing of Gawain: the outcome of the Beheading depends upon the outcome of the Temptation, and this in turn depends upon Gawain himself.

The poet, as we have seen, tells his story in such a way that Gawain's successful fulfilment of his mission is never a foregone conclusion. Above all, the poet is careful to make Gawain very human, in spite of his manifold virtues; and his actions, simply because he is so human, cannot be precisely calculated in advance. He undertakes his mission lightheartedly enough, fortified as he is by strong drink and by the carefree spirit of a New Year's holiday, but it seems a graver thing to him as the year draws to an end. His wild and lonely journey, when he has no one but his horse to keep him company, and no one to talk to but God, tries him severely. The wretched food, the harsh winter weather, the perils he has to face, are bad enough; but the loneliness, as he rides 'Fer floten fro his frendes' (714), is the worst trial of all. We can imagine his relief when he comes out of the deep forest and finds a solid-looking and richly adorned castle looming up in front of him—the symbol to him of civilized social life, warmth and hospitality. The description of the joyous welcome he receives from the lord of the castle, and of the great hall where the fire blazes fiercely on the hearth, makes us feel Gawain's delight at reaching this refuge from the loneliness, danger and bitter cold of the outside world. Gawain is nothing if not a sociable person: 'felawschyp' (652)—love of his fellow men—is one of his outstanding virtues. The frailties he later reveals—his weakness in accepting the lady's belt because he believes it will save him from bodily harm, his failure to surrender the belt to the lord of the castle—all help to make him human. And yet the proof of Gawain's humanity is not limited to one or two major lapses from his high ideals of conduct; it rather consists of innumerable small touches which, all together, give him full membership of the society of ordinary mortals.

Above the very human Gawain towers the marvellous Green Knight, the shape-changer, the instrument of Morgan le Fay's magic, who survives decapitation and later reappears in his own person as Bertilak de Hautdesert. The combat between these two men has been described as 'not the orthodox kind of knightly contest but a kind of ritual contest';[1] and it is at least possible that this combat preserves something of the mythological meaning attributed to the Beheading Test in the ancient Irish saga. The Green Knight appears to have 'the unlimited energy of a symbol',[2] but it would be hazardous to try to pigeon-hole him. Originally he may have been the old sun-god surrendering to the might of the 'yonge sonne', or he may have been the Green Man, whose decapitation and revival represent the annual death and rebirth of vegetation. These meanings will be latent in the poem for some readers but not for others. What is clear in the poem is that the Green Knight, *alias* Sir Bertilak, is an immensely vital person who is closely associated with the life of nature: his greenness, the birds and flies of his decorative embroidery, his beard as great as a bush, the holly branch in his hand, the energy he displays as a huntsman—all give him kinship with the physical world outside the castle.

[1] J. Speirs, *Medieval English Poetry* (London, 1957), p. 220.
[2] F. Berry's essay on 'Sir Gawayne and the Grene Knight', in *The Age of Chaucer* (London, 1954), p. 158.

At every point he is contrasted with Gawain, who comes to life in the hall of the castle, and is most at home in civilized surroundings where courtly behaviour and conversation are the rule. Behind this contrast between the two men is another contrast, which is constantly being made, between the life of court, with its entertainments and feasting, and the life of nature in its harsher aspects. Most of the nature description is related to Gawain, expressing his moods of dejection or symbolizing the dangers he has to overcome. Twice he has to make his way through a 'rough and stubborn forest' reminiscent of Dante's 'dark Wood'. Again, the lord's three hunts are an extension of the three temptations of Gawain by the lady, for both the lord in the wood and his lady in the castle are intent on hunting down their prey and destroying it.

Gawain's land journey in the dead of winter is reminiscent of the sailor's wintry exile on the ice-cold sea in the Old English poem *The Seafarer*. Nature in its winter harshness symbolizes in both poems the sufferings of this world which a man 'proud and flushed with wine' must endure alone before he can attain self-knowledge and humility. The fundamental Christian theme of *Sir Gawain and the Green Knight* is that Gawain's fitness to bear the pentangle, the symbol of bodily and spiritual perfection, is put to the test of suffering and temptation. He does not emerge from his test unscathed.[1] Although he makes a full confession to the priest in Bertilak's castle, he violates the sacrament of penance by wrongfully keeping the belt, and therefore has to undergo a second penance at the edge of the Green Knight's axe. Yet, in spite of his self-abasement, we feel that he is essentially victorious, and we agree with the Green Knight that he is

On the fautlest freke that ever on fote yede. (2363)

As a result of his quest Gawain (like the dreamer in *Pearl*) is spiritually reborn. His spiritual renewal is parallel to the underlying seasonal myth of death and revival, and the poem gains in meaning if we are prepared to believe that pagan myth and Christian doctrine have coalesced in the *Gawain* poet's vision of life in this world.

The blending of old and new, of pagan and Christian, is reflected in the diction and metre of the poem. *Sir Gawain* is full

[1] As J. A. Burrow puts it in his study of the poem, *A Reading of Sir Gawain and the Green Knight*, p. 171, Gawain is 'a superlative hero subjected to, and partly failing, a superlative test'. Other critical studies which have made an important contribution to our understanding of the art of the *Gawain*-poet include those of Spearing, Benson, and Davenport (see Select Bibliography).

of ancient poetic words and phrases which go back to Old English poetry;[1] but it also makes use of the Romance words of chivalry, the technical language of that courtly behaviour which the poet knows as 'frenkysch fare' (1116). Similarly, the metre combines the long unrhymed lines of native descent and the short rhyming lines of French origin.[2] The result of this blending of Germanic and Romance traditions is a remarkably lively and varied diction, and a metrical medium capable of expressing all kinds of different moods, sounds and movements. The rhythmical effects vary from the delicately measured sounds of a winter scene:

> With mony bryddes unblythe upon bare twyges,
> That pitosly ther piped for pyne of the colde (746–7)

to the colloquial abruptness of:

> 'How payes yow this play? Haf I prys wonnen?' (1379)

to the noise and excitement of the boar hunt:

> Thenne such a glaver ande glam of gedered rachches
> Ros that the rocheres rungen aboute. (1426–7)

The *Gawain*-poet, whoever he was, invites comparison with Chaucer, and does not suffer in the process, for 'he seldom wrote a line lacking in zest, or imagination, or rhythm—and Chaucer sometimes did'.[3]

The basic pattern of *Sir Gawain and the Green Knight* is the same as that of *Pearl*: the journey or quest, the test or purgation, and the spiritual renewal. Both poems return to their starting-point—the dreamer in *Pearl* to the grave mound in the garden, Gawain to Arthur's court. Furthermore, although both men come back to where they started from, they have been through an experience which has left its mark on them:

> The forme to the fynisment foldes ful selden. (*Gawain* 499)

[1] J. P. Oakden, op. cit., pp. 179–80, 267–312.
[2] For a note on the metre of *Sir Gawain* see Appendix II.
[3] H. L. Savage, *The Gawain-Poet: Studies in his Personality and Background* (Chapel Hill, 1956), p. 22.

SELECT BIBLIOGRAPHY

The following short list is confined to books only. Comprehensive bibliographies are provided in *The New Cambridge Bibliography of English Literature*, ed. George Watson, vol. I, and *A Manual of the Writings in Middle English*, ed. J. Burke Severs, vol. I (for *Sir Gawain and the Green Knight*), and vol. II (for *Pearl*, *Cleanness* and *Patience*). See also M. Andrew, *The Gawain-Poet: An Annotated Bibliography 1839–1977* (New York, 1979), and R. J. Blanch, *Sir Gawain and the Green Knight: A Reference Guide* (New York, 1983).

MANUSCRIPT

Pearl, Cleanness, Patience, and Sir Gawain, reproduced in facsimile from MS. Cotton Nero A.x in the British Library, with Introduction by I. Gollancz (London, 1923).

EDITIONS AND TRANSLATIONS

The Works of the Gawain-Poet, ed. C. Moorman (Jackson, Miss., 1977).
The Poems of the Pearl Manuscript: Pearl, Cleanness, Patience, Sir Gawain and the Green Knight, ed. M. Andrew and R. A. Waldron (London, 1978).
The Pearl Poems: An Omnibus Edition, ed. W. Vantuono, 2 vols (New York, 1984).
The Complete Works of the Gawain-Poet, trans. (verse) J. Gardner (Chicago, 1965).
The Pearl-Poet, trans. (verse) Margaret Williams (New York, 1967).
Pearl, ed. E. V. Gordon (Oxford, 1953).
—— trans. (verse) B. Stone, in *Medieval English Verse* (London, 1964).
—— trans. (verse) Marie Borroff (New York, 1977).
Purity, ed. R. J. Menner (New Haven, 1920).
Cleanness, ed. I. Gollancz, 2 vols. (London, 1921, 1933); reissued in one vol., with prose trans. by D. S. Brewer. 1974.
—— ed. J. J. Anderson (Manchester, 1977).
—— trans. (verse) B. Stone, in *The Owl and the Nightingale, Cleanness, St. Erkenwald* (London, 1971).
Patience, ed. J. J. Anderson (Manchester, 1969).
—— trans. (verse) B. Stone, in *Medieval English Verse* (London, 1964).
Sir Gawain and the Green Knight, ed. J. R. R. Tolkien and E. V. Gordon (Oxford, 1925); 2nd ed., rev. N. Davis, 1967.
—— ed. I. Gollancz, with introductory essays by Mabel Day and Mary S. Serjeantson (London, 1940).
—— ed. R. A. Waldron (London, 1970).
—— ed. J. A. Burrow (London, 1972; New Haven, 1982).
—— ed. and trans. (prose) W. R. J. Barron (Manchester, 1974).

—— trans. (verse) B. Stone (London, 1959).
—— trans. (verse) Marie Borroff (New York, 1967).
—— ed. T. Silverstein (Chicago, 1984).

STUDIES

Borroff, Marie. *Sir Gawain and the Green Knight: A Stylistic and Metrical Study* (New Haven, 1962).

Benson, L. D. *Art and Tradition in Sir Gawain and the Green Knight* (New Brunswick, N.J., 1965).

Burrow, J. A. *A Reading of Sir Gawain and the Green Knight* (London, 1965).

Kean, Patricia M. *The Pearl: An Interpretation* (London, 1967).

Bishop, I. *Pearl in Its Setting* (Oxford, 1968).

Moorman, C. *The Pearl-Poet* (New York, 1968).

Spearing, A. C. *The Gawain-Poet: A Critical Study* (Cambridge, 1970).

Wilson, E. *The Gawain-Poet* (Leiden, 1976).

Davenport, W. A. *The Art of the Gawain-Poet* (London, 1978).

Barron, W. R. J. *'Trawthe' and Treason: the Sin of Gawain Reconsidered* (Manchester, 1980).

Haines, V. Y. *The Fortunate Fall of Sir Gawain: The Typology of 'Sir Gawain and the Green Knight'* (Washington, DC, 1982).

Bogdanos, Theodore. *Pearl: Image of the Ineffable* (University Park, Pa., and London, 1983).

Elliott, R. W. V. *The Gawain Country* (Leeds, 1984).

Johnson, Lynn S. *The Voice of the Gawain Poet* (Wisconsin, 1984).

Shoaf, R. A. *The Poem as Green Girdle: 'Commercium' in Sir Gawain and the Green Knight* (Florida, 1984).

Nicholls, Jonathan. *The Matter of Courtesy: Medieval Courtesy Books and the Gawain-Poet* (Suffolk, 1985).

Arthur, Ross G. *Medieval Sign Theory and Sir Gawain and the Green Knight* (Toronto, 1987).

COLLECTIONS OF ESSAYS

Sir Gawain and Pearl: Critical Essays, ed. R. J. Blanch (Indiana, 1966).

Critical Studies of Sir Gawain and the Green Knight, ed. D. R. Howard and C. K. Zacher (Notre Dame, 1968).

Twentieth-Century Interpretations of Sir Gawain and the Green Knight, ed. D. Fox (New Jersey, 1968).

The Middle English Pearl: Critical Essays, ed. J. Conley (Notre Dame, 1970).

PEARL

I

Perle, plesaunte to prynces paye
To clanly clos in golde so clere:
Oute of oryent, I hardyly saye,
Ne proved I never her precios pere.
So rounde, so reken in uche araye, *radiant; every setting*
So smal, so smothe her sydes were,
Quere-so-ever I jugged gemmes gaye, *wherever; judged*
I sette hyr sengeley in synglere.
Allas! I leste hyr in on erbere; *lost; a garden*
Thurgh gresse to grounde hit fro me yot. *grass; went*
I dewyne, fordolked of luf-daungere
Of that pryvy perle wythouten spot.

Sythen in that spote hit fro me sprange, *since; place*
Ofte haf I wayted, wyschande that wele,
That wont was whyle devoyde my wrange
And heven my happe and al my hele.
That dos bot thrych my hert thrange,
My breste in bale bot bolne and bele.
Yet thoght me never so swete a sange
As stylle stounde let to me stele.
For sothe ther fleten to me fele,
To thenke hir color so clad in clot.
O moul, thou marres a myry juele,
My privy perle wythouten spotte.

1–4 Pearl, pleasing and delightful for a prince to set flawlessly in gold so bright: among the pearls of orient, I confidently say, I never found her equal.

8 I set her apart as unique.

11–12 I pine away, mortally wounded by the power of my love for my own spotless pearl.

14–23 Often have I watched, longing for that precious thing, which once was wont to drive away my sorrow and heighten my happiness and well-being. This (watching) weighs heavily on my heart, and my breast swells and festers with grief. Yet it seemed to me there was never so sweet a song as the one the quiet hour let steal to me. In truth, many songs flowed into me, as I thought of the fresh colour (of her face) thus wrapped in clay. O earth (of the grave), you spoil a pleasant jewel.

That spot of spyses mot nedes sprede,
Ther such ryches to rot is runne:
Blomes blayke and blwe and rede *yellow*
Ther schynes ful schyr agayn the sunne. *brightly*
Flor and fryte may not be fede *flower; cannot fade*
Ther hit doun drof in moldes dunne;
For uch gresse mot grow of graynes dede—
No whete were elles to wones wonne. *barn; brought*
Of goud uche goude is ay bygonne:
So semly a sede moght fayly not,
That spryngande spyces up ne sponne
Of that precios perle wythouten spotte. *from*

To that spot that I in speche expoun *I describe*
I entred in that erber grene, *into; garden*
In Auguste in a hygh seysoun,
Quen corne is corven wyth crokes kene. *cut*
On huyle ther perle hit trendeled doun
Schadowed this wortes ful schyre and schene—
Gilofre, gyngure and gromylyoun, *gillyflower; gromwell*
And pyonys powdered ay bytwene. *peonies; scattered*
Yif hit was semly on to sene,
A fayr reflayr yet fro hit flot.
Ther wonys that worthyly, I wot and wene,
My precious perle wythouten spot.

Bifore that spot my honde I spenned *clasped*
For care ful colde that to me caght;
A devely dele in my hert denned,
Thagh resoun sette myselven saght.

25–6 That place is bound to be covered with spice plants, where such wealth has gone to decay.

30–1 Where it (i.e. the pearl) sank down into the dark brown earth; for every plant must grow from grains that die. (Cf. John xii. 24–5.)

33–5 From what is good comes every good thing: so fair a seed cannot fail (to be fruitful) nor flourishing spice plants to spring up.

39 *hygh seysoun*, time of festival, possibly the harvest festival of Lammas (1st August).

41–2 On the mound where the pearl had rolled down these bright and beautiful plants cast a shadow.

45–7 If it was fair to look at, no less fair a fragrance came floating from it. There lies that precious one, I know for certain.

50–2 Because of the chilling sorrow that caught hold of me; a desolating grief lay deep in my heart, though reason did its best to reconcile me.

I playned my perle that ther was spenned *mourned; imprisoned*
Wyth fyrce skylles that faste faght;
Thagh kynde of Kryst me comfort kenned,
My wreched wylle in wo ay wraghte.
I felle upon that floury flaght, *turf*
Suche odour to my hernes schot; *rushed; head*
I slode upon a slepyng-slaghte
On that precios perle wythouten spot.

II

Fro spot my spyryt ther sprang in space;
My body on balke ther bod in sweven.
My goste is gon in Godes grace
In aventure ther mervayles meven.
I ne wyste in this worlde quere that hit wace, *knew; was*
Bot I knew me keste ther klyfes cleven.
Towarde a foreste I bere the face, *turned*
Where rych rokkes wer to dyscreven. *splendid; to be seen*
The lyght of hem myght no mon leven, *radiance; believe*
The glemande glory that of hem glent; *gleaming; shone*
For wern never webbes that wyyes weven
Of half so dere adubbement. *glorious; splendour*

Dubbed wern alle tho downes sydes *adorned; hill*
Wyth crystal klyffes so cler of kynde. *clear; by nature*
Holtewodes bryght aboute hem bydes *woods; are set*
Of bolles as blwe as ble of Ynde.
As bornyst sylver the lef onslydes,
That thike con trylle on uch a tynde.
Quen glem of glodes agayns hem glydes,
Wyth schymeryng schene ful schrylle thay schynde.

54–6 With fierce arguments that fought hard. Though the nature of Christ taught me comfort, my wretched self-will still made me suffer sorrow.
59 I slipped into a deep sleep.
61–4 After a while my spirit rose up from that place; my body stayed there sleeping on the mound. By God's grace my spirit went on a quest to where marvellous things exist.
66 But I knew I was set down in a place where cliffs cleave (the sky).
71 For never were fabrics that men weave.
76–80 With trunks as blue as indigo. Like burnished silver the thickset leaves slid open and quivered on every branch. When the light fell on them from clear patches of sky, they shone dazzlingly with a shimmering brightness.

The gravayl that on grounde con grynde *gravel; crunched*
Wern precious perles of oryente,
The sunnebemes bot blo and blynde *dark; dim*
In respecte of that adubbement.

The adubbemente of tho downes dere *hills*
Garten my goste al greffe foryete.
So frech flavores of frytes were,
As fode hit con me fayre refete.
Fowles ther flowen in fryth in fere,
Of flaumbande hwes, bothe smale and grete. *flaming; colours*
Bot sytole-stryng and gyternere
Her reken myrthe moght not retrete;
For quen those bryddes her wynges bete,
Thay songen wyth a swete asent. *sang; harmony*
So gracios gle couthe no mon gete *charming; joy*
As here and se her adubbement.

So al was dubbet on dere asyse
That fryth ther fortwne forth me feres.
The derthe therof for to devyse *glory; describe*
Nis no wyy worthé that tonge beres. *man; worthy*
I welke ay forth in wely wyse; *walked; blissful*
No bonk so byg that did me deres. *harm*
The fyrre in the fryth, the feier con ryse
The playn, the plonttes, the spyse, the peres,
And rawes and randes and rych reveres—
As fyldor fyn her bonkes brent.
I wan to a water by schore that scheres;
Lorde, dere was hit adubbement! *its*

86–9 Made my spirit forget all its grief. So refreshing was the fragrance of the fruits, it restored me as pleasantly as if it were food. Birds flew together in the woodland there.

91–2 But neither citole-string nor player on the cithern could imitate their gay music.

97–8 Thus all adorned in noble fashion was that wood where fortune had transported me.

103–7 The further I went into the wood, the fairer grew the meadow, the shrubs, the spice plants and the pear-trees, the hedgerows, the borders of the streams and the splendid river banks—their steep slopes like fine gold thread. I came to a stream that ran swiftly past its banks.

The dubbemente of tho derworth depe
Wern bonkes bene of beryl bryght.
Swangeande swete the water con swepe,
Wyth a rownande rourde raykande aryght.
In the founce ther stonden stones stepe,
As glente thurgh glas that glowed and glyght,
As stremande sternes, quen strothe-men slepe,
Staren in welkyn in wynter nyght.
For uche a pobbel in pole ther pyght
Was emerad, saffer, other gemme gente,
That alle the loghe lemed of lyght,
So dere was hit adubbement.

III

The dubbement dere of doun and dales,
Of wod and water and wlonk playnes, *lovely; meadows*
Bylde in me blys, abated my bales,
Fordidden my stresse, dystryed my paynes.
Doun after a strem that dryyly hales
I bowed in blys, bredful my braynes.
The fyrre I folwed those floty vales,
The more strenghthe of joye myn herte straynes.
As fortune fares, ther as ho fraynes,
Whether solace ho sende other elles sore,
The wyy to wham her wylle ho waynes
Hyttes to have ay more and more.

109–20 The adornments of those splendid depths were pleasant banks of bright beryl. Swirling sweetly the water swept along, flowing straight on with a murmuring sound. At the bottom stood bright stones that glowed and glinted like a beam of light through glass, or like the streaming stars that shine in the sky on a winter's night, when the men of this world are sleeping. For every pebble set there in the pool was an emerald, sapphire, or noble gem, so that all the pool gleamed with light, so glorious was its splendour.

123–8 Raised up happiness in me, put down my sorrow, removed my anguish, ended my agony. Down beside a stream that flowed ceaselessly on I blissfully made my way, my mind full to overflowing. The further I went along those watery vales, the stronger the joy that stirred my heart.

129–32 Even as fortune, wherever she makes trial (of a person), proceeds to send him pleasure or pain, so the person to whom she grants her favour seeks to have more and still more.

More of wele was in that wyse *joy; of that kind*
Then I cowthe telle thagh I tom hade, *could; leisure*
For urthely herte myght not suffyse
To the tenthe dole of tho gladnes glade.
Forthy I thoght that Paradyse *wherefore*
Was ther over gayn tho bonkes brade. *against*
I hoped the water were a devyse
Bytwene myrthes by meres made.
Byyonde the broke, by slente other slade,
I hoped that mote merked wore.
Bot the water was depe, I dorst not wade,
And ever me longed ay more and more. *I longed*

More and more, and yet wel mare, *still more*
Me lyste to se the broke byyonde;
For if hit was fayr ther I con fare,
Wel loveloker was the fyrre londe.
Abowte me con I stote and stare,
To fynde a forthe faste con I fonde;
Bot wothes mo iwysse ther ware,
The fyrre I stalked by the stronde.
And ever me thoght I schulde not wonde
For wo ther weles so wynne wore.
Thenne nwe note me com on honde
That meved my mynde ay more and more.

More mervayle con my dom adaunt:
I sey byyonde that myry mere *saw; pleasant water*

135–6 For earthly heart would not be adequate for the tenth part of those glad joys.

139–42 I thought the stream was a device (i.e. an artificial conduit) joining pleasure gardens made by the side of pools. Beyond the stream, across hill slope and vale, I believed there would be a walled city built.

146–56 I wished to see beyond the stream; for if it was lovely where I walked, still lovelier was the land on the farther side. I stopped and stared around me, I tried hard to find a ford; but the farther I walked cautiously along the bank, the more dangers there were indeed. And I kept thinking I ought not to shrink from harm where there were such delightful joys (to be gained). Then a new thing came to my notice that stirred my mind more and more.

157 A greater marvel daunted my reason.

A crystal clyffe ful relusaunt; *resplendent*
Mony ryal ray con fro hit rere.
At the fote therof ther sete a faunt, *sat; child*
A mayden of menske, ful debonere;
Blysnande whyt was hyr bleaunt. *gleaming; mantle*
I knew hyr wel, I hade sen hyr ere. *seen; before*
As glysnande golde that man con schere,
So schon that schene anunder shore.
On lenghe I loked to hyr there; *for a long time; at her*
The lenger, I knew hyr more and more.

The more I frayste hyr fayre face, *examined*
Her fygure fyn quen I had fonte,
Suche gladande glory con to me glace
As lyttel byfore therto was wonte.
To calle hyr lyste con me enchace,
Bot baysment gef myn hert a brunt;
I sey hyr in so strange a place, *saw*
Such a burre myght make myn herte blunt.
Thenne veres ho up her fayre frount, *raises; forehead*
Hyr vysayge whyt as playn yvore:
That stonge myn hert ful stray atount,
And ever the lenger, the more and more.

IV

More then me lyste my drede aros.
I stod ful stylle and dorste not calle;
Wyth yyen open and mouth ful clos *eyes*
I stod as hende as hawk in halle. *still*

160 Many a ray of royal splendour sprang from it.
162 A maiden of courteous, gentle bearing.
165–6 Like shining gold cut (into gold thread) by man, so shone that fair maiden at the foot of the cliff.
170–4 When I had observed her exquisite form, a gladdening splendour stole over me as it had seldom been wont to do before. Desire urged me to call her, but bewilderment dealt my heart a blow.
176 A blow (i.e. shock) such as that might well stun my heart.
178 Her face as white as polished ivory.
179 That pierced my heart (and made it) bewildered and confused.
181 Against my will I felt afraid.

I hoped that gostly was that porpose;
I dred onende quat schulde byfalle,
Lest ho me eschaped that I ther chos,
Er I at steven hir moght stalle.
That gracios gay wythouten galle,
So smothe, so smal, so seme slyght,
Ryses up in hir araye ryalle,
A precios pyece in perles pyght.

Perles pyghte of ryal prys,
There moght mon by grace haf sene,
Quen that frech as flor-de-lys
Doun the bonke con bowe bydene.
Al blysnande whyt was hir beau biys,
Upon at sydes and bounden bene
Wyth the myryeste margarys, at my devyse,
That ever I sey yet with myn yyen;
Wyth lappes large, I wot and I wene,
Dubbed with double perle and dyghte;
Her cortel of self sute schene,
Wyth precios perles al umbepyghte.

A pyght coroune yet wer that gyrle
Of mariorys and non other ston,
Highe pynakled of cler quyt perle,
Wyth flurted flowres perfet upon.

185–92 I thought it must have a spiritual meaning; I was afraid of what might happen, (afraid) lest she whom I saw there should escape me before I could stop and meet her. That fair and gracious maiden without spot of impurity, so smooth, so fine, so becomingly slender, rose up in her royal array, a precious person adorned with pearls.

193–204 A setting of pearls of royal excellence, there by grace you could have seen, when that maiden blooming like the fleur-de-lis came straightway down the bank. All gleaming white was her fine linen garment, open at the sides and beautifully trimmed with what, in my opinion, were the loveliest pearls I had ever set eyes on; with broad hanging sleeves, I know for certain, adorned with double rows of pearls; her bright kirtle a perfect match, arrayed all round with precious pearls.

205–16 That girl also wore a crown adorned with pearls and no other precious stones, with high pinnacles of clear white pearls, and exquisite flowers figured on it. She had no other covering on her head. Her face was enclosed all round (i.e. with a wimple), her expression was grave enough for duke or earl, her complexion whiter than ivory. Her hair shone like bright, newly cut gold, and lightly lay unbound on her shoulders. Her deep (white) colouring lacked nothing by comparison with the precious pearls that were set in the embroidered edge (of the wimple).

To hed hade ho non other werle.
Her lere leke al hyr umbegon,
Her semblaunt sade for doc other erle,
Her ble more blaght then whalles bon.
As schorne golde schyr her fax thenne schon,
On schylderes that leghe unlapped lyghte.
Her depe colour yet wonted non
Of precios perle in porfyl pyghte.

Pyght was poyned and uche a hemme
At honde, at sydes, at overture,
Wyth whyte perle and non other gemme,
And bornyste quyte was hyr vesture.
Bot a wonder perle wythouten wemme *wondrous; flaw*
Inmyddes hyr breste was sette so sure: *in the middle of*
A mannes dom moght dryyly demme,
Er mynde moght malte in hit mesure.
I hope no tong moght endure
No saverly saghe say of that syght,
So was hit clene and cler and pure, *bright*
That precios perle ther hit was pyght. *set*

Pyght in perle, that precios pyse
On wyther half water com doun the schore. *the opposite side of*
No gladder gome hethen into Grece
Then I, quen ho on brymme wore. *brink; was*
Ho was me nerre then aunte or nece;
My joy forthy was much the more. *therefore*
Ho profered me speche, that special spyce, *precious; person*
Enclynande lowe in wommon lore,

217–20 Her wristband and every hem were adorned with white pearls at the wrist, at the sides, and at the opening (of the neck), and her raiment was shining white.

223–6 A man's reason would be utterly baffled before his mind could comprehend its size and value. I believe no tongue would be able to find adequate words to describe that vision.

229 Adorned with pearls, that precious person.

231 No happier man from here to Greece.

233 She was more closely related to me than aunt or niece.

236 Bowing low in womanly fashion.

Caghte of her coroun of grete tresore *took off*
And haylsed me wyth a lote lyghte.
Wel was me that ever I was bore
To sware that swete in perles pyghte!

V

'O perle,' quod I, 'in perles pyght,
Art thou my perle that I haf playned, *mourned*
Regretted by myn one on nyghte? *grieved for; on my own*
Much longeyng haf I for the layned,
Sythen into gresse thou me aglyghte.
Pensyf, payred, I am forpayned,
And thou in a lyf of lykyng lyghte,
In Paradys erde, of stryf unstrayned.
What wyrde has hyder my juel vayned, *fate; sent*
And don me in thys del and gret daunger? *put; grief*
Fro we in twynne wern towen and twayned,
I haf ben a joyles juelere.'

That juel thenne in gemmes gente
Vered up her vyse wyth yyen graye,
Set on hyr coroun of perle orient,
And soberly after thenne con ho say: *gravely; said*
'Sir, ye haf your tale mysetente, *told wrongly*
To say your perle is al awaye, *lost*
That is in cofer so comly clente *beautifully; enclosed*
As in this gardyn gracios gaye, *as (to be)*
Hereinne to lenge for ever and play, *dwell; rejoice*
Ther mys nee mornyng com never nere.
Her were a forser for the, in faye,
If thou were a gentyl jueler.

238–40 And greeted me with a joyful cry. I was glad to be alive to answer that sweet person adorned with pearls.
244–8 I have concealed my great longing for you, since you slipped away from me into the grass. I am sorrowful, worn and overcome with pain, and you are settled in a life of pleasure, in the land of Paradise, untouched by strife.
251 Ever since we were severed and parted.
253–4 Then that jewel, in noble gems (arrayed), lifted up her face with its grey-blue eyes.
262–4 Where never loss and grief come near. This would seem a (fitting) casket to you, truly, if you were a noble jeweller.

'Bot, jueler gente, if thou schal lose — *gracious; must*
Thy joy for a gemme that the was lef, — *dear*
Me thynk the put in a mad porpose,
And busyes the aboute a raysoun bref;
For that thou lestes was bot a rose — *that (which); lost*
That flowred and fayled as kynde hyt gef. — *nature; allowed*
Now thurgh kynde of the kyste that hyt con close
To a perle of prys hit is put in pref.
And thou has called thy wyrde a thef,
That oght of noght has mad the cler.
Thou blames the bote of thy meschef; — *remedy for; misfortune*
Thou art no kynde jueler.' — *courteous*

A juel to me then was thys geste, — *newcomer*
And jueles wern hyr gentyl sawes. — *noble; words*
'Iwyse,' quod I, 'my blysfol beste,
My grete dystresse thou al todrawes. — *dispel*
To be excused I make requeste;
I trawed my perle don out of dawes.
Now haf I fonde hyt, I schal ma feste, — *rejoice*
And wony wyth hyt in schyr wod-schawes, — *live; bright groves*
And love my Lorde and al his lawes — *praise*
That has me broght thys blys ner.
Now were I at yow byyonde thise wawes, — *beside you; waves*
I were a joyful jueler.'

'Jueler,' sayde that gemme clene, — *bright*
'Wy borde ye men? So madde ye be! — *jest*
Thre wordes has thou spoken at ene: — *statements; at one time*
Unavysed, for sothe, wern alle thre. — *ill-considered*
Thou ne woste in worlde quat on dos mene;
Thy worde byfore thy wytte con fle.

267–8 I think you have made a mad resolve, and are troubling yourself for a short-lived reason.
271–4 Now through the nature of the chest that encloses it, it has proved to be a pearl of great price. And you have called your fate a thief, which has manifestly made something out of nothing for you .
279 'Indeed,' I said, 'my lovely and dearest one.'
282 I thought my pearl dead (lit. put out of days).
293–4 You haven't the least idea in the world what a single one of them means; your words run ahead of your understanding.

Thou says thou trawes me in this dene, *believe; valley*
Bycawse thou may wyth yyen me se; *eyes*
Another thou says, in thys countré *a second thing*
Thyself schal won wyth me ryght here; *dwell*
The thrydde, to passe thys water fre— *stream; noble*
That may no joyfol jueler.

VI

'I halde that jueler lyttel to prayse *consider; be praised*
That leves wel that he ses wyth yye, *believes*
And much to blame and uncortayse *discourteous*
That leves oure Lorde wolde make a lyye, *lie*
That lelly hyghte your lyf to rayse,
Thagh fortune dyd your flesch to dyye. *caused; die*
Ye setten hys wordes ful westernays
That leves nothynk bot ye hit syye.
And that is a poynt o sorquydryye,
That uche god mon may evel byseme,
To leve no tale be true to tryye
Bot that hys one skyl may dem.

'Deme now thyself if thou con dayly
As man to God wordes schulde heve.
Thou says thou schal won in this bayly; *dwell; domain*
Me thynk the burde fyrst aske leve, *you ought to*
And yet of graunt thou myghtes fayle.
Thou wylnes over thys water to weve; *wish; pass*
Er moste thou cever to other counsayl:
Thy corse in clot mot calder keve.

305 Who faithfully promised to raise you from death to life.
307–12 You twist his words awry who believe nothing unless you see it. And it is an instance of pride, which ill becomes any good man, to believe no statement is true when put to the test unless it be one that his reason alone can judge.
313–14 Consider now whether your idle talk is the way a man should address words to God.
317 And yet you might fail to get permission.
319–20 First you must follow another course of action: your body must sink down cold into the ground.

For hit was forgarte at Paradys greve; *corrupted; garden*
Oure yorefader hit con mysseyeme. *forefather; abused*
Thurgh drwry deth bos uch man dreve,
Er over thys dam hym Dryghtyn deme.'

'Demes thou me,' quod I, 'my swete, *condemn*
To dol agayn, thenne I dowyne. *grief; pine away*
Now haf I fonte that I forlete, *found; lost*
Schal I efte forgo hit er ever I fyne? *again; end (my life)*
Why schal I hit bothe mysse and mete?
My precios perle dos me gret pyne. *pain*
What serves tresor bot gares men grete,
When he hit schal efte wyth tenes tyne?
Now rech I never for to declyne,
Ne how fer of folde that man me fleme.
When I am partles of perle myne, *deprived*
Bot durande doel what may men deme?'

'Thow demes noght bot doel-dystresse,'
Thenne sayde that wyght. 'Why dos thou so? *person*
For dyne of doel of lures lesse
Ofte mony mon forgos the mo.
The oghte better thyselven blesse, *you ought rather*
And love ay God, in wele and wo,
For anger gaynes the not a cresse.
Who nedes schal thole be not so thro.

323–4 Every man must pass through cruel death before the Lord will allow him across this stream.

329 Why must I both find and lose it?

331–4 What is the use of treasure but to make a man weep, if afterwards (i.e. after enjoying possession of it) he must know the bitterness of losing it? Now I don't care how low I fall, nor how far I am banished from the land.

336 What can that be called but lasting grief?

337 You speak of nothing but pain and sorrow.

339–40 Because of noisy lamentation over lesser sorrows many a man often loses sight of the greater.

342–4 And always praise God, come weal or woe, for sorrow is not worth a straw (lit. cress) to you. Anyone who has to suffer should not be so impatient.

For thogh thou daunce as any do, *leap; doe*
Braundysch and bray thy brathes breme,
When thou no fyrre may, to ne fro,
Thou moste abyde that he schal deme.

'Deme Dryghtyn, ever hym adyte,
Of the way a fote ne wyl he wrythe.
Thy mendes mountes not a myte,
Thagh thou for sorwe be never blythe.
Stynt of thy strot and fyne to flyte,
And sech hys blythe ful swefte and swythe. *mercy; swiftly*
Thy prayer may hys pyté byte, *move*
That mercy schal hyr craftes kythe.
Hys comforte may thy langour lythe *suffering; assuage*
And thy lures of lyghtly fleme;
For, marre other madde, morne and mythe,
Al lys in hym to dyght and deme.'

VII

Thenne demed I to that damyselle: *said; damsel*
'Ne worthe no wraththe unto my Lorde,
If rapely I rave, spornande in spelle;
My herte was al wyth mysse remorde,
As wallande water gos out of welle.
I do me ay in hys myserecorde. *put; mercy*
Rebuke me never wyth wordes felle, *cruel*
Thagh I forloyne, my dere endorde, *err; adored (one)*

346–8 Struggle and bray aloud your fierce agony, when you can go no further, backwards or forwards, you must endure what He decrees.

349–54 Judge the Lord, always arraign Him, and He will not turn aside one step (to help you). Your recompense won't be increased a jot, even though your sorrow prevents you from ever being happy. Stop your wrangling, have done with your chiding, and swiftly seek His mercy.

356 So that mercy shall show her power.

358–60 And quickly drive away your sorrows. For, whether you lament and rage, or mourn and conceal your feelings, everything lies with Him to ordain and decree.

362–5 Let it not offend my Lord, if I rashly rave and stumble into speech. My heart was stricken by my loss, like water welling from a spring. (Cf. Ps. xxii. 14.)

Bot kythes me kyndely your coumforde,
Pytosly thenkande upon thysse:
Of care and me ye made acorde,
That er was grounde of alle my blysse.

'My blysse, my bale, ye han ben bothe, *sorrow*
Bot much the bygger yet was my mon; *grief*
Fro thou was wroken fro uch a wothe,
I wyste never quere my perle was gon. *knew*
Now I hit se, now lethes my lothe.
And, quen we departed, we wern at on;
God forbede we be now wrothe, *angry*
We meten so selden by stok other ston.
Thagh cortaysly ye carp con, *speak*
I am bot mol and maneres mysse;
Bot Crystes mersy and Mary and Jon,
Thise arn the grounde of alle my blisse.

'In blysse I se the blythely blent, *joyously; placed*
And I a man al mornyf mate;
Ye take theron ful lyttel tente,
Thagh I hente ofte harmes hate.
Bot now I am here in your presente, *presence*
I wolde bysech, wythouten debate, *argument*
Ye wolde me say in sobre asente
What lyf ye lede erly and late.
For I am ful fayn that your astate *glad; condition*
Is worthen to worschyp and wele iwysse;
Of alle my joy the hyghe gate *highway*
Hit is, and grounde of alle my blysse.'

369 But kindly show me your comfort.
371–2 Of sorrow and me you made companions, you who were once the ground of all my joy.
375 Since you were removed from every peril.
377–8 Now I see it, my grief is softened. When we were parted, we were living in harmony.
380 We meet so seldom anywhere (lit. by tree-trunk or stone).
382–3 I am but dust, and lacking in manners; but the mercy of Christ and Mary and John.
386–8 And I am a man all mournful and dejected. You take very little notice of it, though I often suffer burning sorrow.
394 Has become one of honour and prosperity indeed.

'Now blysse, burne, mot the bytyde,'
Then sayde that lufsoum of lyth and lere,
'And welcum here to walk and byde, *stay*
For now thy speche is to me dere.
Maysterful mod and hyghe pryde, *arrogant; mood*
I hete the, arn heterly hated here. *promise; bitterly*
My Lorde ne loves not for to chyde,
For meke arn alle that wones hym nere; *humble; dwell*
And when in hys place thou schal apere,
Be dep devote in hol mekenesse.
My Lorde the Lamb loves ay such chere, *demeanour*
That is the grounde of alle my blysse. *Who*

'A blysful lyf thou says I lede;
Thou woldes knaw therof the stage. *degree of advancement*
Thow wost wel when thy perle con schede *fell*
I was ful yong and tender of age;
Bot my Lorde the Lombe, thurgh hys godhede,
He toke myȝelf to hys maryage,
Corounde me quene in blysse to brede
In lenghe of dayes that ever schal wage;
And sesed in alle hys herytage
Hys lef is. I am holy hysse:
Hys prese, hys prys, and hys parage
Is rote and grounde of alle my blysse.'

VIII

'Blysful,' quod I, 'may thys be trwe?
Dyspleses not if I speke errour. *do not be displeased*
Art thou the quene of hevenes blwe,
That al thys worlde schal do honour?
We leven on Marye that grace of grewe,
That ber a barne of vyrgyn flour;

397–8 'Now happiness, sir, be yours,' then said that one (so) lovely of limb and face.
406 Be deeply devout in all humility.
414–20 He took me to be His bride, crowned me queen to flourish in bliss for a length of days that shall ever endure; and His beloved is made possessor of all His inheritance. I am wholly His: His worth, His excellence and His noble lineage are the root and ground of all my bliss.
425–6 We believe in Mary from whom grace came, who bore a child in perfect maidenhood.

The croune fro hyr quo moght remwe *take away*
Bot ho hir passed in sum favour?
Now, for synglerty o hyr dousour,
We calle hyr Fenyx of Arraby, *Phoenix*
That freles flewe of hyr fasor,
Lyk to the Quen of cortaysye.' *grace*

'Cortayse Quen,' thenne sayde that gaye, *fair one*
Knelande to grounde, folde up hyr face,
'Makeles Moder and myryest May,
Blessed bygynner of uch a grace!'
Thenne ros ho up and con restay, *paused*
And speke me towarde in that space: *spoke to me then*
'Sir, fele here porchases and fonges pray,
Bot supplantores none wythinne thys place. *usurpers*
That emperise al hevens has,
And urthe and helle in her bayly; *earth; dominion*
Of erytage yet non wyl ho chace,
For ho is Quen of cortaysye.

'The court of the kyndom of God alyve *living*
Has a property in hytself beyng:
Alle that may therinne aryve
Of alle the reme is quen other kyng, *realm: or*
And never other yet schal depryve;
Bot uchon fayn of otheres hafyng,
And wolde her corounes wern worthe tho fyve,
If possyble were her mendyng.
Bot my Lady of quom Jesu con spryng, *was born*
Ho haldes the empyre over uus ful hyghe; *absolute sway*
And that dyspleses non of oure gyng, *company*
For ho is Quene of cortaysye.

428–9 Unless she excelled her in some grace? Now because of her unique sweetness.
431 Which flawless flew from its Creator.
434–6 Kneeling on the ground, her face upturned, 'Peerless Mother and fairest Maiden, blessed source of every grace!'
439 Sir, many here strive for and win a prize.
441 That empress has all heaven.
443 Yet she will oust none from his heritage.
446 Has a special virtue inherent in itself.
449–52 And yet never shall they deprive one another; but each is made happy by what others possess, and would wish their crowns to be five times as precious, if it were possible to improve on them.

'Of courtaysye, as says Saynt Poule, *by grace*
Al arn we membres of Jesu Kryst;
As heved and arme and legg and naule *head; navel*
Temen to hys body ful trwe and tryste,
Ryght so is uch a Krysten sawle *every; soul*
A longande lym to the Mayster of myste.
Thenne loke what hate other any gawle
Is tached other tyyed thy lymmes bytwyste:
Thy heved has nauther greme ne gryste,
On arme other fynger thagh thou ber byghe.
So fare we alle wyth luf and lyste
To kyng and quene by cortaysye.' *towards*

'Cortaysé,' quod I, 'I leve, *believe*
And charyté grete, be yow among.
Bot my speche that yow ne greve,
. . . . .

Thyself in heven over hygh thou heve,
To make the quen that was so yonge.
What more honour moghte he acheve
That hade endured in worlde stronge,
And lyved in penaunce hys lyves longe, *all life long*
Wyth bodyly bale hym blysse to byye?
What more worschyp moght he fonge
Then corounde be kyng by cortaysé?

IX

'That cortaysé is to fre of dede,
Yyf hyt be soth that thou cones saye. *true; you say*

460 Are joined loyally and faithfully to the body.
462–7 A limb belonging to the Master of spiritual union. Next consider what hatred or rancour exists (lit. is attached or fastened) between your limbs: your head feels no anger or resentment because you wear a ring on your arm or finger. In the same way we all behave with love and joy.
471 But don't let my words offend you.
473–4 You exalt yourself too high in heaven by making yourself a queen, you who were so young.
476 Who had continued steadfast in the world.
478–80 So as to buy himself bliss at the price of bodily torment? What greater honour could he receive than to be crowned king by grace?
481 That grace is too lavish in performance

Thou lyfed not two yer in oure thede; *land*
Thou cowthes never God nauther plese ne pray, *could*
Ne never nawther Pater ne Crede—
And quen mad on the fyrst day!
I may not traw, so God me spede,
That God wolde wrythe so wrange away.
Of countes, damysel, par ma fay,
Wer fayr in heven to halde asstate,
Other elles a lady of lasse aray.
Bot a quene!—hit is to dere a date.'

'Ther is no date of hys godnesse,' *limit to*
Then sayde to me that worthy wyghte, *noble; maiden*
'For al is trawthe that he con dresse, *ordains*
And he may do nothynk bot ryght.
As Mathew meles in your messe,
In sothfol gospel of God almyght,
In sample he can ful graythely gesse,
And lyknes hit to heven lyghte:
"My regne," he says, "is lyk on hyght
To a lorde that hade a vyne, I wate.
Of tyme of yere the terme was tyght,
To labor vyne was dere the date.

"That date of yere wel knawe thys hyne.
The lorde ful erly up he ros
To hyre werkmen to hys vyne, *for*
And fyndes ther summe to hys porpos. *purpose*
Into acorde thay con declyne
For a pené on a day, and forth thay gos, *penny; go*

485 Nor (did you ever know) either the Paternoster or Creed.

487–92 I cannot believe, so help me God, that He would turn aside so unjustly (from the true course). Upon my word, young lady, it would be fine in heaven to hold the position of countess, or else of a lady of lesser rank. But a queen!—that is too noble a goal.

496–504 And He can do nothing but what is right. As St Matthew tells you in your mass, in the true gospel of Almighty God, He aptly conceives it in the form of a parable and likens it to bright heaven: 'My kingdom on high,' He says, 'is like a lord who had a vineyard. The right time of the year had come, and the season was good for cultivating the vine.'

505 The workmen knew very well what season of the year it was.

509 They come to an agreement.

Wrythen and worchen and don gret pyne,
Kerven and caggen and man hit clos.
Aboute under the lorde to marked tos,
And ydel men stande he fyndes therate.
'Why stande ye ydel?' he sayde to thos;
'Ne knawe ye of this day no date?'

"'Er date of daye hider arn we wonne;'
So was al samen her answar soght.
'We haf standen her syn ros the sunne, *stood; since*
And no mon byddes uus do ryght noght.'
'Gos into my vyne, dos that ye conne,' *go; do what*
So sayde the lorde, and made hit toght. *made a firm agreement*
'What resonabele hyre be naght be runne
I yow pay in dede and thoghte.'
Thay wente into the vyne and wroghte, *worked*
And al day the lorde thus yede his gate, *went his way*
And nw men to hys vyne he broghte
Welnegh wyl day was passed date.

"At the date of day of evensonge, *hour*
On oure byfore the sonne go doun, *one hour*
He sey ther ydel men ful stronge *saw*
And sade to hem wyth sobre soun, *said; a serious voice*
'Wy stonde ye ydel thise dayes longe?' *all day long*
Thay sayden her hyre was nawhere boun.
'Gos to my vyne, yemen yonge, *yeomen*
And wyrkes and dos that at ye moun.' *do what you can*

511–13 To work and toil and take great pains, to prune and bind and make all secure. About the third hour (i.e. 9 a.m.) the lord goes to the market-place.

516 Do you think the day will never end?

517–18 'We came here before the beginning of the day.' This was the answer they all gave.

520 And no one asks us to do anything at all.

523–4 Whatever reasonable wages have mounted up by night time I will pay you in full (lit. in deed and thought).

528 Until the end of the day was nearly past.

534 They said they could find no employment anywhere.

Sone the worlde bycom wel broun; *very dark*
The sunne was doun and hit wex late. *grew*
To take her hyre he mad sumoun;
The day was al apassed date.

X

"The date of the daye the lorde con knaw, *knew*
Called to the reve: 'Lede, pay the meyny.
Gyf hem the hyre that I hem owe, *wages*
And fyrre, that non me may reprené, *further; reprove*
Set hem alle upon a rawe *in a row*
And gyf uchon inlyche a peny. *alike*
Bygyn at the laste that standes lowe, *at the bottom*
Tyl to the fyrste that thou atteny.' *reach*
And thenne the fyrst bygonne to pleny *complain*
And sayden that thay hade travayled sore: *toiled hard*
'These bot on oure hem con streny;
Uus thynk uus oghe to take more.

"'More haf we served, uus thynk so, *deserved*
That suffred han the dayes hete,
Thenn thyse that wroght not houres two,
And thou dos hem uus to counterfete.'
Thenne sayde the lorde to on of tho: *one of them*
'Frende, no waning I wyl the yete;
Take that is thyn owne, and go.
And I hyred the for a peny agrete,
Quy bygynnes thou now to threte? *complain*
Was not a pené thy covenaunt thore? *then*
Fyrre then covenaunde is noght to plete.
Wy schalte thou thenne ask more?

539–40 He had them summoned to receive their wages; the end of the day was past.
542 Called to his steward: 'My good man, pay the labourers.'
551–2 These others have exerted themselves for just one hour; we think we ought to receive more.
556 And (yet) you make them equal to us.
558 Friend, I don't want to make any reduction (of what is due to you).
560 Seeing that I hired you all for a penny.
563 You have no right to claim anything over and above the covenant.

"'More, wether louyly is me my gyfte,
To do wyth myn quat-so me lykes?
Other elles thyn yye to lyther is lyfte
For I am goude and non byswykes?'
"Thus schal I," quod Kryste, "hit skyfte: *arrange*
The laste schal be the fyrst that strykes, *who comes*
And the fyrst the laste, be he never so swyft;
For mony ben called, thagh fewe be mykes."
Thus pore men her part ay pykes, *share; get*
Thagh thay com late and lyttel wore; *unimportant*
And thagh her sweng wyth lyttel atslykes,
The merci of God is much the more.

'More haf I of joye and blysse hereinne,
Of ladyschyp gret and lyves blom,
Then alle the wyyes in the worlde myght wynne *people*
By the way of ryght to aske dome.
Whether welnygh now I con bygynne—
In eventyde into the vyne I come—
Fyrst of my hyre my Lorde con mynne:
I was payed anon of al and sum.
Yet other ther werne that toke more tom,
That swange and swat for long yore,
That yet of hyre nothynk thay nom,
Paraunter noght schal to-yere more.'

Then more I meled and sayde apert: *spoke; plainly*
'Me thynk thy tale unresounable. *words*
Goddes ryght is redy and evermore rert, *justice; supreme*
Other Holy Wryt is bot a fable. *or*

565–8 Moreover, is it not lawful for me to give away or do what else I like with my own property? Or is your eye turned to evil because I am good and cheat no one?
572 *mykes*, friends (of the Lord).
575 And though their efforts are spent with little result.
578 Of queenly rank and perfection of life.
580–8 If they ask for an award to be made according to strict justice. And though I began only a short time ago—it was evening when I came into the vineyard—my Lord remembered my wages first: I was immediately paid in full. Yet there were others who had spent more time (than I had), who had toiled and sweated for long enough, and yet they received none of their wages, and perhaps will not for years to come.

In Sauter is sayd a verce overte *Psalter; plain to see*
That spekes a poynt determynable:
"Thou quytes uchon as hys desserte,
Thou hyghe kyng ay pretermynable."
Now he that stod the long day stable,
And thou to payment com hym byfore,
Thenne the lasse in werke to take more able,
And ever the lenger the lasse, the more.'

XI

'Of more and lasse in Godes ryche,'
That gentyl sayde, 'lys no joparde, *there is no question*
For ther is uch mon payed inlyche, *alike*
Whether lyttel other much be hys rewarde.
For the gentyl Cheventayn is no chyche,
Quether-so-ever he dele nesch other harde:
He laves hys gyftes as water of dyche,
Other gotes of golf that never charde.
Hys fraunchyse is large that ever dard
To Hym that mas in synne rescoghe.
No blysse bes fro hem reparde,
For the grace of God is gret inoghe.

'Bot now thou motes, me for to mate,
That I my peny haf wrang tan here;
Thou says that I that come to late
Am not worthy so gret fere. *high rank*

594–600 Which makes a definite statement on this point: 'You reward everyone according to his deserts, you high King ever pre-ordaining.' Now if you came for payment before him who stood steadfast all day long, then (it would follow that) the less work you did the more you would be able to earn; and so it would go on—the less work, the more pay.

605–11 For the noble Chieftain is no niggard, whether He metes out a pleasant or a hard fate. He pours out His gifts like water from a dike, or streams from a chasm that never stop flowing. His generosity is abundant to those who have always stood in fear of Him who rescues sinners. No happiness is withheld from them.

613–14 But now you are arguing, in order to shame me, that I have received my penny unjustly.

Where wystes thou ever any bourne abate
Ever so holy in hys prayere
That he ne forfeted by sumkyn gate
The mede sumtyme of hevenes clere?
And ay the ofter, the alder thay were,
Thay laften ryght and wroghten woghe.
Mercy and grace moste hem then stere, *guide*
For the grace of God is gret innoghe.

'Bot innoghe of grace has innocent.
As sone as thay arn borne, by lyne *in regular order*
In the water of babtem thay dyssente: *baptism; descend*
Then arne thay boroght into the vyne.
Anon the day, wyth derk endente,
The niyght of deth dos to enclyne.
That wroght never wrang er thenne thay wente,
The gentyle Lorde thenne payes hys hyne.
Thay dyden hys heste; thay wern thereine.
Why schulde he not her labour alow, *give credit for*
Yys, and pay hem at the fyrst fyne?
For the grace of God is gret innoghe.

'Inoghe is knawen that mankyn grete
Fyrste was wroght to blysse parfyt;
Oure forme fader hit con forfete *first father; forfeited*
Thurgh an apple that he upon con byte.
Al wer we dampned for that mete *food*
To dyye in doel, out of delyt,
And sythen wende to helle hete, *hell's heat*
Therinne to won wythoute respyt. *dwell*

617–22 Where did you ever hear of any man who always lived such a holy and prayerful life that he never once forfeited in some way or other the reward of bright heaven? And the older they are, the more often they forsake the right and do the wrong.
625 But an innocent person has grace enough.
628 Then they are brought into the vineyard (i.e. the Church).
629–33 Quickly the day, inlaid with darkness, sinks towards the night of death. Those who never did evil before they departed, the noble Lord then pays as His workmen. They kept His commandment; they were in it (i.e. His vineyard).
635 Yes, and pay them first in full?
637–8 It is well known that noble mankind was first created for perfect bliss.
642 To die in grief, deprived of joy.

Bot theron com a bote astyt:
Ryche blod ran on rode so roghe, *cross; cruel*
And wynne water then at that plyt;
The grace of God wex gret innoghe. *grew*

'Innoghe ther wax out of that welle, *flowed*
Blod and water of brode wounde: *from; broad*
The blod uus boght fro bale of helle *redeemed; torment*
And delyvered uus of the deth secounde;
The water is baptem, the sothe to telle, *truth*
That folwed the glayve so grymly grounde,
That wasches away the gyltes felle *sins; deadly*
That Adam wyth inne deth uus drounde.
Now is ther noght in the worlde rounde *nothing*
Bytwene uus and blysse bot that he wythdrow,
And that is restored in sely stounde;
And the grace of God is gret innogh.

XII

'Grace innogh the mon may have
That synnes thenne new, yif him repente, *anew; if he repent*
Bot wyth sorw and syt he mot hit crave, *sorrow; grief*
And byde the payne therto is bent.
Bot resoun, of ryght that con noght rave,
Saves evermore the innossent;
Hit is a dom that never God gave, *judgment*
That ever the gyltles schulde be schente. *destroyed*

645 But after that quickly came a remedy.

647 And then precious water in that time of peril.

654 That followed the spear so cruelly sharpened.

656 With which Adam drowned us in death.

658–9 Between us and bliss that He has not withdrawn, and that (bliss) is restored in a blessed hour.

664–6 And endure the penalty attached to it (i.e. do satisfaction for his sins). But reason, which cannot swerve from what is just, will always save the innocent.

The gyltyf may contryssyoun hente
And be thurgh mercy to grace thryght; *brought*
Bot he to gyle that never glente,
As inoscente, is saf and ryghte.

'Ryght thus I knaw wel in this cas *even so*
Two men to save is god by skylle:
The ryghtwys man schal se hys face,
The harmles hathel schal com hym tylle. *innocent man; to*
The Sauter hyt sas thus in a pace:
"Lorde, quo schal klymbe thy hygh hylle,
Other rest wythinne thy holy place?"
Hymself to onsware he is not dylle:
"Hondelynges harme that dyt not ille,
That is of hert bothe clene and lyght,
Ther schal hys step stable stylle."
The innosent is ay saf by ryght.

'The ryghtwys man also sertayn *certainly*
Aproche he schal that proper pyle,
That takes not her lyf in vayne,
Ne glaveres her nieghbor wyth no gyle. *deceives*
Of thys ryghtwys sas Salamon playn
How Koyntise onoure con aquyle;
By wayes ful streght ho con hym strayn,
And scheued hym the rengne of God awhyle,
As quo says: "Lo, yon lovely yle! *(one) who; domain*
Thou may hit wynne if thou be wyghte." *valiant*
Bot, hardyly, wythoute peryle, *assuredly*
The innosent is ay save by ryghte.

669 The guilty can find contrition.
671–2 But he who has never deviated into guile is, as an innocent, redeemed and justified (by grace).
674 It is good and reasonable to believe that two kinds of men shall be saved.
677 The Psalter expresses it thus in a certain passage.
680–4 He is not slow to give the answer Himself: 'He who has not wrongfully done evil with his hands, and who is both clean and pure in heart, there shall his footstep stand firm for ever.' The innocent person is always redeemed by justifying grace.
686–7 Shall come to that fair castle, who does not spend his life here foolishly.
689–92 Concerning this righteous man Solomon says plainly how Wisdom obtained honour for him; she guided him in right paths, and showed him awhile the kingdom of God.

'Anende ryghtwys men yet says a gome,
David in Sauter, if ever ye sey hit:
"Lorde, thy servaunt draw never to dome, *bring; judgment*
For non lyvyande to the is justyfyet."
Forthy to corte quen thou schal com, *and so*
Ther alle oure causes schal be tryed, *where; cases*
Alegge the ryght, thou may be innome
By thys ilke spech I have asspyed.
Bot he on rode that blody dyed, *bloodily*
Delfully thurgh hondes thryght, *grievously; pierced*
Gyve the to passe, when thou arte tryed,
By innocens and not by ryghte.

'Ryghtwysly quo con rede,
He loke on bok and be awayed
How Jesus hym welke in arethede,
And burnes her barnes unto hym brayde.
For happe and hele that fro hym yede
To touch her chylder thay fayr hym prayed.
His dessypeles wyth blame let be hem bede,
And wyth her resounes ful fele restayed.
Jesus thenne hem swetely sayde:
"Do way, let chylder unto me tyght; *come*
To suche is hevenryche arayed."
The innocent is ay saf by ryght.

XIII

'Jesus con calle to hym hys mylde, *gentle (disciples)*
And sayde hys ryche no wyy myght wynne *kingdom; man*

697-700 Furthermore, concerning righteous men, a certain person, David in the Psalter, says, if ever you should see it: 'Lord, never bring thy servant to judgment, for no living man is justified before thee.'

703-4 If you plead salvation as a right, you may be refuted by the very words I have pointed out.

707 May allow you to go free, when you are brought to trial.

709-16 He who can read aright, let him look at the Bible and be taught how Jesus walked among the people of olden times, and how parents brought their children to Him. Because of the happiness and health that came from Him they asked Him courteously to touch their children. His disciples, with rebukes, commanded them to stop, and deterred many of them by what they said.

719 For such is prepared the kingdom of Heaven.

Bot he com thyder ryght as a chylde,
Other elles nevermore com therinne.
Harmles, trwe, and undefylde, *innocent; faithful*
Wythouten mote other mascle of sulpande synne—
Quen such ther cnoken on the bylde, *knock; dwelling*
Tyt schal hem men the yate unpynne. *quickly; unfasten*
Ther is the blys that con not blynne *cease*
That the jueler soghte thurgh perré pres,
And solde alle hys goud, bothe wolen and lynne,
To bye hym a perle was mascelles. *spotless*

'This makelles perle, that boght is dere, *matchless*
The joueler gef fore alle hys god,
Is lyke the reme of hevenesse clere: *kingdom; heaven*
So sayde the Fader of folde and flode; *land; sea*
For hit is wemles, clene, and clere, *spotless; pure*
And endeles rounde, and blythe of mode,
And commune to alle that ryghtwys were. *belonging equally*
Lo, even inmyddes my breste hit stode. *exactly in the middle*
My Lorde the Lombe, that schede hys blode,
He pyght hit there in token of pes. *set; peace*
I rede the forsake the worlde wode *advise; mad*
And porchace thy perle maskelles.' *acquire*

'O maskeles perle in perles pure,
That beres,' quod I, 'the perle of prys, *wear*
Quo formed the thy fayre fygure? *for you*
That wroght thy wede, he was ful wys. *raiment*
Thy beauté com never of nature; *by*
Pymalyon paynted never thy vys, *Pygmalion; face*
Ne Arystotel nawther by hys lettrure
Of carped the kynde these propertés.

726 Without spot or stain of polluting sin.
730–1 That the jeweller sought with precious jewels, and sold all his goods, both linen and wool.
734 The jeweller gave all his goods in exchange for it.
738 And perfectly round, and serene in character.
751–2 Nor did Aristotle, for all his learning, speak of the nature of these attributes.

Thy colour passes the flour-de-lys, *surpasses*
Thyn angel-havyng so clene cortes.
Breve me, bryght, quat kyn offys
Beres the perle so maskelles?'

'My makeles Lambe that al may bete,' *peerless; amend*
Quod scho, 'my dere destyné,
Me ches to hys make, althagh unmete
Sumtyme semed that assemblé.
When I wente fro yor worlde wete, *dank*
He calde me to hys bonerté: *beatitude*
"Cum hyder to me, my lemman swete, *beloved one*
For mote ne spot is non in the." *stain*
He gef me myght and als bewté; *also*
In hys blod he wesch my wede on dese,
And coronde clene in vergynté, *crowned; pure*
And pyght me in perles maskelles.' *adorned*

'Why, maskelles bryd, that bryght con flambe,
That reiates has so ryche and ryf,
Quat kyn thyng may be that Lambe *kind of*
That the wolde wedde unto hys vyf? *as His wife*
Over alle other so hygh thou clambe *have climbed*
To lede wyth hym so ladyly lyf. *so ladylike a*
So mony a comly onunder cambe
For Kryst han lyved in much stryf;
And thou con alle tho dere out dryf
And fro that maryag al other depres,
Al only thyself so stout and styf,
A makeles may and maskelles.'

754–5 Your angelic demeanour so wholly gracious. Tell me, fair maid, what kind of office.

759–60 Chose me as His bride, although that union would once have seemed unfitting (i.e. while she was still alive).

766 In His blood He washed my raiment on the (heavenly) dais.

769–70 Why, spotless bride, who shine so brightly, and have royal dignities so noble and abundant.

775 So many fair ladies (lit. many a fair one under comb).

777–80 And you have driven away all those worthy ladies and vanquished all other pretenders to that marriage, yourself alone so valiant and strong, a peerless and spotless maiden.

XIV

'Maskelles,' quod that myry quene, *lovely*
'Unblemyst I am, wythouten blot, *stain*
And that may I wyth mensk menteene; *honour*
Bot "makeles quene" thenne sade I not. *said*
The Lambes vyves in blysse we bene, *wives*
A hondred and forty fowre thowsande flot, *company*
As in the Apocalyppes hit is sene:
Sant John hem syy al in a knot
On the hyl of Syon, that semly clot; *fair; hill*
The apostel hem segh in gostly drem *saw; spiritual*
Arayed to the weddyng in that hyl-coppe,
The nwe cyté o Jerusalem. *of*

'Of Jerusalem I in speche spelle. *tell*
If thou wyl knaw what kyn he be, *kind*
My Lombe, my Lorde, my dere juelle,
My joy, my blys, my lemman fre, *beloved one; noble*
The profete Ysaye of hym con melle *spoke*
Pitously of hys debonerté: *compassionately; gentleness*
"That gloryous gyltles that mon con quelle *innocent (one); killed*
Wythouten any sake of felonye,
As a schep to the slaght ther lad was he; *slaughter*
And, as lombe that clypper in hande nem, *shearer; took hold of*
So closed he hys mouth fro uch query, *against; complaint*
Quen Jues hym jugged in Jerusalem."

'In Jerusalem was my lemman slayn
And rent on rode wyth boyes bolde. *cross; ruffians*
Al oure bales to bere ful bayn, *sorrows; willing*
He toke on hymself oure cares colde. *grievous*
Wyth boffetes was hys face flayn *buffets; torn*
That was so fayr on to byholde.

788 Saint John saw the whole throng of them (Rev. xiv. 1)
791 Arrayed for the wedding on that hill top.
797 *Ysaye*, Isa. liii. 7.
800 Without any criminal charge proved against Him.

For synne he set hymself in vayn,
That never hade non hymself to wolde.
For uus he lette hym flyye and folde
And brede upon a bostwys bem;
As meke as lomp that no playnt tolde, *lamb*
For uus he swalt in Jerusalem. *died*

'In Jerusalem, Jordan, and Galalye,
Ther as baptysed the goude Saynt Jon,
His wordes acorded to Ysaye. *agreed with*
When Jesus con to hym warde gon, *went to him*
He sayde of hym thys professye: *prophecy*
"Lo, Godes Lombe as trwe as ston, *steadfast*
That dos away the synnes dryye *heavy*
That alle thys worlde has wroght upon.
Hymself ne wroght never yet non;
Whether on hymself he con al clem.
Hys generacyoun quo recen con, *declare*
That dyyed for uus in Jerusalem?"

'In Jerusalem thus my lemman swete
Twyes for lombe was taken thare,
By trw recorde of ayther prophete,
For mode so meke and al hys fare.
The thryde tyme is therto ful mete,
In Apokalypes wryten ful yare:
Inmydes the trone, there saayntes sete, *in the midst of; sat*
The apostel John hym saw as bare, *quite clearly*
Lesande the boke with leves sware *opening; square*
There seven syngnettes wern sette in seme;
And at that syght uche douth con dare *all men; cowered*
In helle, in erthe, and Jerusalem.

811–14 For our sin He sacrificed Himself, He who had never committed any sin Himself. For us He let Himself be scourged and bent and stretched upon a cumbrous cross.
824 That all mankind have helped to commit.
826 And yet He took them all upon Himself.
830–4 Was twice there taken as a lamb, by the true testimony of each Prophet (i.e. Isaiah and John the Baptist), because of His gentle disposition and demeanour. The third occasion, clearly described in the Apocalypse, is also pertinent (Rev. v. 6).
838 To the border of which seven seals were attached.

XV

'Thys Jerusalem Lombe hade never pechche
Of other huee bot quyt jolyf,
That mot ne masklle moght on streche,
For wolle quyte so ronk and ryf.
Forthy uche saule that hade never teche	*and so; stain*
Is to that Lombe a worthyly wyf;	*honoured*
And thagh uch day a store he feche,	*large number; bring*
Among uus commes nouther strot ne stryf,	*dispute*
Bot uchon enlé we wolde were fyf—
The mo the myryer, so God me blesse.
In compayny gret our luf con thryf	*thrives*
In honour more and never the lesse.

'Lasse of blysse may non uus bryng
That beren thys perle upon oure bereste,	*breast*
For thay of mote couthe never mynge	*quarrelling; think*
Of spotles perles that beren the creste.	*crown*
Althagh oure corses in clottes clynge,
And ye remen for rauthe wythouten reste,
We thurghoutly haven cnawyng;
Of on dethe ful oure hope is drest.
The Lombe uus glades, oure care is kest;	*gladdens; removed*
He myrthes uus alle at uch a mes.
Uchones blysse is breme and beste,	*glorious*
And never ones honour yet never the les.

'Lest les thou leve my tale farande,
In Appocalyppece is wryten in wro:	*corner*
"I seghe," says John, "the Loumbe hym stande	*saw*
On the mount of Syon ful thryven and thro,	*fair; noble*

841–4 This Lamb of Jerusalem never had a speck of any colour but brilliant white, on which neither spot nor stain could spread because the white fleece was so thick and abundant.
849 But we wish that every single one were five.
857–60 Although our bodies shrivel in the earth, and you cry out incessantly with grief, we have perfect understanding; from a single death our hope is fully drawn.
862 He delights us all at every mass.
864 And yet no one's honour is any the less.
865 Lest you believe my goodly words less (than you should).

And wyth hym maydennes an hundrethe thowsande,
And fowre and forty thowsande mo. *more*
On alle her forhedes wryten I fande *found*
The Lombes nome, hys Faderes also. *name*
A hue from heven I herde thoo, *shout; then*
Lyk flodes fele laden runnen on resse,
And as thunder throwes in torres blo—
That lote, I leve, was never the les.

"'Nautheles, thagh hit schowted scharpe, *sharply*
And ledden loude althagh hit were, *voice*
A note ful nwe I herde hem warpe, *song; sing*
To lysten that was ful lufly dere.
As harpores harpen in her harpe,
That nwe songe thay songen ful cler *clearly*
In sounande notes a gentyl carpe;
Ful fayre the modes thay fonge in fere.
Ryght byfore Godes chayere, *throne*
And the fowre bestes that hym obes, *do obeisance to*
And the aldermen so sadde of chere,
Her songe thay songen never the les. *sang*

"'Nowthelese non was never so quoynt,
For alle the craftes that ever thay knewe,
That of that songe myght synge a poynt,
Bot that meyny the Lombe that swe;
For thay arn boght fro the urthe aloynte
As newe fryt to God ful due, *first fruits*
And to the gentyl Lombe hit arn anjoynt, *they are; joined*
As lyk to hymself of lote and hwe, *aspect; colour*

874–6 A voice like many rivers rushing in full spate, or like thunder rolling in the dark blue hills—that sound, I believe, was in no way less.

880 That was delightful and precious to listen to.

883–4 A noble discourse set to sonorous notes; together they caught the melody most beautifully.

887 And the elders so grave of face.

889–93 Nevertheless there is none so skilful, in spite of all the arts they ever knew, who could sing a phrase of that song, save only that company who follow the Lamb. For they are redeemed and far removed from the earth.

For never lesyng ne tale untrwe — *lie*
Ne towched her tonge for no dysstresse.
That moteles meyny may never remwe
Fro that maskeles mayster, never the les."'

'Never the les let be my thonc,'
Quod I, 'my perle, thagh I appose.
I schulde not tempte thy wyt so wlonc,
To Krystes chambre that art ichose.
I am bot mokke and mul among,
And thou so ryche a reken rose,
And bydes here by thys blysful bonc — *dwell; bank*
Ther lyves lyste may never lose.
Now, hynde, that sympelnesse cones enclose,
I wolde the aske a thynge expresse, — *plainly*
And thagh I be bustwys as a blose, — *rude; churl*
Let my bone vayl neverthelese. — *prayer; prevail*

XVI

'Neverthelese cler I yow bycalle, — *call upon*
If ye con se hyt be to done;
As thou art gloryous wythouten galle, — *spot of impurity*
Wythnay thou never my ruful bone. — *refuse; piteous*
Haf ye no wones in castel-walle, — *dwellings*
Ne maner ther ye may mete and won? — *mansion; dwell*
Thou telles me of Jerusalem the ryche ryalle, — *royal*
Ther David dere was dyght on trone; — *set*
Bot by thyse holtes hit con not hone, — *woods; be situated*
Bot in Judee hit is, that noble note. — *Judaea; structure*
As ye ar maskeles under mone,
Your wones schulde be wythouten mote. — *stain*

898–900 Came near their tongue, whatever the compulsion. That spotless company can never be parted from that spotless Master, notwithstanding.
901–6 'Let not my gratitude be thought less,' I said, 'although, my pearl, I question you. I ought not to test the noble wisdom of you who are chosen for Christ's bridal chamber. I am nothing but a mixture of muck and dust, and you are so fair and fresh a rose.'
908–9 Where the joy of life can never fade. Now, gracious maid, in whom simplicity is contained.
914 If you can see your way to do it.
923 As you are altogether spotless (lit. spotless under moon).

'Thys moteles meyny thou cones of mele,
Of thousandes thryght so gret a route,
A gret cité, for ye arn fele,
Yow byhod have, wythouten doute.
So cumly a pakke of joly juele
Wer evel don schulde lyy theroute;
And by thyse bonkes ther I con gele — *slopes; linger*
I se no bygyng nawhere aboute. — *dwelling*
I trowe alone ye lenge and loute
To loke on the glory of thys gracious gote. — *stream*
If thou has other bygynges stoute, — *stately*
Now tech me to that myry mote.'

'That mote thou menes in Judy londe,'
That specyal spyce then to me spakk, — *precious; person*
'That is the cyté that the Lombe con fonde — *visited*
To soffer inne sor for manes sake—
The olde Jerusalem to understonde;
For there the olde gulte was don to slake.
Bot the nwe, that lyght of Godes sonde,
The apostel in Apocalyppce in theme con take.
The Lompe ther wythouten spottes blake — *Lamb; black*
Has feryed thyder hys fayre flote; — *conveyed; company*
And as hys flok is wythouten flake, — *blemish*
So is hys mote wythouten moote. — *city; stain*

'Of motes two to carpe clene—
And Jerusalem hyght bothe nawtheles—

925–30 For this spotless retinue you speak of, so great a company of thousands thronged together, you would need to have a great city, without doubt, because there are so many of you. It would be wrong for such a beautiful assembly of bright jewels to sleep out of doors.
933 I think you stay and walk alone.
936 Now show me the way to that pleasant city.
937 That city you refer to in the land of Judaea.
940–4 To suffer sorrow in for mankind's sake—that is to say, the old Jerusalem; for there the old sin (of Adam and Eve) was brought to an end. But the new city, which came down (from heaven) and was of God's sending, the apostle has taken as his theme in the Apocalypse.
949–55 To speak correctly of these two cities—and both alike are called Jerusalem—the name means nothing more than 'city of God' or 'vision of peace'. In the one our peace was made complete; the Lamb chose it as the place to suffer in with pain. In the other there is nothing to glean but peace.

That nys to yow no more to mene
Bot "cetè of God" other "syght of pes".
In that on oure pes was mad at ene;
Wyth payne to suffer the Lombe hit chese.
In that other is noght bot pes to glene
That ay schal laste wythouten reles. *without ceasing*
That is the borgh that we to pres
Fro that oure flesch be layd to rote,
Ther glory and blysse schal ever encres *where; increase*
To the meyny that is wythouten mote.' *for*

'Moteles may so meke and mylde,' *spotless; maid*
Then sayde I to that lufly flor, *flower*
'Bryng me to that bygly bylde *pleasant; dwelling*
And let me se thy blysful bor.' *abode*
That schene sayde: 'That God wyl schylde; *fair (maiden); forbid*
Thou may not enter wythinne hys tor, *stronghold*
Bot of the Lombe I have the aquylde *obtained permission*
For a syght therof thurgh gret favor.
Utwyth to se that clene cloystor
Thou may, bot inwyth not a fote;
To strech in the strete thou has no vygour, *walk; power*
Bot thou wer clene wythouten mote. *unless*

XVII

'If I this mote the schal unhyde, *reveal*
Bow up towarde thys bornes heved,
And I anendes the on this syde *opposite*
Schal sue, tyl thou to a hil be veved.' *follow; come*
Then wolde I no lenger byde,
Bot lurked by launces so lufly leved,
Tyl on a hyl that I asspyed
And blusched on the burghe, as I forth dreved,

957–8 That is the city we hasten to after our flesh is laid in the ground to rot.

969–70 From outside you may see that fair enclosure, but not (go) one foot inside.

974 Go up towards the head of this stream.

978–83 But made my way under boughs so beautifully in leaf, till from a hill I caught sight of the city and gazed upon it, as I hurried along, sunk down beyond the brook away from me, and shining with beams of light brighter than the sun. The fashion of it is shown in the Apocalypse (Rev. xxi. 2).

Byyonde the brok fro me warde keved,
That schyrrer then sunne wyth schaftes schon.
In the Apokalypce is the fasoun preved,
As devyses hit the apostel Jhon. *describes*

As John the apostel hit syy wyth syght, *saw it*
I syye that cyty of gret renoun,
Jerusalem so nwe and ryally dyght, *royally; adorned*
As hit was lyght fro the heven adoun. *descended*
The borgh was al of brende golde bryght
As glemande glas burnist broun,
Wyth gentyl gemmes anunder pyght;
Wyth banteles twelve on basyng boun—
The foundementes twelve of riche tenoun—
Uch tabelment was a serlypes ston;
As derely devyses this ilk toun
In Apocalyppes the apostel John.

As John thise stones in writ con nemme, *scripture; named*
I knew the name after his tale. *according to; enumeration*
Jasper hyght the fyrst gemme *was called*
That I on the fyrst basse con wale: *base; discerned*
He glente grene in the lowest hemme;
Saffer helde the secounde stale;
The calsydoyne thenne wythouten wemme
In the thryd table con purly pale;
The emerade the furthe so grene of scale;
The sardonyse the fyfthe ston; *sardonyx*
The sexte the rybé he con hit wale *sixth; ruby*
In the Apocalyppce, the apostel John.

Yet joyned John the crysolyt, *added; chrysolite*
The seventhe gemme in fundament; *foundation*

989–96 The city was all of bright gold, burnished like gleaming glass, adorned below with noble gems; with twelve tiers built at the base—the twelve foundations tenoned admirably—each tier garnished with separate stones; as the apostle John has splendidly described this city in the Apocalypse.

1001–5 It glinted green in the lowest tier; sapphire held the second place; the flawless chalcedony in the third tier showed pale and clear; fourth was the emerald with surface so green.

The aghtthe the beryl cler and quyt;
The topasye twynne-hew the nente endent;
The crysopase the tenthe is tyght,
The jacynght the enleventhe gent;
The twelfthe, the gentyleste in uche a plyt,
The amatyst purpre wyth ynde blente.
The wal abof the bantels bent
O jasporye, as glas that glysnande schon.
I knew hit by his devysement *description*
In the Apocalyppes, the apostel John.

As John devysed yet saw I thare:
Thise twelve degres wern brode and stayre; *steps; steep*
The cyté stod abof ful sware, *square*
As longe as brode as hyghe ful fayre; *exactly*
The stretes of golde as glasse al bare, *lustrous*
The wal of jasper that glent as glayre;
The wones wythinne enurned ware *adorned*
Wyth alle kynnes perré that moght repayre.
Thenne helde uch sware of this manayre
Twelve forlonge space, er ever hit fon,
Of heght, of brede, of lenthe, to cayre,
For meten hit syy the apostel John. *measured; saw*

XVIII

As John hym wrytes yet more I syye:
Uch pane of that place had thre yates, *side; gates*

1012–18 The double-coloured topaz was set in the ninth; the chrysoprase adorned the tenth, the noble jacinth the eleventh; the twelfth, most excellent in every peril, was the amethyst of purple blended with indigo. The wall set firmly on the tiers (of the foundation) was of jasper that shone like gleaming glass.

1026 The wall of jasper that glinted like the white of egg (used in illuminating manuscripts).

1028–31 With precious stones of every kind that could be brought together there. Moreover each square side of this mansion filled the space of twelve furlongs in height, breadth and length before it came to an end. (*fon . . . to cayre*, 'ceased to go'.)

1033 I saw still more of what John described.

So twelve in poursent I con asspye,
The portales pyked of rych plates,
And uch yate of a margyrye,
A parfyt perle that never fates. *fades*
Uchon in scrypture a name con plye
Of Israel barnes, folewande her dates,
That is to say, as her byrth-whates:
The aldest ay fyrst theron was done. *oldest; inscribed*
Such lyght ther lemed in alle the strates *shone; streets*
Hem nedde nawther sunne ne mone. *they needed*

Of sunne ne mone had thay no nede;
The self God was her lambe-lyght,
The Lombe her lantyrne, wythouten drede; *doubt*
Thurgh hym blysned the borgh al bryght.
Thurgh wowe and won my lokyng yede,
For sotyle cler noght lette no lyght.
The hyghe trone ther moght ye hede *observe*
Wyth alle the apparaylmente umbepyghte,
As John the appostel in termes tyghte;
The hyghe Godes self hit set upone. *sat*
A rever of the trone ther ran outryghte
Was bryghter then bothe the sunne and mone.

Sunne ne mone schon never so swete
As that foysoun flode out of that flet; *copious; ground*
Swythe hit swange thurgh uch a strete *swiftly; rushed*
Wythouten fylthe other galle other glet. *or impurity; slime*
Kyrk therinne was non yete,
Chapel ne temple that ever was set: *built*

1035–7 So I saw twelve in the whole surrounding wall, the gateways adorned with splendid plates of metal, and each gate with a pearl.
1039–41 Each (gate) had inscribed on it the name of one of the children of Israel in chronological order, that is to say, according to the dates of their birth.
1046 God Himself was their lamplight.
1048–50 Because of Him the city shone all brightly. My gaze penetrated wall and dwelling-place, for all was transparent and clear and nothing obstructed the light.
1052–3 With all its array of adornments, as John the apostle plainly described it.
1055 A river flowed straight out from the throne.
1061 Yet there was no church in that place.

The Almyghty was her mynster mete; *church; noble*
The Lombe, the sakerfyse, ther to refet.
The yates stoken was never yet, *shut*
Bot evermore upen at uche a lone; *open; roadway*
Ther entres non to take reset *refuge*
That beres any spot anunder mone.

The mone may therof acroche no myghte;
To spotty ho is, of body to grym, *ugly*
And also ther ne is never nyght.
What schulde the mone ther compas clym
And to even wyth that worthly lyght
That schynes upon the brokes brym? *river's*
The planetes arn in to pover a plyght, *poor*
And the self sunne ful fer to dym. *all too*
Aboute that water arn tres ful schym, *bright*
That twelve frytes of lyf con bere ful sone;
Twelve sythes on yer thay beren ful frym,
And renowles nwe in uche a mone.

Anunder mone so great merwayle *marvel*
No fleschly hert ne myght endeure, *endure*
As quen I blusched upon that bayle,
So ferly therof was the fasure. *marvellous; form*
I stod as stylle as dased quayle *quail*
For ferly of that freuch fygure,
That felde I nawther reste ne travayle, *so that I felt; toil*
So was I ravyste wyth glymme pure. *enraptured; radiance*
For I dar say wyth conciens sure, *conviction*
Hade bodyly burne abiden that bone,
Thagh alle clerkes hym hade in cure,
His lyf were loste anunder mone.

1064 The Lamb, the sacrifice, was there for (the soul's) refreshment.
1068 That has any blemish on this earth (lit. under the moon).
1069 The moon can steal no light from there.
1072–3 Why should the moon make her circuit there and vie with that glorious light.
1078–80 That quickly bear twelve fruits of life; twelve times a year they bear abundantly, and every month renew themselves.
1083 As (I saw) when I gazed at that city (lit. outer wall).
1086 In amazement at that frail vision.
1090–2 If mortal man had endured that favour (granted to me), his life would have been utterly lost, though all the learned men had taken care of him.

XIX

Ryght as the maynful mone con rys
Er thenne the day-glem dryve al doun,
So sodanly on a wonder wyse — *marvellous; manner*
I was war of a prosessyoun. — *aware*
This noble cité of ryche enpryse — *glorious; renown*
Was sodanly ful wythouten sommoun — *summons*
Of such vergynes in the same gyse — *guise*
That was my blysful anunder croun;
And coronde wern alle of the same fasoun, — *crowned*
Depaynt in perles and wedes qwyte; — *adorned; garments*
In uchones breste was bounden boun — *fastened; firmly*
The blysful perle wyth gret delyt.

Wyth gret delyt thay glod in fere — *glided; together*
On golden gates that glent as glasse. — *streets*
Hundreth thowsandes I wot ther were, — *know*
And alle in sute her livrés wasse;
Tor to knaw the gladdest chere.
The Lombe byfore con proudly passe — *went*
Wyth hornes seven of red golde cler; — *bright*
As praysed perles his wedes wasse.
Towarde the throne thay trone a tras. — *they made their way*
Thagh thay wern fele, no pres in plyt,
Bot mylde as maydenes seme at mas,
So drow thay forth wyth gret delyt. — *moved*

Delyt that hys come encroched — *coming; brought*
To much hit were of for to melle. — *to tell of*
Thise aldermen, quen he aproched, — *the elders*
Grovelyng to his fete thay felle. — *prostrate*
Legyounes of aungeles togeder voched — *summoned*
Ther kesten ensens of swete smelle. — *scattered*

1093–4 Even as the mighty moon rises before the light of day has fully gone.
1100 As was my blissful maiden beneath her crown.
1108–9 And their garments were all alike; it was hard to tell who looked the happiest.
1112 His raiment was like precious pearls.
1114 Though they were many, there was no crowding in their array.

Then glory and gle was nwe abroched;
Al songe to love that gay juelle. *sang; praise*
The steven moght stryke thurgh the urthe to helle *sound*
That the Vertues of heven of joye endyte.
To love the Lombe his meyny in melle
Iwysse I laght a gret delyt.

Delit the Lombe for to devise
Wyth much mervayle in mynde went. *wonder*
Best was he, blythest, and moste to pryse,
That ever I herde of speche spent;
So worthly whyt wern wedes hys, *gloriously; garments*
His lokes symple, hymself so gent. *unassuming; gracious*
Bot a wounde ful wyde and weete con wyse *wet; showed*
Anende hys hert, thurgh hyde torente.
Of his quyte syde his blod outsprent. *gushed out*
Alas, thoght I, who did that spyt? *outrage*
Ani breste for bale aght haf forbrent
Er he therto hade had delyt.

The Lombe delyt non lyste to wene.
Thagh he were hurt and wounde hade,
In his sembelaunt was never sene, *demeanour*
So wern his glentes gloryous glade.
I loked among his meyny schene *retinue; shining*
How thay wyth lyf wern laste and lade;
Then saw I ther my lyttel quene
That I wende had standen by me in sclade.

1123 Then praise and joy were uttered anew.
1126–8 That the heavenly Virtues (i.e. one of the nine orders of angels) made for sheer joy. Indeed I took a great delight in praising the Lamb, among His retinue.
1129 My delight in gazing upon the Lamb.
1131–2 He was the noblest, gentlest and most praiseworthy that ever I heard tell of.
1136 Close to His heart, through His cruelly torn skin.
1139–40 Any breast should have burnt up with sorrow rather than take delight in such a thing.
1141 None wished to doubt the Lamb's delight.
1144 So gloriously happy were His looks.
1146 (And saw) how they were charged and laden with (eternal) life.
1148–9 That I thought had stood near me in the valley. Lord, how greatly she rejoiced.

Lorde, much of mirthe was that ho made
Among her feres that was so quyt! *companions*
That syght me gart to thenk to wade
For luf-longyng in gret delyt.

XX

Delyt me drof in yye and ere,
My manes mynde to maddyng malte.
Quen I sey my frely, I wolde be there, *saw; fair (one)*
Byyonde the water thagh ho were walte. *kept*
I thoght that nothyng myght me dere *harm*
To fech me bur and take me halte,
And to start in the strem schulde non me stere,
To swymme the remnaunt, thagh I ther swalte.
Bot of that munt I was bitalt. *intention; shaken*
When I schulde start in the strem astraye,
Out of that caste I was bycalt; *purpose; summoned*
Hit was not at my Prynces paye. *to; liking*

Hit payed hym not that I so flonc
Over mervelous meres, so mad arayde.
Of raas thagh I were rasch and ronk,
Yet rapely therinne I was restayed.
For, ryght as I sparred unto the bonc,
That braththe out of my drem me brayde.
Then wakned I in that erber wlonk; *garden; lovely*
My hede upon that hylle was layde

1151–2 That sight made me resolve to wade (across the river) because of my great joy and love-longing.
1153–4 Delight assailed both eye and ear, and my mortal mind was reduced to frenzy.
1158–60 By fetching me a blow and making me halt, and that none would prevent me from plunging into the stream and swimming the rest of the way, even though I died in the attempt.
1162 When I was about to rush astray into the stream.
1165–70 It did not please Him that I should fling myself across those marvellous waters in so mad a fashion. Though I was rash and impetuous in my headlong haste, yet I was quickly checked in what I did. For, just as I rushed forward to the bank, that impetuous action startled me from my dream.

Ther as my perle to grounde strayd. *slipped away*
I raxled, and fel in gret affray,
And, sykyng, to myself I sayd: *sighing*
'Now al be to that Prynces paye.'

Me payed ful ille to be outfleme
So sodenly of that fayre regioun,
Fro alle tho syghtes so quyke and queme. *vivid; pleasant*
A longeyng hevy me strok in swone,
And rewfully thenne I con to reme: *sorrowfully; cried out*
'O perle,' quod I, 'of rych renoun, *glorious*
So was hit me dere that thou con deme
In this veray avysyoun.
If hit be veray and soth sermoun *true; statement*
That thou so stykes in garlande gay, *are set*
So wel is me in thys doel-doungoun
That thou art to that Prynses paye.'

To that Prynces paye hade I ay bente,
And yerned no more then was me gyven, *desired*
And halden me ther in trwe entent,
As the perle me prayed that was so thryven, *fair*
As helde, drawen to Goddes present,
To mo of his mysterys I hade ben dryven.
Bot ay wolde man of happe more hente *good fortune; seize*
Then moghte by ryght upon hem clyven. *belong to them*
Therfore my joye was sone toriven, *shattered*
And I kaste of kythes that lastes aye.
Lorde, mad hit arn that agayn the stryven, *they are*
Other proferen the oght agayn thy paye.

1174 I stretched myself, and suddenly felt a great dismay.
1177 It greatly displeased me to be an exile.
1180 A heavy longing overcame me (lit. struck me down in a swoon).
1183–4 It was so precious to me what you spoke of in this true vision.
1187 Then I am happy in this dungeon of sorrow.
1189 If I had always submitted to that Prince's will.
1191 And restrained myself with steadfast purpose.
1193–4 As likely as not, led into God's presence, I would have been brought to more of His mysteries.
1198 And I cast out from regions that endure for ever.
1200 Or propose anything to you against your will.

To pay the Prince other sete saghte
Hit is ful ethe to the god Krystyin; *easy; Christian*
For I haf founden hym, bothe day and naghte, *night*
A God, a Lorde, a frende ful fyin. *most true*
Over this hyul this lote I laghte,
For pyty of my perle enclyin, *lying prostrate*
And sythen to God I hit bytaghte
In Krystes dere blessyng and myn, *remembrance*
That in the forme of bred and wyn
The preste uus schewes uch a daye. *every*
He gef uus to be his homly hyne
Ande precious perles unto his pay.
Amen. Amen.

1201 To please or propitiate the Prince.
1205 Upon this mound I had this fortune.
1207 And afterwards I committed it (i.e. the Pearl) to God.
1211–12 May He allow us to be His household servants and precious pearls for His pleasure.

CLEANNESS

I

Clannesse who-so kyndly cowthe comende,
And rekken up alle the resouns that ho by right askes,
Fayre formes myght he fynde in forthering his speche,
And in the contraré kark and combraunce huge.

For wonder wroth is the wyy that wroght alle thinges
Wyth the freke that in fylthe folwes hym after,
As renkes of relygioun that reden and syngen — *men; read in church*
And aprochen to hys presens, and prestes arn called.

Thay teen unto his temmple and temen to hymselven;
Reken with reverence thay rychen his auter; — *suitably; prepare*
Thay hondel ther his aune body, and usen hit bothe. — *partake of it also*
If thay in clannes be clos, thay cleche gret mede,

Bot if they conterfete crafte and cortaysye wont, — *virtue; lack*
As be honest utwyth and inwith alle fylthes,
Then ar thay synful hemself, and sulped altogeder
Bothe God and his gere, and hym to greme cachen.

He is so clene in his courte, the kyng that al weldes, — *rules*
And honeste in his housholde, and hagherlych served — *fittingly*
With angeles enourled in alle that is clene — *by; steeped in*
Bothe withinne and withouten, in wedes ful bryght.

1–6 He who was able to praise cleanness appropriately, and reckon up all the justifications that are hers as of right, might expect to find excellent examples to help him in his discourse, and in doing the contrary great trouble and difficulty. For the One who made all things is very angry with the man who serves Him in a state of filth.
9 They go to His temple and attach themselves to Him.
12 If they are full of cleanness, they obtain great reward.
14–16 As to be clean outwardly, and inwardly all filthiness, then they (themselves) are sinful, and both God and His vessels are utterly defiled, and they drive Him to anger.
20–4 Both inside and outside, dressed in bright clothes. If He were not

Nif he nere scoymus and skyg and non scathe lovied,
Hit were a mervayl to much, hit moght not falle.
Kryst kydde hit hymself in a carp ones,
Ther as he hevened aght happes and hyght hem her medes.

Me mynes on one amonge other, as Mathew recordes, *I remember*
That thus of clannesse uncloses a ful cler speche: *sets forth*
'The hathel clene of his hert hapenes ful fayre,
For he schal loke on oure Lorde with a loue chere.' *humble countenance*

As so says, to that syght seche schal he never
That any unclannesse has on, auwhere abowte;
For he that flemus uch fylthe fer fro his hert
May not byde that burre, that hit his body neghe.

Forthy hyy not to heven in hateres totorne,
Ne in the harlates hod and handes unwaschen. *beggar's hood*
For what urthly hathel that hygh honour haldes *earthly; rank*
Wolde lyke if a ladde com lytherly attyred, *badly*

When he were sette solempnely in a sete ryche, *seated*
Abof dukes on dece, with dayntys served? *dais*
Then the harlot with haste helded to the table *if then; went*
With rent cokres at the kne, and his clutte trasches,

And his tabarde totorne, and his totes oute,
Other ani on of alle thyse, he schulde be halden utter, *or; one* / *thrown out*
With mony blame ful bygge, a boffet peraunter,
Hurled to the halle dore and harde theroute schowved,

fastidious and particular and loved no wrong, it would be too great a marvel, it might not be. Christ made it clear Himself in a speech once, where He exalted eight blessed states and assigned them their rewards.

27 The man clean of heart gains good fortune.

29–33 That is to say that the man who has any uncleanness on him, anywhere about him, shall never come to that sight; for He who drives all filth far from His heart may not endure the shock of its coming near His person. Therefore do not hasten to Heaven in torn clothes.

40–1 With leggings torn at the knee, and his patched old shoes, and his tabard torn, and the toes of his shoes out of shape.

43 With many a sharp rebuke, perhaps a blow.

And be forbode that borghe, to bowe thider never,
On payne of enprysonment and puttyng in stokkes;
And thus schal he be schent for his *punished*
schrowde feble, *clothes*
Thagh never in talle ne in tuch he trespas more.

And if unwelcum he were to a worthlych prynce, *noble*
Yet hym is the hyghe kyng harder in heven; *on him*
As Mathew meles in his masse of that man ryche
That made the mukel mangerye to marie his here dere,

And sende his sonde then to say that thay samne schulde,
And in comly quoyntis to com to his feste: *fine clothes*
'For my boles and my bores arn bayted and slayne,
And my fedde foules fatted with sclaght;

My polyle that is penne-fed, and partrykes bothe,
Wyth scheldes of wylde swyn, swanes, and *shoulders*
crones, *cranes*
Al is rotheled and rosted ryght to the sete;
Comes cof to my corte, er hit colde worthe.' *quickly; gets*

When thay knewen his cal that thider com schulde,
Alle excused hem by the skyly he scape by moght.
On hade boght hym a borgh, he sayde by hys trawthe:
'Now turne I theder als tyd the toun to byholde.'

45 And be forbidden to go to that great house ever again.
48 Though he should never again offend either in general appearance or in detail of dress.
51–3 As Matthew speaks in his gospel (read at mass) of that rich man who made the great banquet to marry his dear son, and then sent his messengers to say that men should assemble.
55–7 For my bulls and my boars are baited (by dogs, to improve the flavour of the meat) and killed, and my well-fed fowls are fattened for slaughter; my poultry that is fed in a pen, and partridges as well.
59 Everything is broiled and roasted ready for the men to sit down.
61–4 When those who were invited received his summons, each man excused himself by a pretext which enabled him to escape. One had bought himself an estate, he said on his honour: 'Now I am going there at once to see the property.'

Another nayed also and nurned this cawse: *refused; offered*
'I haf yerned and yat yokkes of oxen, *desired; got*
And for my hywes hem boght, to bowe haf I mester;
To see hem pulle in the plow aproche me byhoves.' *I must*

'And I haf wedded a wyf,' so wer hym the thryd, *excused*
'Excuse me at the court, I may not com there.'
Thus thay drow hem adrey with daunger uchone,
That non passed to the place, thagh he prayed were.

Thenne the ludych lorde lyked ful ille,
And hade dedayn of that dede—ful dryyly he carpes.
He says: 'Now for her owne sorwe thay forsaken habbes;
More to wyte is her wrange then any wylle gentyl.

Thenne gos forth, my gomes, to the grete streetes, *servants; roads*
And forsettes on uche a syde the ceté aboute
The wayferande frekes, on fote and on hors, *people*
Bothe burnes and burdes, the better and the wers. *men; women*

Lathes hem alle luflyly to lenge at my fest,
And brynges hem blythly to borghe as barounes thay were, *graciously*
So that my palays platful be pyght al aboute;
Thise other wreches iwysse worthy noght wern.' *indeed; not*

Then thay cayred and com that the cost waked,
Broghten bachleres hem wyth that thay by bonkes metten,
Swyeres that swyftly swyed on blonkes,
And also fele upon fote, of fre and of bonde.

67 And because my servants bought them, I need to go.
71–6 Thus each one of them drew back disdainfully, so that none, though entreated, went to the house. Then the noble lord was much displeased, and took offence at their behaviour—most gravely he spoke. He says: 'Now it is to their own sorrow that they have refused; their wrongdoing is more to be blamed than any gentile wilfulness.'
78 And waylay on every side of the city.
81 Invite them all courteously to be present at my feast.
83 So that every part of my palace will be filled to overflowing.
85–8 Then they went to and fro, rousing the countryside, brought young knights with them that they met by the way, squires who came swiftly on horses, and also many on foot, bondmen and free.

When thay com to the courte, keppte wern thay fayre, *received*
Styghtled with the stewarde, stad in the halle,
Ful manerly with marchal mad for to sitte,
As he was dere of degré dressed his seete.

Thenne segges to the soverayn sayden therafter: *servants; lord*
'Lo, lorde, with your leve, at your lege heste *sovereign command*
And at thi banne we haf broght, as thou beden habbes,
Mony renischche renkes, and yet is roum more.' *outlandish men*

Sayde the lorde to tho ledes: 'Laytes yet ferre,
Ferre out in the felde, and feches mo gestes;
Waytes gorstes and greves, if ani gomes lygges;
What kyn folk so ther fare, feches hem hider.

Be thay fers, be thay feble, forlotes none,
Be thay hol, be thay halt, be thay on-yyed,
And thagh thay ben bothe blynde and balterande cruppeles, *hobbling*
That my hous may holly by halkes by fylled.

For certes thyse ilk renkes that me renayed habbe,
And denounced me noght now at this tyme, *honoured*
Schul never sitte in my sale my soper to fele, *hall; taste*
Ne suppe on sope of my seve, thagh thay swelt schulde.'

Thenne the sergauntes at that sawe swengen theroute,
And diden the dede that demed as he devised hade,

90–2 Looked after by the steward, given a place in the hall, most courteously made to sit down by the marshal (the officer in charge of the feast), a man's place at table being assigned him according to his rank.
95 And by your edict we have brought, as you have asked.
97–102 Said the lord to those servants: 'Search still further afield, far out in the countryside, and bring more guests; search scrublands and thickets, to see if any men lie hidden; whatever people are there, bring them to this place. Be they bold, be they timid, overlook none, be they sound, be they lame, be they one-eyed.'
104–5 So that my house may be filled completely, every corner of it. For certainly these men who have refused me.
108–10 'Nor swallow one mouthful of my stew, though they should die.' Then the servants at that command went swiftly outside and performed the task, making proclamation as he had ordained.

And with peple of alle plytes the palays thay fyllen; *kinds*
Hit weren not alle on wyves sunes, wonen with on fader.

Whether thay wern worthy other wers, wel *or not so worthy*
  wern thay stowed, *seated*
Ay the best byfore and bryghtest atyred, *always; in front*
The derrest at the hyghe dese, that dubbed wer fayrest,
And sythen on lenthe biloogh ledes inogh;

And ay a segge soberly semed by her wedes.
So with marschal at her mete mensked *by; meal; honoured*
  thay were;
Clene men in compaynye forknowen wern lyte,
And yet the symplest in that sale was served to the fulle,

Bothe with menske and with mete and mynstrasy noble,
And alle the laykes that a lorde aght in londe schewe;
And thay bigonne to be glad that god drink haden,
And uch mon with his mach made hym at ese. *companion*

Now inmyddes the mete the mayster hym bithoght *decided*
That he wolde se the semblé that samned *assembly; gathered*
  was there,
And rehayte rekenly the riche and the pover,
And cherisch hem alle with his cher, and chaufen her joye.

Then he bowes from his bour into the brode halle,
And to the best on the bench, and bede hym be myry,
Solased hem with semblaunt and syled fyrre,
Tron fro table to table and talkede ay myrthe.

112 They were not all one wife's sons, begotten by one father (i.e. they were many and varied).

115–17 The noblest, who were best dressed, on the high dais, and then men in plenty down the hall below; and each man looked dignified in his dress.

119–22 Well-bred men in that company were by no means neglected, and yet the most lowly man in the hall was served unstintingly, with honours and food and excellent minstrelsy, and all the diversions that it was proper for a lord to provide.

127–38 And courteously pay his respects to the rich and the poor, and be hospitable towards them all, and encourage their merrymaking. Then he went from his chamber into the great hall, to the noblest at the table, and bade them be merry, cheered them with his friendliness and passed on, went from table to table always talking pleasantly. But as he moved over the floor he noticed that there was a fellow not properly dressed for a festival, poorly clothed in the midst of the throng; (he wore) no festive

Bot as he ferked over the flor he fande with his yye
Hit was, not for a halyday honestly arayed,
A thral thryght in the throng, unthryvandely clothed,
Ne no festival frok, bot fyled with werkkes.

The gome was ungarnyst with god men to dele,
And gremed therwith the grete lorde, and greve hym he thoght.
'Say me, frende,' quoth the freke, with a felle chere, *grim countenance*
Hou wan thou into this won in wedes so fowle? *came; house*

The abyt that thou has upon, no halyday hit menskes; *garment; have on*
Thou, burne, for no brydale art busked in wedes.
How was thou hardy this hous for thyn unhap neghe,
In on so ratted a robe, and rent at the sydes? *so very ragged a*

Thow art a gome ungoderly in that goun febele; *vile*
Thou praysed me and my place ful pover and ful nede,
That was so prest to aproche my presens hereinne. *quick*
Hopes thou I be a harlot, thi erigaut to prayse?'

That other burne was abayst of his brothe wordes, *abashed at; angry*
And hurkeles doun with his hede, the urthe he biholdes; *hangs*
He was so scoumfit of his scylle, lest he skathe hent,
That he ne wyst on worde what he warp schulde.

Then the lorde wonder loude laled and cryed, *very; spoke*
And talkes to his tormenttoures: 'Takes hym,' he biddes, *torturers*
'Byndes byhynde at his bak bothe two his handes,
And felle fetteres to his fete festenes bylyve; *at once*

garment, but one stained by labours. The man was not suitably dressed for dealing with decent men, and the great lord was angry on that account, and thought to punish him.

142–3 You, sir, are dressed for no wedding feast. How dared you come near this house, to your misfortune?

146 You set a very poor and meagre value on me and my house.

148 Do you take me for a beggar, (that you expect me) to admire your garment?

151–2 He was so scared out of his wits, lest he should come to harm, that he might not find a single word to say.

Stik hym stifly in stokes, and stekes hym therafter *securely; confine*
Depe in my doungoun ther doel ever dwelles, *where misery*
Greving and gretyng and gryspyng harde
Of tethe tenfully togeder, to teche hym be quoynt.'

Thus comparisunes Kryst the kyndom of heven *compares*
To this frelych feste that fele arn to called;
For alle arn lathed luflyly, the luther and the better,
That ever wern fulwed in font that fest to have. *baptised*

Bot war the wel, if thou wylt, thy wedes ben clene, *take care*
And honest for the halyday, lest thou harme lache; *suitable* *come to*
For aproch thou to that prynce of parage noble,
He hates helle no more then hem that ar sowle. *filthy*

Wich arn thenne thy wedes thou wrappes the inne,
That schal schewe hem so schene, schrowde of the best?
Hit arn thy werkes wyterly that thou wroght haves,
And lyned with the lykyng that lyye in thyn hert,

That tho be frely and fresch fonde in thy lyve,
And fetyse of a fayr forme to fote and to honde,
And sythen alle thyn other lymes lapped ful clene;
Thenne may thou se thy Savior and his sete ryche. *throne*

For fele fautes may a freke forfete his blysse, *many*
That he the Soverayn ne se; then for slauthe one,
As for bobaunce and bost and bolnande priyde,
Throly into the develes throte man thrynges bylyve;

159–60 Wailing and weeping and bitter gnashing of teeth in anguish, to teach him to be well-dressed.

162–3 To this splendid feast to which many are summoned; for all are courteously invited, the better and the worse.

167 For should you approach that prince of noble rank.

170–5 That must look so bright, the best of clothes? To be sure they are your deeds which you have performed, and (which you have) lined with the good disposition of your heart, so that they should be found fair and fresh in your life, neat and of attractive appearance for the hands and feet, and then all your other parts brightly attired.

178–86 So that he does not see the Sovereign; thus for sloth alone, just as for vanity and boasting and overweening pride, a man at once hurtles

For covetyse and colwarde and croked dedes,
For monsworne and mensclaght and to much drynk,
For thefte and for threpyng, unthonk may mon have,
For roborrye and riboudrye and resounes untrwe,

And dysheriete and depryve dowrie of wydoes,
For marryng of maryages and mayntnaunce of schrewes,
For traysoun and trichcherye and
tyrauntyre bothe, *tyranny also*
And for fals famacions and fayned lawes. *rumours; spurious*

Man may mysse the myrthe that much is *bliss*
to prayse *be prized*
For such unthewes as thise, and thole much payne, *sins; endure*
And in the Creatores cort com never more,
Ne never see hym with syght, for such sour tournes. *vile doings*

Bot I have herkned and herde of mony hyghe clerkes,
And als in resounes of ryght red hit myselven, *true writings*
That that ilk proper prynce that Paradys weldes *excellent; rules*
Is displesed at uch a poynt that plyes to scathe;

Bot never yet in no boke breved I herde
That ever he wrek so wytherly on werk that he made,
Ne venged for no vilté of vice ne synne,
Ne so hastyfly was hot for hatel of his wylle,

Ne never so sodenly soght unsoundely to weng,
As for fylthe of the flesch that foles han used;
For, as I fynde, ther he foryet alle his fre thewes,
And wex wod to the wrache for wrath at his hert.

violently into the Devil's throat; for covetousness and villainy and unjust deeds, for perjury and manslaughter and too much drink, for theft and for quarrelling, one may incur displeasure, for robbery and loose living and false statements, and misappropriating and stealing widows' dowers, for adultery and supporting evildoers.

193 But I have heard from many great scholars.

196–204 Is displeased at everything that has to do with sin; but I have not yet found written down in any book that He ever punished His creation so fiercely, or exacted retribution (so fiercely) for any abomination of vice or sin, or was so precipitately violent for the hatred in His mind, or was ever so abruptly concerned to take drastic vengeance, as for filth of the flesh that fools have indulged in; for I find that then He abandoned all His gracious ways, and became furious for revenge for the anger in His heart.

For the fyrste felonye the falce fende wroght, *Devil*
Whyl he was hyghe in the heven, hoven upon lofte, *raised up*
Of alle thyse athel aungeles attled the fayrest, *glorious; created*
And he unkyndely as a karle kydde a reward.

He sey noght bot hymself, how semly he were, *saw*
Bot his Soverayn he forsoke and sade thyse wordes: *said*
'I schal telde up my trone in the tramountayne, *raise; North*
And by lyke to that Lorde that the lyft made.' *be; heavens*

With this worde that he warp the wrake on hym lyght;
Dryghtyn with his dere dom hym drof to the abyme.
In the mesure of his mode his mes never-the-lasse;
Bot ther he tynt the tythe dool of his tour ryche.

Thagh the feloun were so fers for his fayre wedes, *proud*
And his glorious glem that glent so bryght, *radiance; shone*
As sone as Dryghtynes dome drof to hymselven, *reached him*
Thikke thowsandes thro thrwen theroute;

Fellen fro the fyrmament fendes ful blake, *black*
Sweved at the fyrst swap as the snaw thikke,
Hurled into helle-hole as the hyve swarmes. *hurtled*
Fylter fenden folk forty dayes lencthe,

Er that styngande storme stynt ne myght;
Bot as smylt mele under smal sive smokes for thikke,
So fro heven to helle that hatel schor laste,
On uche syde of the worlde aywhere ilyche.

208 And he responded as ungratefully as a churl.
213–16 With this speech that he uttered the vengeance fell on him; the Lord with His stern judgement drove him to the pit. Nevertheless His blow was in keeping with the moderation of His nature; He struck down on that occasion only the tenth part of His splendid entourage.
220 Teeming thousands were violently flung out.
222 Fell at the first blow like thick snow.
224–31 The fiendish creatures tumbled for the space of forty days, before that venomous storm was allowed to cease; but as refined meal smokes thickly under a fine sieve, so that hateful shower reached from Heaven to Hell, everywhere the same on all sides of the universe. This was a fearful calamity and a mighty vengeance; and yet the man (i.e. God) did not become angry, nor did the wretch make his peace, or ever wish to acknowledge his glorious God, on account of his wilfulness.

This hit was a brem brest and a byge wrache;
And yet wrathed not the wyy, ne the wrech saghtled,
Ne never wolde for wylnesful his worthy God knawe,
Ne pray hym for no pité, so proud was his wylle.

Forthy thagh the rape were rank, the rawthe was lyttel;
Thagh he be kest into kare, he kepes no better.
Bot that other wrake that wex, on wyyes hit lyght,
Thurgh the faut of a freke that fayled in trawthe, *loyalty*

Adam inobedyent, ordaynt to blysse, *appointed*
Ther pryvely in Paradys his place was devised, *apart; ordained*
To lyve ther in lykyng the lenthe of a terme, *in pleasure for a while*
And thenne enherite that home that aungeles forgart. *forfeited*

Bot thurgh the eggyng of Eve he ete of an apple *urging*
That enpoysened alle peples that parted fro hem bothe, *descended*
For a defence that was dyght of Dryghtyn selven,
And a payne theron put and pertly halden.

The defence was the fryt that the freke towched, *fruit*
And the dom is the dethe that drepes uus alle; *strikes down*
Al in mesure and methe was mad the vengiaunce,
And efte amended with a mayden that make had never.

Bot in the thryd was forthrast al that thryve schuld;
Ther was malys mercyles and mawgré much scheued.
That was for fylthe upon folde that the folk used *earth* *indulged in*
That then wonyed in the worlde withouten any maysters. *lived*

233–5 And so though the fall was great, the remorse was small; though he is thrown into misfortune, he looks for nothing better. But the second vengeance that took place fell on men.

243–4 On account of a prohibition that was ordained by the Lord Himself, and a penalty put on it and manifestly kept to.

247–50 The vengeance was taken in all measure and moderation, and afterwards mitigated by a maiden who was without peer. But in the third (vengeance), everything that had life was destroyed; there merciless anger and great hostility were displayed.

Hit wern the fayrest of forme and of face als, *they were*
The most and the myriest that maked wern ever, *mightiest; most excellent*
The styfest, the stalworthest that stod ever on fete, *strongest*
And lengest lyf in hem lent of ledes alle other.

For hit was the forme foster that the folde bred,
The athel aunceteres sunes that Adam was called,
To wham God hade geven alle that gayn were, *good*
Alle the blysse boute blame that bodi myght have. *blameless; a man*

And those lykkest to the lede that lyved next after;
Forthy so semly to see sythen wern none.
Ther was no law to hem layd bot loke to kynde,
And kepe to hit and alle hit cors clanly fulfylle.

And thenne founden thay fylthe in fleschlych dedes, *but*
And controeved agayn kynde contraré werkes,
And used hem unthryftyly uchon on other,
And als with other, wylsfully, upon a wrange wyse.

So ferly fowled her flesch that the fende loked
How the deghter of the douthe wern derelych fayre,
And fallen in felawschyp with hem on folken wyse,
And engendered on hem jeauntes with her japes ille. *giants* *tricks; vile*

Those wern men metheles and maghty on urthe, *violent; mighty*
That for her lodlych laykes alosed thay were;

256–8 And (they were) the most long-lived of all men. For they were the first offspring that the earth bred, sons of the noble forefather named Adam.
261–4 And those who lived immediately after him (Adam) were most like him; and so there were none afterwards so seemly to look upon. There was no law imposed on them except to pay heed to nature, and keep to it and perform its functions in a clean manner.
266–71 And contrived immoral acts against nature, and practised them wantonly one on another, and also with other creatures, wilfully, in a perverted way. So thoroughly was their flesh defiled that the devils saw the daughters of men as exceedingly beautiful, and coupled with them in human fashion.
274–6 Who were renowned for their hateful practices; he who best loved strife was reputed good, and always the man most prominent in evil-doing was reckoned the best.

He was famed for fre that feght loved best,
And ay the bigest in bale the best was halden.

And thenne eveles on erthe ernestly grewen, *in earnest*
And multyplyed monyfolde inmonges mankynde, *many times*
For that the maghty on molde so marre thise other
That the wyye that all wroght ful wrothly bygynnes.

When he knew uche contré coruppte in hitselven, *country*
And uch freke forloyned fro the ryght wayes, *gone astray*
Felle temptande tene towched his hert; *fierce distressing anger*
As wyye wo hym withinne werp to hymselven:

'Me forthynkes ful much that ever I mon made; *I repent*
Bot I schal delyver and do away that doten on this molde,
And fleme out of the folde al that flesch weres,
Fro the burne to the best, fro bryddes to fysches. *man; beast*

Al schal doun and be ded and dryven out of erthe
That ever I sette saule inne, and sore hit me rwes *I regret deeply*
That ever I made hem myself; bot if I may herafter,
I schal wayte to be war her wrenches to kepe.'

Thenne in worlde was a wyye wonyande on lyve, *living*
Ful redy and ful ryghtwys, and rewled hym fayre;
In the drede of Dryghtyn his dayes he uses, *fear; passes*
And ay glydande wyth his God his grace was the more.

Hym was the name Noe, as is innogh knawen; *his name was*
He had thre thryven sunes, and thay thre wyves; *grown*
Sem sothly that on, that other hyght Cam,
And the jolef Japheth was gendered the thryd.

279–80 Inasmuch as the mighty ones on the earth so corrupt the others that the One who created all things begins to speak most angrily.
284 As one anguished inwardly He said to Himself.
286–7 But I shall purge and do away with those who act senselessly on this earth, and banish from the world everything that has flesh.
292 I shall try to be careful to observe their tricks.
294 Most zealous and righteous, and he conducted himself properly.
296 And his grace (received from God) was the greater in that he was always walking with his God.
299–310 The first indeed was Shem, the second was called Ham, and the third-born was the worthy Japheth. Now God in fury spoke wild vengeful

Now God in nwy to Noe con speke
Wylde wrakful wordes, in his wylle greved:
'The ende of alle kynes flesch that on urthe meves
Is fallen forthwyth my face, and forther hit I thenk.

With her unworthelych werk me wlates withinne;
The gore therof me has greved and the glette nwyed;
I schal strenkle my distresse and strye al togeder,
Bothe ledes and londe and alle that lyf habbes.

Bot make to the a mancioun, and that is my wylle,
A cofer closed of tres clanlych planed;
Wyrk wones therinne for wylde and for tame, *rooms; wild animals*
And thenne cleme hit with clay comly withinne, *caulk; well*

And alle the endentur dryven daube withouten.
And thus of lenthe and of large that lome thou make: *breadth; vessel*
Thre hundred of cupydes thou holde to the lenthe, *cubits; allow*
Of fyfty fayre overthwert forme the brede,

And loke even that thyn ark have of heghthe thretté,
And a wyndow wyd uponande wroght upon lofte,
In the compas of a cubit kyndely sware,
A wel dutande dor don on the syde.

Haf halles therinne and halkes ful mony, *large rooms; cubicles*
Bothe boskes and boures and wel bounden penes;

words to Noah, His mind full of anger: 'The end of creatures of all kinds that move on the earth has come before me, and I intend to hasten it. In my heart I am disgusted with their shameful behaviour; the vileness of it has angered me and the filth has distressed me. I shall put forth my power and destroy all at once, both people and land and everything that has life. But make a house for yourself, and that is my will, a closed-in Ark of smoothly-planed boards.'

313 And daub on the outside all the riveted jointing.

316–20 Make the width exactly fifty (cubits) across, and see to it that your Ark has a height of exactly thirty, with a window that opens wide constructed above, exactly a cubit square, (and) a properly-closing door made in the side.

322 Cow-houses and stalls and well-secured pens.

For I schal waken up a water to wasch alle the worlde, *deluge*
And quelle alle that is quik with quavende flodes.

Alle that glydes and gos and gost of lyf habbes,
I schal wast with my wrath, that wons upon urthe;
Bot my forwarde with the I festen on this wyse,
For thou in reysoun has rengned and ryghtwys ben ever:

Thou schal enter this ark with thyn athel barnes, *fine sons*
And thy wedded wyf with the thou take,
The makes of thy myry sunes—this meyny of aghte
I schal save of monnes saules, and swelt those other.

Of uche best that beres lyf busk the a cupple; *has; take*
Of uche clene comly kynde enclose seven makes,
Of uche horwed in ark halde bot a payre, *unclean*
For to save me the sede of alle ser kyndes; *various*

And ay thou meng with the males the mete ho-bestes,
Uche payre by payre, to plese ayther other. *each other*
With alle the fode that may be founde frette thy cofer, *stock*
For sustnaunce to yowself and also those other.'

Ful graythely gos this god-man and dos Godes hestes, *promptly* *commands*
In dryy dred and daunger, that durst do non other.
Wen hit was fettled and forged and to the fulle graythed,
Thenn con Dryghttyn hym dele dryyly thyse wordes:

324–8 And kill all live things with surging floods. I shall destroy in my anger everything that lives on the earth, that walks and moves and has the breath of life; but I shall make my agreement with you as follows, because you have lived by reason and have always been righteous.

331–2 (And) the wives of your worthy sons—this company of eight I shall save from amongst mankind, and destroy the rest.

334 Take in seven of each clean seemly species.

337 And always put in with the males the appropriate she-animals.

342–4 In great fear and awe, not daring to do otherwise. When it was prepared and built and quite made ready, then the Lord gravely spoke these words to him.

'Now, Noe,' quoth oure Lorde, 'art thou al redy?
Hast thou closed thy kyst with clay alle aboute?' *caulked; Ark*
'Ye, Lorde, with thy leve,' sayde the lede thenne, *man*
'Al is wroght at thi worde, as thou me wyt lantes.' *gave me skill*

'Enter in thenn,' quoth he, 'and haf thi wyf with the,
Thy thre sunes withouten threp, and her thre wyves; *question*
Bestes, as I bedene have, bosk therinne als, *commanded; drive*
And when ye arn staued styfly, stekes yow therinne.

Fro seven dayes ben seyed I sende out bylyve
Such a rowtande ryge that rayne schal swythe,
That schal wasch alle the worlde of werkes of fylthe;
Schal no flesch upon folde by fonden on lyve, *be found*

Outtaken yow aght in this ark staued, *except for*
And sed that I wyl save of thyse ser bestes.' *seed; various*
Now Noe never styntes—that niyght he bygynnes— *pauses*
Er al wer stawed and stoken as the steven wolde.

Thenne sone com the seventhe day, when samned wern alle,
And alle woned in the whichche, the wylde and the tame.
Then bolned the abyme and bonkes con ryse;
Waltes out uch walle-heved in ful wode stremes.

Was no brymme that abod unbrosten bylyve;
The mukel lavande logh to the lyfte rered.
Mony clustered clowde clef alle in clowtes,
Torent uch a rayn ryfte and rusched to the urthe,

352–5 And when you are securely housed, shut yourselves up in it. After seven days have passed I shall send out straightway a most violent storm, with heavy rain, that will cleanse all the world of deeds of filth.

360–8 Until all were housed and confined as the command required. Then quickly came the seventh day, by which time all were assembled, and all dwelt in the Ark, wild animals and tame. Then the depths of the earth swelled and the land rose up; each spring gushed out in raging streams. Soon there was no bank that remained unbroken; the great surging flood rose to the sky. Many a massed cloud split into shreds, every cataract burst open and poured to the earth.

Fon never in forty dayes, and then the flod ryses, *stopped*
Overwaltes uche a wod and the wyde feldes; *rolls over; wood*
For when the water of the welkyn with the worlde mette, *sky*
Alle that deth moght dryye drowned therinne. *who were subject to death*

Ther was moon for to make when meschef was cnowen,
That noght dowed bot the deth in the depe stremes.
Water wylger ay wax, wones that stryede,
Hurled into uch hous, hent that ther dowelled.

Fyrst feng to the flyght alle that fle myght;
Uuche burde with her barne the byggyng thay leves
And bowed to the hygh bonk ther brentest hit wern,
And heterly to the hyghe hylles thay aled on faste.

Bot al was nedles her note, for never cowthe stynt
The roghe raynande ryg, the raykande wawes,
Er uch bothom was brurdful to the bonkes egges,
And uche a dale so depe that demmed at the brynkes.

The moste mountaynes on mor thenne were no more dryye,
And theron flokked the folke for ferde of the wrake.
Sythen the wylde of the wode on the water flette;
Summe swymmed theron that save hemself trawed, *thought to*

Summe styye to a stud and stared to the heven, *climbed; high place*
Rwly wyth a loud rurd rored for drede; *pitifully; noise*
Hares, herttes also, to the hyghe runnen, *harts; high ground*
Bukkes, bausenes, and bules to the bonkkes hyyed, *badgers; bulls*

373–87 There was lamentation to be made when the worst was known, that nothing had power but death in the deep streams. The water grew ever wilder, destroying dwellings, rushed into each house, seized those who lived there. First all who were able to flee took to flight; each woman with her child left her home and went to the high slopes where they were steepest, hurried on with all speed to the high hills. But all their effort was useless, for the furious rainstorm, the advancing waves showed no signs of abating till each valley was brimful to the tops of its slopes, and all the deepest dales were overflowing at the brink. The greatest mountains on earth were then no longer secure, but the people flocked onto them for fear of the vengeance. Then the wild creatures of the wood floated on the water.

And alle cryed for care to the kyng of heven; *distress*
Recoverer of the Creator thay cryed uchone. *relief; cried for*
That amounted the mase, his mercy was passed, *was pointless*
And alle his pyté departed fro peple that he hated.

Bi that the flod to her fete flowed and waxed,
Then uche a segge sey wel that synk hym byhoved;
Frendes fellen in fere and fathmed togeder,
To dryy her delful deystyné and dyyen alle samen;

Luf lokes to luf, and his leve takes, *lover*
For to ende alle at ones and for ever twynne. *part*
By forty dayes wern faren, on folde no flesch styryed
That the flod nade al freten with feghtande wawes;

For hit clam uche a clyffe cubites fyftene, *climbed up*
Over the hyghest hylle that hurkled on erthe. *stood*
Thenne mourkne in the mudde most ful nede *rot; must needs*
Alle that spyrakle inspranc—no sprawlyng awayled—

Save the hathel under hach and his here straunge,
Noe that ofte nevened the name of oure Lorde, *called on*
Hym aghtsum in that ark, as athel God lyked,
Ther alle ledes in lome lenged druye.

The arc hoven was on hyghe with hurlande gotes,
Kest to kythes uncouthe the clowdes ful nere;
Hit waltered on the wylde flod, went as hit lyste, *rolled; pleased*
Drof upon the depe dam—in daunger hit semed, *drove over; sea*

397–400 When the flood ran and rose to their feet, then each man saw clearly that he must sink; friends came together and embraced each other, to meet their wretched fate and die all together.

403–4 By the time that forty days had passed, no creature stirred on the earth that the flood had not devoured with turbulent waves.

408–9 Everything in which sprang the breath of life—no death-throes availed—except for the man on shipboard and his strange household.

411–14 Him and seven others in that Ark, as glorious God desired, there in that vessel where all (men) remained dry. The Ark was raised on high by surging swells, hurled to unknown regions close to the clouds.

Withouten mast other myke other myry bawelyne,
Kable other capstan to clyppe to her ankres, *attach*
Hurrok, other hande-helme hasped on rother,
Other any sweande sayl to seche after haven.

Bot flote forthe with the flyt of the felle wyndes; *it drifted; brawling*
Whederwarde-so the water wafte, hit rebounde. *wherever; surged*
Ofte hit roled on rounde and rered on ende; *spun about*
Nyf oure Lorde hade ben her lodesmon, hem had lumpen harde.

Of the lenthe of Noe lyf to lay a lel date:
The sex hundreth of his age and none odde yeres,
Of secounde monyth the seventethe day ryghtes,
Towalten alle thyse welle-hedes and the water flowed, *burst out*

And thryes fyfty the flod of folwande dayes.
Uche hille was ther hidde with ythes ful graye; *waves*
Al was wasted that ther wonyed the worlde withinne,
Ther ever flote, other flwe, other on fote yede.

That roghly was the remnaunt that the rac dryves,
That alle gendres so joyst wern joyned wythinne.
Bot quen the Lorde of the lyfte lyked hymselven *heavens; was pleased*
For to mynne on his mon his meth that abydes,

417 Without mast or crutch (for mast when lowered) or goodly bowline.
419–20 Rudder-band, or tiller fastened to the rudder, or any speeding sail with which to seek out harbour.
424–7 If our Lord had not been their steersman, they would have fared badly. To assign an exact date (for the beginning of the Flood) in terms of Noah's age: (in) the six hundredth year of his age, with none left over, (on) precisely the seventeenth day of the second month.
429 And the flood (flowed) for the next one hundred and fifty days.
431–4 Everything was destroyed that lived there in the world, (that) ever swam there, or flew, or went on foot. All that remained was that troubled vessel that the storm drove, in which all species were so tightly packed.
436 To remember His servant who hopes for His mercy.

Then he wakened a wynde on watteres to blowe; *raised*
Thenne lasned the llak that large was are;
Then he stac up the stanges, stoped the welles,
Bed blynne of the rayn—hit batede as fast.

Thenne lasned the logh, lowkande togeder, *flood; contracting*
After harde dayes wern out an hundreth and fyfté. *over*
As that lyftande lome luged aboute
Where the wynde and the weder warpen hit wolde,

Hit saghtled on a softe day, synkande to grounde; *settled; pleasant*
On a rasse of a rok hit rest at the laste, *crevice*
On the mounte of Ararach, of Armene hilles, *Armenian*
That otherwayes on Ebru hit hat the Thanes.

Bot thagh the kyste in the crages were closed to byde,
Yet fyned not the flod, ne fel to the bothemes; *ended*
Bot the hyghest of the egges unhuled wern a lyttel, *edges; uncovered*
That the burne bynne borde byhelde the bare erthe. *man on board*

Thenne wafte he upon his wyndowe and wysed theroute
A message fro that meyny, hem moldes to seche.
That was the raven so ronk, that rebel was ever; *wilful*
He was colored as the cole, corbyal untrwe. *raven*

And he fonges to the flyght and fannes on the wyndes,
Hales hyghe upon hyght to herken tythynges;
He croukes for comfort when carayne he fyndes, *carrion*
Kast up on a clyffe ther costes lay drye. *land*

438–40 Then the flood, that was immense before, subsided; then He closed the cataracts, stopped up the wells, ordered the rain to cease—it abated instantly.

443–4 As that heaving vessel lurched about wherever the wind and the weather would drive it.

448–9 Which alternatively, in Hebrew, is called Thanes. But though the Ark was lodged in the crags.

453–4 Then he swung open his window and sent out a messenger from that company, to look for land for them.

457–8 And he takes flight and glides on the winds, soars to a great height to survey the scene.

He hade the smelle of the smach and *stench*
smoltes theder sone, *goes there at once*
Falles on the foule flesch and fylles his wombe, *stomach*
And sone yederly foryete yisterday steven,
How the chevetayn hym charged that the kyst yemed.

The raven raykes hym forth that reches ful lyttel
How alle fodes ther fare, elles he fynde mete;
Bot the burne bynne borde, that bod to hys *awaited*
come, *coming*
Banned hym ful bytterly, with bestes alle samen. *cursed; together*

He seches another sondesmon and settes *messenger; chooses*
on the dove,
Brynges that bryght upon borde, blessed, and *fair one; deck*
sayde:
'Wende, worthelych wyght, uus wones to seche.
Dryf over this dymme water; if thou druye fyndes,

Bryng bodworde to bot, blysse to uus alle. *message; boat*
Thagh that fowle be false, fre be thou ever.' *bird; true*
Ho wyrles out on the weder on wynges ful scharpe,
Dreyly alle alonge day that dorst never lyght.

And when ho fyndes no folde her fote on to pyche, *land; set*
Ho umbekestes the coste and the kyst seches. *circles; region*
Ho hittes on the eventyde and on the ark sittes; *finds it*
Noe nymmes hir anon and naytly hir staues.

Noe on another day nymmes efte the dove, *again*
And byddes hir bowe over the borne efte bonkes to seche;

463–6 And soon entirely forgot the command of a short time before, how the lord who ruled the Ark had enjoined him. Off goes the raven, caring little how all the creatures there get on, so long as he might find food.
471–2 Go, noble creature, to look for a place for us to live. Press on over this dark water; if you should find dry land.
475–6 She flies out into the sky on swift wings, on and on all through the day, never daring to alight.
480 Noah takes her at once and lodges her well.
482–4 And bids her go over the water to look for land again; and she moves swiftly about in the sky and scouts around until it is almost nightfall, and then she seeks out Noah.

And ho skyrmes under skwe and skowtes aboute
Tyl hit was nyghe at the naght, and Noe then seches.

On ark on an eventyde hoves the dowve; *alights*
On stamyn ho stod and stylle hym abydes.
What! ho broght in hir beke a bronch of olyve, *look!*
Gracyously umbegrouen al with grene leves. *attractively covered*

That was the syngne of savyté that sende hem oure Lorde, *salvation*
And the saghtlyng of hymself with tho sely bestes. *reconciliation* *innocent*
Then was ther joy in that gyn, where jumpred er dryyed,
And much comfort in that cofer that was clay-daubed. *Ark*

Myryly on a fayr morn, monyth the fyrst,
That falles formast in the yer, and the fyrst day,
Ledes loghen in that lome, and loked theroute
How that watteres wern woned and the worlde dryed.

Uchon loved oure Lorde, bot lenged ay stylle, *praised; remained*
Tyl thay had tythyng fro the tolke that tyned hem therinne.
Then Godes glam to hem glod that gladed hem alle,
Bede hem drawe to the dor, delyver hem he wolde. *bade; go*

Then went thay to the wykket, hit walt upon sone;
Bothe the burne and his barnes bowed theroute;
Her wyves walkes hem wyth, and the wylde after, *animals*
Throly thrublande in thronge, throwen ful thykke.

486 She perched on the prow and quietly waited for him.
491 Then there was joy in that vessel, where the motley company had suffered before.
493–6 On a fair morning, the first day of the first month of the year, men laughed happily in that vessel, and saw how outside the waters were diminished and the world was made dry.
498–9 Until they had word from the One who had confined them there. Then God's speech came to them, cheering them all.
501–2 Then they went to the door, it swung open at once; the man and his children went outside.
504–6 Impatiently jostling in a throng, pressed together tightly. But Noah picked out (a single) one of each clean species, and raised up an altar and consecrated it properly.

Bot Noe of uche honest kynde nem out an odde,
And hevened up an auter and halwed hit fayre,
And sette a sakerfyse theron of uch a ser kynde *different*
That was comly and clene—God kepes non other. *seemly; recognises*

When bremly brened those bestes and the brethe rysed,
The savour of his sacrafyse soght to hym even
That al spedes and spylles; he spekes with that ilke,
In comly comfort ful clos and cortays wordes:

'Now, Noe, no more nel I never wary *will not; curse*
Alle the mukel mayny-molde for no mannes synnes; *great world*
For I se wel that hit is sothe that alle segges wyttes *true; men's*
To unthryfte arn alle thrawen with thoght of her herttes, *folly; turned*

And ay has ben and wyl be yet fro her barnage; *childhood*
Al is the mynde of the man to malyce enclyned. *evil*
Forthy schal I never schende so schortly at ones
As dysstrye al for manes synne, dayes of this erthe.

Bot waxes now and wendes forth and worthes to monye;
Multyplyes on this molde, and menske yow bytyde.
Sesounes schal yow never sese of sede ne of hervest,
Ne hete ne no harde forst, umbre ne droghthe,

Ne the swetnesse of somer, ne the sadde wynter, *dismal*
Ne the nyght, ne the day, ne the newe yeres, *succeeding*
Bot ever renne restles—rengnes ye therinne.'
Therwyth he blesses uch a best and bytaght hem this erthe. *gave*

509–12 When those beasts were burning vigorously and the smoke rose, the smell of His sacrifice went right up to the One who makes and mars everything; He speaks with that man, full of seemly cheer and courteous words.

519–24 Therefore I shall never, on account of man's sin, punish so decisively as to destroy all at once, for as long as the earth shall last. But prosper now and go forth and increase in numbers; multiply on the earth, and may grace befall you. Seasons of seed-time and of harvest shall never cease for you, neither heat nor hard frost, dull weather nor drought.

527 But they shall run ever-changing—hold sway therein (i.e. on earth).

Then was a skylly skyvalde, quen scaped alle the wylde;
Uche fowle to the flyght that fytheres myght serve, *wings*
Uche fysch to the flod that fynne couthe nayte, *water; use*
Uche beste to the bent that bytes on erbes. *field; grass*

Wylde wormes to her won wrythes in the erthe,
The fox and the folmarde to the fryth wyndes,
Herttes to hyghe hethe, hares to gorstes, *scrublands*
And lyounes and lebardes to the *leopards*
lake ryftes. *river-valleys*

Hernes and havekes to the hyghe roches, *eagles; hawks; crags*
The hole-foted fowle to the flod hyyes, *web-footed; hastens*
And uche best at a brayde ther hym best lykes;
The fowre frekes of the folde fonges the empyre.

Lo, suche a wrakful wo, for wlatsum dedes,
Parformed the hyghe Fader on folke that he made; *inflicted*
That he chysly hade cherisched he chastysed ful hardee,
In devoydynge the vylanye that venkquyst his thewes.

Forthy war the now, wyye, that worschyp desyres
In his comlych courte that kyng is of blysse, *seemly*
In the fylthe of the flesch that thou be founden never,
Tyl any water in the worlde to wasche the fayly.

529 Then there was a clear splitting-up, when all the animals escaped.

533–4 Wild snakes slither to their dwelling in the earth, the fox and the polecat go to the wood.

539–41 And each animal (hastens) forthwith to where it pleases him best; the four men assume the rule of the earth. Look, such a bitter misfortune, on account of loathsome deeds.

543–5 Those whom He had lovingly cherished He chastised most severely, in purging the evil that had overcome His good nature. Therefore take care now, sir, you who desire honour.

548–56 To the extent that any water in the world should fail to cleanse you. For there is no man under the sun so seemly in his manners (but that) if he is polluted by sin that remains uncleansed, one speck of a spot may be enough to (make him) forfeit the sight of the Sovereign who sits so high. For he who will make an appearance in those bright houses must be as clean as the burnished beryl, which is perfect everywhere and has no seam, without spot or blemish, like the pearl.

For is no segge under sunne so seme of his craftes,
If he be sulped in synne that syttes unclene,
On spec of a spote may spede to mysse
Of the syghte of the Soverayn that syttes so hyghe.

For that schewe me schale in tho schyre howses
As the beryl bornyst byhoves be clene,
That is sounde on uche a syde and no sem habes,
Withouten maskle other mote, as margerye-perle.

II

Sythen the Soverayn in sete so sore forthoght
That ever he man upon molde merked to lyvy. *gave life to*
For he in fylthe was fallen, felly he venged, *because; fiercely*
Quen fourferde alle the flesch that he formed hade. *perished*

Hym rwed that he hem uprerde and raght hem lyflode,
And efte that he hem undyd, hard hit hym thoght;
For quen the swemande sorwe soght to his hert, *painful; touched*
He knyt a covenaunde cortaysly with monkynde there, *made; graciously*
In the mesure of his mode and methe of his wylle,
That he schulde never for no syt smyte al at ones, *evil*
As to quelle alle quykes, for qued that myght falle,
Whyl of the lenthe of the londe lastes the terme.

That ilke skyl for no scathe ascaped hym never;
Wheder wonderly he wrak on wykked men after,
Ful felly for that ilk faute forferde a kyth ryche,
In the anger of his ire that arwed mony. *terrified*

557 Then the Sovereign on His throne repented very deeply.
561–2 He regretted that He had raised them up and given them sustenance, but afterwards it seemed to Him hard that He had destroyed them.
565 In the moderation of His nature and the mildness of His heart.
567–71 So as to kill all living things, whatever mischief occurred, for as long as the world lasted. That purpose never left Him, not for any sin; yet afterwards He punished wicked men exceedingly, fiercely destroyed a mighty people for that same offence.

And al was for this ilk evel, that unhappen glette, *accursed sin*
The venym and the vylanye and the vycios fylthe
That bysulpes mannes saule in unsounde hert, *defiles*
That he his Saveour ne see with syght of his yyen. *eyes*

Thus alle illes he hates as helle that stynkkes; *evils*
Bot non nuyes hym, on naght ne never upon dayes,
As harlottrye unhonest, hethyng of selven;
That schames for no schrewedschyp, schent mot he worthe!

Bot savour, mon, in thyself, thagh thou a *consider*
sotte lyvie, *idiot*
Thagh thou bere thyself babel, bythenk the sumtyme
Whether he that stykked uche a stare in uche steppe yye,
Yif hymself be bore blynde, hit is a brod wonder,

And he that fetly in face fettled alle eres, *skilfully; fixed*
If he has losed the lysten, hit lyftes mervayle;
Traue thou never that tale, untrwe thou hit fyndes. *believe*
Ther is no dede so derne that dittes his yyen;

Ther is no wyye in his werk so war ne so stylle
That hit ne thrawes to hym thro er he hit thoght have;
For he is the gropande God, the grounde of *searching*
alle dedes,
Rypande of uche a ring the reynyes and hert.

And there he fyndes al fayre a freke wythinne, *where*
That hert honest and hol, that hathel he *whole; man*
honoures,

578–80 But none angers Him, neither by night nor by day, so much as unclean lewdness, contempt for one's person; he who is ashamed of no depravity, let him be destroyed!
582–4 Though you behave foolishly, take thought for once that if He who put the power of sight in each bright eye should Himself be born blind, that would be a great wonder.
586 If He has lost the power of hearing, that would be a marvellous thing.
588–90 There is no deed so hidden that He is prevented from seeing it (lit. that closes His eyes); there is no man so careful or secretive in what he does but that it flies to Him swiftly before he has so much as thought of it.
592 Probing the reins and heart (i.e. innermost being) of every man.

Sendes hym a sad syght, to se his auen face, *solemn; own*
And harde honyses thise other and of his erde flemes.

Bot of the dome of the douthe for dedes of schame,
He is so skoymos of that skathe he scarres bylyve;
He may not dryye to draw allyt bot drepes in hast,
And that was schewed schortly by a scathe ones. *disaster*

Olde Abraham in erde ones he syttes, *at home*
Even byfore his hous dore, under an oke grene. *directly*
Bryght blykked the bem of the brode heven; *shone; sun's rays*
In the hyghe hete therof Abraham bides. *intense; sits*

He was schunt to the schadow under schyre leves;
Thenne was he war on the waye of wlonk wyyes thrynne;
If thay wer farande and fre and fayre to beholde, *handsome; noble*
Hit is ethe to leve by the last ende.

For the lede that ther laye the leves anunder, *man*
When he hade of hem syght he hyyes bylyve, *hastens*
And as to God the good-mon gos hem agaynes, *towards*
And haylsed hem in onhede, and sayde: 'Hende Lorde,

Yif ever thy mon upon molde merit disserved, *reward*
Lenge a lyttel with thy lede, I lowly biseche;
Passe never fro thi povere, yif I hit pray durst,
Er thou haf biden with thi burne and under boghe restted.

596–9 And harshly spurns the rest and drives them from His dwelling. But concerning the punishment of men for deeds of shame, He is so revolted by that sin that He takes alarm at once; He cannot bear to hold back but kills in haste.
605–6 He had retreated to the shade under the bright leaves. Then he became aware of three lordly men on the road.
608 It is easy to conclude from the sequel.
612 And greeted them as one, and said: 'Gracious Lord.'
614–16 Stay for a little with your servant, I humbly beseech; do not leave your lowly one, if I dare entreat it, until you have sat with your servant and rested under the boughs.

And I schal wynne yow wyght of water a lyttel, *bring; quickly*
And fast aboute schal I fare your fette wer waschene;
Resttes here on this rote and I schal rachche after *root; go to get*
And brynge a morsel of bred to baume your hertte.' *cheer*

'Fare forthe,' quoth the frekes, 'and fech as thou segges;
By bole of this brode tre we byde the here.'
Thenne orppedly into his hous he hyyed to Sare, *quickly; Sarah*
Comaunded hir to be cof and quyk *prompt*
at this ones: *for this once*

'Thre mettes of mele menge, and ma kakes;
Under askes ful hote happe hem bylive;
Quyl I fete sumquat fat, thou the fyr bete,
Prestly, at this ilke poynte, sum polment to make.'

He cached to his couhous and a calf brynges *went*
That was tender and not toghe, bed tyrve of the hyde,
And sayde to his servaunt that he hit sethe faste; *cook*
And he dervely at his dome dyght hit bylyve.

The burne to be bare-heved buskes hym thenne,
Cleches to a clene clothe and kestes on the grene,
Thrwe thryftyly theron tho thre therve-kakes,
And brynges butter wythal and by the bred settes. *sets it*

Mete messes of mylke he merkkes bytwene,
Sythen potage and polment in plater honest;

618 And I shall busy myself to wash your feet.
621–2 'Go forth,' said the men, 'and fetch them as you say; we shall wait for you here by the trunk of this great tree.'
625–8 Mix three measures of meal, and make loaves; cover them quickly under hot ashes; while I fetch an animal which has been fattened (for the table), you kindle the fire promptly, now at this very moment, to make a stew.
630 Ordered the hide to be stripped off.
632–5 And at his bidding he prepared it at once with all speed. The man then hastens to be bare-headed, takes up a clean cloth and throws it on the grass, swiftly and with propriety places the three unleavened loaves on it.
637–40 He placed appropriate milk dishes here and there, then pottage and stew in a worthy platter; in fitting manner, like a servant at table, he served them fully with such as he had, with dignified and pleasant bearing.

As sewer in a gud assyse he served hem fayre,
Wyth sadde semblaunt and swete, of such as he hade.

And God as a glad gest mad god chere,
That was fayn of his frende and his fest praysed; *pleased with*
Abraham, al hodles, with armes upfolden, *uplifted (in prayer)*
Mynystred mete byfore tho men that myghtes al weldes.

Thenne thay sayden as thay sete samen alle *together*
thrynne, *three*
When the mete was remued and thay of
mensk speken: *made polite conversation*
'I schal efte hereaway, Abram,' thay sayden, *again come here*
'Yet er thy lyves lyght lethe upon erthe; *is extinguished*

And thenne schal Sare consayve and a sun bere,
That schal be Abrahames ayre, and after hym *heir*
wynne *beget*
With wele and wyth worschyp the worthely peple
That schal halde in heritage that I haf men yarked.'

Thenne the burde byhynde the dor for busmar *woman; scorn*
laghed,
And sayde sotyly to hirself Sare the madde: *slyly; foolish*
'May thou traw for tykle that thou teme moghtes,
And I so hyghe out of age, and also my lorde?' *much over age*

For sothely, as says the Wryt, hit wern of sadde elde,
Bothe the wyye and his wyf, such werk was hem fayled;
Fro mony a brod day byfore ho barayn ay had bene, *long*
That selve Sare withouten sede into that same tyme. *up to*

644 Served food before those men who wield all powers.
651–2 In blessedness and honour the noble race which shall inherit that which I have granted to men (i.e. in the Covenant).
655 Can you believe that you will conceive through wantonness.
657 For truly, as the Bible says, they were of advanced age.
658 Such activity had come to an end for them.

Thenne sayde oure Syre ther he sete: 'Se! so Sare laghes,
Not trawande the tale that I the to schewed. *matter; disclosed*
Hopes ho oght may be harde my hondes to work?
And yet I avow verayly the avaunt that I made;

I schal yeply ayayn and yelde that I hyght,
And sothely sende to Sare a soun and an hayre.' *indeed*
Thenne swenged forth Sare and swer by hir trawthe *rushed: swore*
That for lot that thay laused ho laghed never. *words; uttered*

'Now innogh, hit is not so,' thenne nurned the Dryghtyn, *declared* *Lord*
'For thou laghed alow, bot let we hit one.' *quietly; let it pass*
With that thay ros up radly as thay rayke schulde,
And setten toward Sodamas her syght alle at ones.

For that cité therbysyde was sette in a vale, *nearby*
No myles fro Mambre mo then tweyne,
Where-so wonyed this ilke wyy that wendes with oure Lorde
For to tent hym with tale and teche hym the gate.

Then glydes forth God, the godmon hym folwes;
Abraham heldes hem wyth, hem to conveye *goes; escort*
In towarde the cety of Sodamas that synned had thenne
In the faute of this fylthe; the Fader hem thretes, *threatens*

And sayde thus to the segg that sued hym after: *man; attended*
'How myght I hyde myn hert fro Habraham the trwe,
That I ne dyscovered to his corse my counsayl so dere,
Sythen he is chosen to be chef chyldryn fader,

663–5 Does she think anything is difficult for my hands to do? But nevertheless I emphatically affirm the vow that I made: I shall quickly return and perform what I promised.
671–2 With that they stood up quickly in readiness to go, and together turned their eyes towards Sodom.
674–7 No more than two miles from Mamre, where this same man lived who goes with our Lord to engage Him in conversation and show Him the way. Then God goes forth, the master of the house follows Him.
683–8 And not reveal to him my most stern purpose, since he is chosen to be the first father of the children of Israel, from whom people shall spring so as to fill all the world, and (since) each nation shall be blessed through him? I must tell that man of the anger in my mind, and disclose all my intention to Abraham at once.

That so folk schal falle fro to flete alle the worlde,
And uche blod in that burne blessed schal worthe?
Me bos telle to that tolk the tene of my wylle,
And alle myn atlyng to Abraham unhaspe bilyve.

The grete soun of Sodamas synkkes in myn eres, *clamour*
And the gult of Gomorre gares me to wrath;
I schal lyght into that led and loke myselven *go down; people*
If thay haf don as the dyne dryves on lofte.

Thay han lerned a lyst that lykes me ille, *practice; pleases*
That thay han founden in her flesch of fautes the werst; *in that*
Uch male mas his mach a man as hymselven,
And fylter folyly in fere on femmales wyse.

I compast hem a kynde crafte and kende hit hem derne,
And amed hit in myn ordenaunce oddely dere,
And dyght drwry therinne, doole alther-swettest;
And the play of paramores I portrayed myselven,

And made therto a maner myriest of other.
When two true togeder had tyyed hemselven,
Bytwene a male and his make such merthe schulde come, *mate; pleasure*
Welnyghe pure Paradys moght preve no better. *itself; prove*

Elles thay moght honestly ayther other welde,
At a stylle stollen steven unstered wyth syght,
Luf-lowe hem bytwene lasched so hote
That alle the meschefes on mold moght hit not sleke.

690 And the sin of Gomorrah makes me angry.
692 To see if they have behaved as the noise is raised on high.
695–702 Each male takes as his mate a man like himself, and they join together wantonly in female fashion. I devised for them a natural skill and taught it to them privately, and valued it exceptionally highly in my plan of creation, establishing love, the sweetest of all gifts, in that skill; and I devised the dalliance of lovers, and contrived in that regard the most pleasant practice of all. Whenever two virtuous people joined themselves together.
705–8 As long as they used each other decently, at a quiet private meeting with none to look on, the fire of love might flare up between them so hotly that all the misfortunes in the world would be unable to extinguish it.

Now haf thay skyfted my skyl and scorned natwre, *altered; purpose*
And henttes hem in hethyng an usage unclene; *adopt in contempt*
Hem to smyte for that smod smartly I thenk, *filth*
That wyyes schal be by hem war worlde withouten ende.' *warned*

Thenne arwed Abraham, and alle his mod chaunged, *was afraid; mood*
For hope of the harde hate that hyght has oure Lorde.
Al sykande he sayde: 'Sir, with yor leve, *sighing*
Schal synful and sakles suffer al on payne? *innocent; one penalty*

Wether ever hit lyke my Lorde to lyfte such domes,
That the wykked and the worthy schal on wrake suffer, *punishment*
And weye upon the worre half that wrathed the never?
That was never thy won that wroghtes uus alle. *custom*

Now fyfty fyn frendes wer founde in yonde toune,
In the cety of Sodamas, and also Gomorre,
That never lakked thy laue, bot loved ay trauthe, *offended against; law*
And reghtful wern and resounable and redy the to serve, *righteous*

Schal thay falle in the faute that other frekes wroght,
And joyne to her juggement, her juise to have?
That nas never thyn note, unnevened hit worthe,
That art so gaynly a God and of goste mylde.' *gracious; nature*

714 In expectation of the severe punishment that our Lord had promised.
717 Does it please my Lord to pronounce such judgements?
719 And to weigh on the wrong side (of the balance) those who never angered you?
721 If now fifty worthies were found in that town.
726–7 And be included in your judgement of them (i.e. the guilty), to share their doom? That was never your way, may it (i.e. the judgement) be retracted.

'Nay, for fyfty,' quoth the Fader, 'and thy fayre speche,
And thay be founden in that folk of her fylthe clene, *if; free*
I schal forgyve allé the gylt thurgh my grace one, *alone*
And let hem smolt al unsmyten smothely at ones.'

'Aa! blessed be thow,' quoth the burne, 'so boner and thewed, *kind gracious*
And al haldes in thy honde, the heven and the erthe; *you hold*
Bot, for I haf this talke, tas to non ille
Yif I mele a lyttel more, that mul am and askes.

What if fyve faylen of fyfty the noumbre, *are wanting*
And the remnaunt be reken, how restes thy wylle?' *honest; stands*
'And fyve wont of fyfty,' quoth God, 'I schal foryete alle, *if pardon*
And wythhalde my honde for hortyng on lede.'

'And quat if faurty be fre and fauty thyse other?
Schalt thow schortly al schende and schape non other?'
'Nay, thagh faurty forfete, yet fryst I a whyle,
And voyde away my vengaunce, thagh me vyl thynk.'

Then Abraham obeched hym and lowly him thonkkes: *bowed to; humbly*
'Now sayned be thou, Saviour, so symple in thy wrath. *blessed; mild*
I am bot erthe ful evel and usle so blake, *vile; ashes*
For to mele wyth such a mayster as myghtes has alle. *powers*

Bot I have bygonnen wyth my God, and he hit gayn thynkes; *if; good*
Yif I forloyne as a fol, thy fraunchyse may serve.

732 And let them go in peace at once, quite unharmed.
735–6 But, since I am engaged in this conversation, do not take it amiss if I speak a little more, I who am dust and ashes.
740–4 'And restrain my hand, so as not to hurt a single person.' 'And what if forty be good, and the others sinful, will you destroy all directly and have it no other way?' 'No, if forty are to be lost, I shall still hold back, and forego my vengeance, disgusted though I am.'
750–1 If I should go astray like a fool, your generosity will serve. What if thirty worthy men should be punished in those towns?

What if thretty thryvande be thrad in yon tounes?
What shall I leve of my Lorde, if he hem lethe wolde?' *think; save*

Thenne the godlych God gef hym onsware: *gracious*
'Yet for thretty in throng I schal my thro steke, *wrath* *restrain*
And spare spakly of spyt, in space of my thewes,
And my rankor refrayne four thy reken wordes.' *restrain; for*

'What for twenty,' quoth the tolke, 'untwynes thou hem thenne?'
'Nay, yif thou yernes hit, yet yark I hem grace. *grant*
If that twenty be trwe, I tene hem no more, *harm*
Bot relece alle that regioun of her ronk werkkes.' *absolve; vile*

'Now, athel Lorde,' quoth Abraham, 'ones a speche, *noble* *once more*
And I schal schape no more tho schalkkes to helpe. *endeavour; men*
If ten trysty in toune be tan in thi werkkes,
Wylt thou mese thy mode and menddyng abyde?'

'I graunt,' quoth the grete God. 'Graunt mercy,' that other; *consent* *thank you*
And thenne arest the renk and raght no fyrre.
And Godde glydes his gate by those grene wayes, *departs along*
And he conveyen hym con with cast of his yye.

And als he loked along there as oure Lorde passed,
Yet he cryed hym after with careful steven: *anxious voice*
'Meke mayster, on thy mon to mynne if the lyked,
Loth lenges in yon leede, that is my lef brother.

755 And willingly refrain from anger, in the generosity of my good nature.
757 'What shall you do for twenty,' said the man, 'will you then destroy them?'
763–4 If ten true men in the town should be found engaged in your works, will you moderate your anger and wait for improvement?
766 And then the man stopped and went no further.
768–9 And he followed Him with his glance; and as he looked to where our Lord passed.
771–2 Merciful Lord, if it should please you to remember your servant, Lot, who is my dear kinsman, lives amongst that people.

He syttes ther in Sodomis, thy servaunt so povere, *dwells; lowly*
Among tho mansed men that han the much *accursed*
greved; *angered*
Yif thou tynes that toun, tempre thyn yre *will overthrow*
As thy mersy may malte, thy meke to spare.'

Then he wendes his way, wepande for care,
Towarde the mere of Mambre, mornande for sorewe; *border*
And there in longyng al nyght he lenges in wones,
Whyl the Soverayn to Sodamas sende to spye. *sent messengers*

His sondes into Sodamas was sende in that tyme, *embassy*
In that ilk eventyde, by aungels tweyne,
Mevande mekely togeder as myry men yonge, *briskly*
As Loot in a loge dor lened hym alone,

In a porche of that place pyght to the yates,
That was ryal and ryche, so was the renkes selven.
As he stared into the strete, ther stout men played,
He syye ther swey in asent swete men tweyne.

Bolde burnes wer thay bothe, with berdles chynnes,
Royl rollande fax to raw sylk lyke, *splendid flowing hair*
Of ble as the brere-flour, where-so the bare scheweed.
Ful clene was the countenaunce of her cler yyen; *bright; glance*

Wlonk whit was her wede, and wel hit hem semed;
Of alle fetures ful fyn, and fautles bothe;
Was non aucly in outher, for aungels hit wern,
And that the yep underyede that in the yate syttes.

776 As much as your mercy is able to soften it, to spare your humble one.
779 And there he remains at home, in anxiety all night.
784–8 As Lot sat alone in the doorway of a lodge, in a gatehouse next to the gates of that city, which was splendid and rich, as the man was himself. As he looked into the road, where proud men came and went, he saw two comely men there, moving together.
791 Of complexion like the briar-rose, wherever the bare skin was revealed.
793–6 Their dress was of rich white, and well it suited them; they were pleasing in every feature, and faultless as well; there was no blemish in either, for they were angels, and the alert man who sat in the gateway realized that.

He ros up ful radly and ran hem to mete, *swiftly*
And lowe he loutes hem to, Loth, to the grounde; *bows*
And sythen soberly: 'Syres, I yow byseche *earnestly*
That ye wolde lyght at my loge and lenge therinne.

Comes to your knaves kote, I crave at this ones;
I schal fette yow a fatte your fette for to wasche; *fetch; tub*
I norne yow bot for on nyght neghe me to lenge, *ask; with*
And in the myry mornyng ye may your waye take.' *bright*

And thay nay that thay nolde negh no howses,
Bot stylly ther in the strete, as thay stadde wern,
Thay wolde lenge the long naght, and logge theroute;
Hit was hous innoghe to hem the heven upon lofte.

Loth lathed so longe wyth luflych wordes, *urged; courteous*
That thay hym graunted to go, and grught no lenger. *agreed; refused*
The bolde to his byggyng brynges hem bylyve, *house; quickly*
That was ryally arayed, for he was ryche ever. *exceedingly*

The wyyes wern welcom as the wyf couthe;
His two dere doghteres devoutly hem haylsed, *greeted*
That wer maydenes ful meke, maryed not yet,
And thay wer semly and swete and swythe wel arayed. *very*

Loth thenne ful lyghtly lokes hym aboute, *quickly*
And his men amonestes mete for to dyght: *charges; prepare*
'Bot thenkkes on hit be threfte, what thynk so ye make,
For wyth no sour ne no salt serves hym never.' *leaven*

800–1 That you would stop at my house and lodge there. Come to your servant's cottage, I beg you, for this once.
805–7 But they said they would not go near any houses, but would stay there quietly in the road all night, and lodge in the open as they found themselves.
813 The men were made welcome by his wife to the best of her ability.
819 But take care that it be unleavened, whatever you make.

Bot yet I wene that the wyf hit wroth to dyspyt,
And sayde softely to hirself: 'This unsaveré hyne *unseasoned fellows*
Loves no salt in her sauce, yet hit no skyl were
That other burne be boute, thagh bothe be nyse.'

Thenne ho saveres with salt her seves uchone, *seasons; sauces*
Agayne the bone of the burne that hit forboden hade, *command*
And als ho scelt hem in scorne that wel her skyl knewen.
Why was ho, wrech, so wod? Ho wrathed oure Lorde. *mad; angered*

Thenne seten thay at the soper, wern served bylyve,
The gestes gay and ful glad, of glam debonere, *speech; courteous*
Wela wynnely wlonk, tyl thay waschen hade,
The trestes tylt to the wowe, and the table bothe.

Fro the segges haden souped, and seten bot a whyle,
Er ever thay bosked to bedde, the borgh was al up, *went; town*
Alle that weppen myght welde, the wakker and the stronger, *wield*
To umbelyye Lothes hous, the ledes to take. *surround; men*

In grete flokkes of folk thay fallen to his yates; *rush at*
As a scowte-wach scarred so the asscry rysed;
With kene clobbes of that clos thay clater on the wowes,
And wyth a schrylle scharp schout thay schewe thys worde: *utter*

'If thou lovyes thy lyf, Loth, in thyse wones, *this place*
Yete uus out those yong men that yorewhyle here entred, *get; recently*
That we may lere hym of lof, as oure lyst biddes, *teach; desire*
As is the asyse of Sodomas to segges that passen.' *custom*

821 But yet I fancy that the woman took it amiss.
823–4 But it would not be reasonable that others should be without, though they are both ill-bred.
827 And in this way she scorned those who well knew her purpose.
831–3 Most excellently polite, until they had washed (i.e. at the end of the meal), the trestles having been tilted against the wall, and the table as well. After the men had eaten supper, and had sat but a short while.
838 Clamour rose up as from a startled sentry-patrol; with great clubs they beat on the walls of that house.

Whatt! thay sputen and speken of so spitous fylthe;
What! thay yeyed and yolped of yestande sorwe,
That yet the wynd and the weder and the worlde stynkes *air*
Of the brych that upbraydes those brothelych wordes.

The godman glyfte with that glam and gloped for noyse;
So scharpe schame to hym schot, he schrank at the hert.
For he knew the costoum that kythed those wreches; *observed*
He doted never for no doel so depe in his mynde.

'Allas!' sayd hym thenne Loth, and lyghtly he ryses, *to himself*
And bowes forth fro the bench into the brode yates.
What! he wonded no wothe of wekked knaves
That he ne passed the port the peril to abide.

He went forthe at the wyket and waft hit hym after, *swung*
That a clyket hit cleght clos hym byhynde.
Thenne he meled to tho men mesurable wordes, *moderate*
For harlotes with his hendelayk he hoped to chast:

'Oo, my frendes so fre, your fare is to strange;
Dos away your derf dyn, and deres never my gestes.
Avoy! hit is your vylaynye, ye vylen yourselven;
And ye ar jolyf gentylmen, your japes ar ille.

Bot I schal kenne yow by kynde a crafte that is better;
I haf a tresor in my telde of tow my fayre deghter,

845–6 Listen! they talked together and spoke of such shameful sin; listen! they shouted and boasted of festering filth.
848–50 Of the sin which throws up those wild words. The master of the house winced at that uproar and was aghast at the noise; such deep shame came over him that he recoiled inwardly.
852 Never for any distressing event was he in such great confusion (of mind).
854–6 And goes forth from his seat into the main gateway. Look! he feared no harm from evil men that would stop him passing through the gate to face the danger.
858 So that a catch fastened it firmly behind him.
860–6 For he hoped to chasten the lechers by his courtesy. 'Oh my most noble friends, your behaviour is too unnatural; cease your great clamour, and do not harm my guests. For shame! it is to your disgrace, you degrade yourselves; if you are worthy gentlemen, your tricks are vile. But I shall teach you a better skill, according to nature; I have a treasure in my house, my two fair daughters.'

That ar maydenes unmard for alle men yette; *undefiled*
In Sodamas, thagh I hit say, non semloker burdes. *prettier women*

Hit arn ronk, hit arn rype, and redy to manne;
To samen wyth tho semly the solace is better;
I schal biteche yow tho two that tayt arn and quoynt,
And laykes wyth hem as yow lyst, and letes my gestes one.'

Thenne the rebaudes so ronk rerd such a noyse,
That awly hurled in his eres her harlotes speche: *fearsomely rang*
'Wost thou not wel that thou wones here a wyye strange,
An outcomlyng, a carle?—we kylle of thyn heved!

Who joyned the be jostyse, oure japes to blame,
That com a boy to this borgh, thagh thou be burne ryche?'
Thus thay throbled and throng and thrwe umbe his eres,
And distresed hym wonder strayt with strenkthe in the prece,

Bot that the yonge men so yepe yornen theroute, *bold; ran*
Wapped upon the wyket and wonnen hem tylle,
And by the hondes hym hent and horyed hym withinne, *took; hurried*
And steken the yates ston-harde wyth stalworth barres. *fastened; very firmly*

Thay blwe a boffet in blande that banned peple,
That thay blustered as blynde as Bayard was ever.

869–73 'They are grown, they are ripe, and ready to be mastered; there is better pleasure in consorting with those pretty ones; I shall give the two of them to you, lively and attractive as they are, and play with them as it pleases you, and leave my guests alone.' Then the vile scoundrels raised such a din.

875–80 'Do you not know well that you live here as a foreigner, an alien, a churl—we shall knock off your head! Who appointed you to be a judge, to find fault with our games, you who came to this town as a man of no account, though you are now a rich man?' Thus they jostled and pushed and crowded close about him, and would have hurt him very severely by their violence in the press.

882 Flung open the wicket and made their way to them.

885–6 They blew a blast amongst that accursed people, so that they stumbled about as blind as Bayard (a proverbially blind horse) ever was.

Thay lest of Lotes logging any lysoun to fynde, *failed; opening*
Bot nyteled ther alle the nyght for noght at the last. *blundered*

Thenne uch tolke tyght hem that hade of tayt fayled,
And uchon rotheled to the rest that he reche moght; *staggered; get*
Bot thay wern wakned awrank that ther in won lenged,
Of on the uglokest unhap ever on erd suffred.

Ruddon of the day-rawe ros upon ughten,
When merk of the mydnyght moght no more last. *darkness*
Ful erly those aungeles this hathel thay ruthen, *man; rouse*
And glopnedly, on Godes halve, gart hym upryse.

Fast the freke ferkes up, ful ferd at his hert;
Thay comaunded hym cof to cach that he hade: *quickly; take*
'Wyth thy wyf and thy wyyes and thy wlonc deghtters, *fair*
For we lathe the, sir Loth, that thou thy lyf have. *urge; save*

Cayre tid of this kythe, er combred thou worthe,
With alle thi here upon haste, tyl thou a hil fynde; *household*
Foundes faste on your fete, bifore your face lokes, *go on*
Bot bes never so bolde to blusch yow bihynde. *do not dare; look*

And loke ye stemme no stepe, bot streches on faste;
Til ye reche to a reset, rest ye never; *refuge*
For we schal tyne this toun and traythely disstrye,
Wyth alle thise wyyes so wykke wyghtly devoyde,

889 Then each man went away, having failed to find pleasure.
891–3 But they were wretchedly awakened, those who lived there in that town, by the very worst disaster ever experienced on earth. The redness of first light came up at daybreak.
896–7 And in alarming fashion they ordered him to get up, in God's name. Quickly the man starts up, very frightened at heart.
901 Go quickly from this land, before you are overwhelmed.
905 And see to it that you do not stop, but move on quickly.
907–9 For we shall overthrow this town and pitilessly destroy it, do away with it in a moment together with all these evil men, and all the land with its people we shall ruin all at once.

And alle the londe with thise ledes we losen at ones;
Sodomas schal ful sodenly synk into grounde,
And the grounde of Gomorre gorde into helle, *foundations; plunge*
And uche a koste of this kyth clater upon hepes.' *part*

Then laled Loth: 'Lorde, what is best? *spoke*
If I me fele upon fote that I fle moght,
Hou schulde I huyde me from hym that has his hate kynned,
In the brath of his breth that brennes alle thinkes?

To crepe fro my Creatour and know not wheder,
Ne whether his fooschip me folwes bifore other bihynde!'
The freke sayde: 'No foschip oure Fader has the schewed,
Bot highly hevened thi hele fro hem that arn combred.

Nou wale the a wonnyng that the warisch myght,
And he schal save hit for thy sake that has uus sende hider;
For thou art oddely thyn one out of this fylthe,
And als Abraham thyn eme hit at himself asked.'

'Lorde, loved he worthe,' quoth Loth, 'upon erthe! *may He be praised*
Ther is a cité herbisyde that Segor hit hatte; *which is called*
Hereutter on a rounde hil hit hoves hit one.
I wolde, if his wylle wore, to that won scape.'

'Thenn fare forth,' quoth that fre, 'and fyne thou never,
With those ilk that thow wylt, that threnge the after,
And ay goande on your gate wythouten agayntote;
For alle this londe schal be lorne longe er the sonne rise.' *lost*

914–18 If I should go forward on foot in order to escape, how should I hide myself from Him who has kindled His anger, who consumes all things in the violence of His fury? To steal away from my Creator and not know where to go, nor whether His enmity will seek me out from in front or behind!

920–1 But (He has) specially exalted your safety above those who are overwhelmed. Now choose a place for yourself which can protect you.

923–4 For you are absolutely the only one untouched by this filth, and also Abraham your uncle asked it of Him.

927–31 'It stands on its own on a round hill outside this place. I would like to escape to that town, if it were His will.' 'Then go forth,' said that noble one, 'and do not stop, with those whom you want with you, who owe allegiance to you, always going on your way without a backward glance.'

The wyye wakened his wyf and his wlonk deghteres,
And other two myri men tho maydenes schulde wedde;
And thay token hit as tayt and tented hit lyttel, *joke; heeded*
Thagh fast lathed hem Loth, thay leyen ful stylle. *earnestly urged*

The aungeles hasted thise other and awly hem thratten, *fearsomely threatened*
And enforsed alle fawre forth at the yates. *drove*
Tho wern Loth and his lef, his luflyche deghter; *dear one (wife)*
Ther soght no mo to savement of cities athel fyve.

Thise aungeles hade hem by hande out at the yates, *brought*
Prechande hem the perile, and beden hem passe fast: *bade; go*
'Lest ye be taken in the teche of tyrauntes here, *sin; evil men*
Loke ye bowe now bi bot, bowes fast hence.'

And thay kayre ne con and kenely flowen;
Erly, er any heven-glem, thay to a hil comen. *glimmer of dawn*
The grete God in his greme bygynnes on lofte *anger*
To wakan wederes so wylde—the wyndes he calles, *storms*

And thay wrothely upwafte and wrastled togeder, *fiercely rose*
Fro fawre half of the folde, flytande loude;
Clowdes clustered bytwene, kesten up torres,
That the thik thunder-thrast thirled hem ofte.

The rayn rueled adoun, ridlande thikke, *poured; sifting*
Of felle flaunkes of fyr and flakes of soufre,
Al in smolderande smoke, smachande ful ille, *smothering; smelling*
Swe aboute Sodamas and hit sydes alle, *fell; its environs*

934 And two other worthy men whom those maidens were to wed.
940 No more reached safety from the five proud cities.
944–5 'See that you go now quickly, go fast from this place.' And they did not hesitate but swiftly fled.
950–2 From the four corners of the earth, contending loudly; clouds clustered at intervals, threw up hill-like masses, which the ever-present lightning often pierced.
954 Of terrible sparks of fire and lumps of sulphur.

Gorde to Gomorra that the grounde laused,
Abdama and Syboym—thise ceteis alle faure
Al birolled wyth the rayn, rostted and brenned,
And ferly flayed that folk that in those fees lenged.

For when that the helle herde the houndes of heven, *when Hell*
He was ferlyly fayn, unfolded bylyve;
The grete barres of the abyme he barst up at ones,
That alle the regioun torof in riftes ful grete, *broke up*

And cloven alle in lyttel cloutes the clyffes aywhere,
As lauce leves of the boke that lepes in twynne.
The brethe of the brynston bi that hit blende were,
Al tho citees and her sydes sunkken to helle.

Rydelles wern tho grete rowtes of renkkes withinne,
When thay wern war of the wrake that no wyye achaped;
Such a yomerly yarm of yellyng ther rysed, *doleful clamour*
Therof clatered the cloudes, that Kryst myght *resounded*
haf rawthe. *pity*

The segge herde that soun to Segor that yede, *sound; went*
And the wenches hym wyth that by the way folwed;
Ferly ferde was her flesch that flowen ay ilyche,
Trynande ay a hyghe trot that torne never dorsten.

Loth and tho luly-whit, his lefly two deghter,
Ay folwed here face, bifore her bothe yyen;

957–8 Beat on Gomorrah so that the ground gave way, on Admah and Zeboim.

959–60 Were all enveloped by the rain, were roasted and burned, and the people who dwelt in those towns were exceedingly frightened.

962–3 He was utterly delighted, opened quickly; he burst the great bars of the abyss all at once.

965–70 And the cliffs everywhere shattered all in little pieces, as leaves fly from a book that springs apart. By the time that the stench of the brimstone had spread, all those cities and their environs were sinking to Hell. The great crowds of people in those places were in despair, when they became aware of the vengeance that no man might escape.

974–83 And the girls with him, following along the road; they were thoroughly frightened, fleeing ever onwards, always going at a fast pace, never daring to turn round. Lot and those lily-white ones, his two lovely daughters, went ever forward, both eyes before them; but the wretched

Bot the balleful burde, that never bode keped,
Blusched byhynden her bak that bale for to herkken.

Hit was lusty Lothes wyf, that over her lyfte schulder
Ones ho bluschet to the burghe; bot bod ho no lenger
That ho nas stadde a stiffe ston, a stalworth image,
Also salt as ani se—and so ho yet standes. *as; sea*

Thay slypped bi and syye hir not that wern hir samenferes, *saw* *companions*
Tyl thay in Segor wern sette, and sayned our Lorde; *arrived; blessed*
Wyth lyght loves uplyfte thay loved hym swythe,
That so his servauntes wolde see and save of such wothe.

Al was dampped and don and drowned by thenne; *damned; destroyed*
The ledes of that lyttel toun wern lopen out for drede *people; had rushed*
Into that malscrande mere, marred bylyve, *charmed sea; killed*
That noght saved was bot Segor that sat on a lawe, *so that; hill*

The thre ledes therin, Loth and his deghter.
For his make was myst, that on the mount lenged
In a stonen statue that salt savor habbes,
For two fautes that the fol was founde in mistrauthe:

On, ho served at the soper salt bifore Dryghtyn, *firstly* *the Lord*
And sythen ho blusched hir bihynde, thagh hir forboden were.
For on ho standes a ston, and salt for that other, *the one*
And alle lyst on hir lik that arn on launde bestes.

woman, who never did as she was told, looked behind her back to see that disaster. That was worthy Lot's wife, who looked once at the town over her left shoulder; but the moment she did so she was turned into a hard stone, a solid image.

987–8 With eager hands uplifted they praised Him devoutly, He who would so look after His servants and save them from such danger.

994–6 For his wife was missing, remaining on the mountain as a stone statue which has a salt taste, for two offences in which the foolish woman was found to be faithless.

998 And then she looked behind her, though she was forbidden to do so.

1000 And all the beasts of the earth desire to lick her.

Abraham ful erly was up on the morne,
That alle naght much niye hade nomen in his hert, *anguish; endured*
Al in longing for Loth leyen in a wache;
Ther he lafte hade oure Lorde he is on lofte wonnen.

He sende towards Sodomas the syght of his yyen, *sent*
That ever hade ben an erde of erthe the swettest,
As aparaunt to Paradis that plantted the Dryghtyn;
Nou is hit plunged in a pit like of pich fylled. *as though*

Suche a rothum of a reche ros fro the blake,
Askes upe in the ayre and uselles ther flowen, *ashes; cinders*
As a fornes ful of flot that upon fyr boyles, *scum*
When bryght brennande brondes ar bet theranunder. *kindled*

This was a vengaunce violent that voyded thise places, *laid waste*
That foundered has so fayr a folk and the folde sonkken. *engulfed*
There fyve citees wern set nou is a see called,
That ay is drovy and dym, and ded in hit kynde;

Blo, blubrande, and blak, unblythe to neghe,
As a stynkande stanc that stryed synne,
That ever of synne and of smach smart is to fele;
Forthy the dẹrk dede see hit is demed evermore. *and so; called*

For hit dedes of dethe duren there yet; *its; continue*
For hit is brod and bothemles, and bitter as the galle,
And noght may lenge in that lake that any lyf beres, *stay*
And alle the costes of kynde hit combres uchone.

1003–4 Had lain awake in great anxiety for Lot; he went up to (the place) where he had left our Lord.
1006–7 That had always been a region which was the most pleasant on earth, in that it was like Paradise which the Lord created.
1009 Such a pall of red smoke rose from the blackness.
1015–19 The place where five cities were situated is now a sea, which is always murky and dark, and dead in its nature; livid, bubbling, and black, unpleasant to approach—a stinking pool which destroyed sin, which in its sin and its savour is always bitter to taste.
1024 And it overturns all of the laws of nature.

For lay theron a lump of led and hit on loft fletes, *surface*
And folde theron a lyght fyther and hit to founs synkkes; *place; bottom*
And ther water may walter to wete any erthe,
Schal never grene theron growe, gresse ne wod nawther.

If any schalke to be schent wer schowved therinne, *man; killed*
Thagh he bode in that bothem brothely a monyth,
He most ay lyve in that loghe, in losying evermore,
And never dryye no dethe to dayes of ende.

And as hit is corsed of kynde, and hit coostes als,
The clay that clenges therby arn corsyes strong,
As alum and alkaran, that angré arn bothe, *bitumen; caustic*
Soufre sour and saundyver and other such mony;

And ther waltes of that water, in waxlokes grete,
The spumande aspaltoun that spyseres sellen.
And suche is alle the soyle by that se halves, *sea's shores*
That fel fretes the flesch and festres bones. *cruelly devours; rots*

And ther ar tres by that terne of traytoures, *lake; evildoers*
And thay borgounes and beres blomes ful fayre, *flourish*
And the fayrest fryt that may on folde growe,
As orenge and other fryt and apple-garnade, *pomegranate*

Al so red and so ripe and rychely hwed *coloured*
As any dom myght device, of dayntyes oute;
Bot quen hit is brused other broken other byten in twynne,
No worldes goud hit wythinne, bot wyndowande askes.

1027–8 And wherever the water flows to wet a piece of ground, vegetation will never grow there, neither grass nor trees.

1030–4 Though he should remain wretchedly in that pit for a month, he must live on in that sea, in perdition for ever, and never suffer death till the end of the world. And as it is cursed in its nature, and its shores as well, the clay that clings there consists of strong corrosives.

1036–8 Bitter sulphur and glass-gall and many other such; and there the foaming asphalt that apothecaries sell is flung from that water in great wax-like curls.

1046 As any wit might conceive, attractive on the outside.

1048–50 No goodness inside it at all, only swirling ashes. All these are signs and tokens to take note of still, and evidence of that evil behaviour, and the vengeance afterwards.

Alle thyse ar teches and tokenes to trow upon yet,
And wittnesse of that wykked werk, and the wrake after
That oure Fader forthered for fylthe of those ledes; *executed*
Thenne uch wyye may wel wyt that he the wlonk lovies.

And if he lovyes clene layk that is oure Lorde *conduct*
ryche, *noble*
And to be couthe in his courte thou coveytes *known; desire*
thenne,
To se that semly in sete and his swete face, *seemly one; throne*
Clerrer counsayl con I non bot that thou clene worthe. *know; be*

For Clopyngnel in the compas of his clene Rose,
Ther he expounes a speche to hym that spede wolde
Of a lady to be loved: 'Loke to hir sone
Of wich beryng that ho be, and wych ho best lovyes;

And be ryght such in uch a borghe, of body and of dedes,
And folw the fet of that fere that thou fre haldes.
And if thou wyrkkes on this wyse, thagh *act*
ho wyk were, *hostile*
Hir schal lyke that layk that lyknes hir tylle.'

If thou wyl dele drwrye wyth Dryghtyn *have love-dealings*
thenne,
And lelly lovy thy Lorde and his leef worthe, *truly; dear one*
Thenne confourme the to Kryst, and the clene make, *be like*
That ever is polyced als playn as the perle selven. *smooth*

For loke, fro fyrst that he lyght withinne the lel mayden,
By how comly a kest he was clos there,

1052 And so all may see well that He loves what is clean.
1057–62 For Clopinel (Jean de Meun) in his clean Rose (*Le Roman de la Rose*) sets forth there a speech for the man who would succeed in love with a lady: 'Look to her without delay to see what her disposition is, and what she likes best; and in every place be just like her, in appearance and actions, and follow the footsteps of the mistress whom you hold dear.'
1064 That conduct which copies her will be pleasing to her.
1069–70 For see, from the moment He alighted within the true maiden, by how seemly a contrivance He was enclosed there.

When venkkyst was no vergynyté, ne vyolence maked, *vanquished* *done*
Bot much clener was hir corse God kynned therinne.

And efte when he borne was in Bethelen the ryche, *again*
In wych purytć thay departed, thagh thay pover were.
Was never so blysful a bour as was a bos thenne, *manger*
Ne no schroude-hous so schene as a schepon thare,

Ne non so glad under God as ho that grone schulde;
For ther was seknesse al sounde that sarrest is halden,
And ther was rose reflayr where rote has ben ever, *scent; rottenness*
And ther was solace and songe wher sorw has ay cryed. *joy*

For aungelles with instrumentes of organes and pypes,
And rial ryngande rotes, and the reken fythel,
And alle hende that honestly moght an hert glade,
Aboutte my lady was lent, quen ho delyver were. *present; delivered*

Thenne was her blythe barne burnyst so clene *fair child*
That bothe the ox and the asse hym hered at ones; *worshipped together*
Thay knewe hym by his clannes for kyng of nature,
For non so clene of such a clos com never er thenne. *dwelling*

And yif clanly he thenne com, ful cortays therafter, *well-bred*
That alle that longed to luther ful lodly he hated;
By nobleye of his norture he nolde never towche *nobility*
Oght that was ungoderly other ordure was inne.

1072 But much cleaner was her body in that God was conceived in it.
1074 In what purity they parted from each other, though they were poor.
1076–8 Nor any sacristy so beautiful as a cow-shed was there, nor anyone so glad on God's earth as she who must groan (in childbirth); for there that sickness, which is considered the most severe, was fully healed.
1082–3 And rich resonant stringed instruments, and the noble violin, and everything pleasant that might worthily gladden the heart.
1090 In that everything that pertained to vileness He hated with great loathing.
1092–7 Anything that was bad or had filth inside it. Yet loathsome people came to that Lord, such as many who were sick, some leprous, some lame,

Yet comen lodly to that lede, as lazares monye,
Summe lepre, summe lome, and lomerande blynde,
Poysened and parlatyk and pyned in fyres,
Drye folk and ydropike, and dede at the laste.

Alle called on that cortayse and claymed his grace;
He heled hem wyth hynde speche of that thay ask after; *gracious* *about*
For what-so he towched also tyd tourned to hele,
Wel clanner then any crafte cowthe devyse.

So clene was his hondelyng uche ordure hit schonied,
And the gropyng so goud of God and man bothe
That for fetys of his fyngeres fonded he never *skill; troubled*
Nauther to cout ne to kerve with knyf ne wyth egge. *blade*

Forthy brek he the bred blades wythouten, *and so; broke*
For hit ferde freloker in fete in his fayre honde,
Displayed more pryvyly when he hit part schulde
Thenne alle the toles of Tolowse moght tyght hit to kerve.

Thus is he kyryous and clene that thou his cort askes;
Hou schulde thou com to his kyth bot if thou clene were? *kingdom*
Nou ar we sore and synful and souly uchone,
How schulde we se, then may we say, that Syre upon throne?

Yis, that mayster is mercyable, thagh thou be man fenny,
And al tomarred in myre whyl thou on molde lyvyes; *astray; earth*

and the stumbling blind, (some) poisoned and palsied and consumed by fevers, dry-humoured people and dropsical, and finally the dead. All appealed to that courteous one and claimed His grace.

1099–102 For whatever He touched became sound at once, much cleaner than any art could make it. So clean was His handling that every filthy thing fled from it, and so good was the touching of Him who was both God and man.

1106–9 For it fared better, indeed, in His fair hand, fell apart more cleanly when He came to divide it than all the tools of Toulouse might manage to cut it. Thus He whose court you seek is fastidious and clean.

1111 Since we are vile and sinful and filthy, each one of us.

1113 Yes we may, (for) that Lord is merciful, though you be foul.

Thou may schyne thurgh schryfte, thagh *confession*
thou haf schome served, *given yourself to*
And pure the with penaunce tyl thou a perle *purify*
worthe. *become*

Perle praysed is prys ther perré is schewed,
Thagh ho not derrest be demed to dele for penies;
Quat may the cause be called bot for hir clene hwes,
That wynnes worschyp abof alle whyte stones? *honour*

For ho schynes so schyr that is of schap rounde, *brightly*
Wythouten faut other fylthe, yif ho fyn were; *impurity; fine*
And wax ho ever in the worlde in weryng so olde,
Yet the perle payres not whyle ho in pyese lasttes.

And if hit cheve the chaunce uncheryst ho worthe,
That ho blyndes of ble in bour ther ho lygges,
Nobot wasch hir wyth wourchyp in wyn, as ho askes;
Ho by kynde schal becom clerer then are.

So if folk be defowled by unfre chaunce,
That he be sulped in sawle, seche to schryfte;
And he may polyce hym at the prest, by penaunce taken,
Wel bryghter then the beryl other browden perles. *linked*

Bot war the wel, if thou be waschen wyth water *take good care*
of schryfte,
And polysed als playn as parchmen *smooth; parchment*
schaven, *scraped*
Sulp no more thenne in synne thy saule therafter,
For thenne thou Dryghtyn dyspleses with dedes *the Lord*
ful sore, *vile*

1117–19 The pearl is deemed precious where jewels are displayed, though it is not considered to have the highest money-value; what may be the reason unless on account of its clean colouring?

1123–31 And, however long it may be worn (in the world), yet the pearl does not deteriorate during its lifetime. And if it happens to be uncared for, so that it loses colour in the chamber where it lies, just wash it with respect in wine, as it requires; by its nature it will then become brighter than before. So if through evil fortune a man should be defiled, so that he is corrupted in his soul, let him resort to confession; and he may cleanse himself at the hands of the priest, by penance received.

And entyses hym to tene more traythly then ever,
And wel hatter to hate then hade thou not waschen; *more hotly*
For when a sawele is saghtled and sakred to Dryghtyn, *reconciled*
He holly haldes hit his, and have hit he wolde. *wholly counts*

Thenne efte lastes hit likkes, he loses hit ille,
As hit were rafte wyth unryght and robbed wyth thewes.
War the thenne for the wrake, his wrath is achaufed,
For that that ones was his schulde efte be unclene.

Thagh hit be bot a bassyn, a bolle other a scole, *bowl; cup*
A dysche other a dobler, that Dryghtyn ones served, *platter*
To defowle hit ever upon folde fast he forbedes,
So is he scoymus of scathe that scylful is ever.

And that was bared in Babyloyn in Baltazar tyme, *shown*
Hou harde unhap ther hym hent, and hastyly sone,
For he the vesselles avyled that vayled in the temple *defiled; were used*
In servyse of the Soverayn sumtyme byfore.

Yif ye wolde tyght me a tom, telle hit I wolde, *grant; opportunity*
Hou charged more was his chaunce that hem cherych nolde
Then his fader forloyné, that feched hem wyth strenthe,
And robbed the relygioun of relykes alle. *faith; sacred objects*

1137 And you incite Him to be more violently angry than ever.
1141–4 If then it tastes sins again, He takes its loss badly, as if it were wrongfully carried off and plundered by thieves. Look out then for vengeance, His anger is kindled, that what was once His should again be unclean.
1147–8 Sternly He forbids it to be defiled in any way at all, so revolted is He by sin, He who is ever righteous.
1150 How dire disaster overtook him there, and very speedily.
1154–5 How the fate of that man who would not respect them was more grievous than that of his erring father, who carried them off by force.

III

Danyel in his dialokes devysed symtyme,
As yet is proved expresse in his profecies,
Hou the gentryse of Juise and Jherusalem the ryche
Was disstryed wyth distres and drawen to the erthe.

For that folke in her fayth was founden untrwe,
That haden hyght the hyghe God to halde of hym ever;
And he hem halwed for his, and help at her nede
In mukel meschefes mony that mervayl were to here.

And thay forloyne her fayth and folwed other goddes, *but; stray from*
And that wakned his wrath and wrast hit so hyghe *worked it up*
That he fylsened the faythful in the falce lawe *helped; religion*
To forfare the falce in the faythe trwe. *destroy*

Hit was sen in that sythe that Zedethyas rengned *time; Zedekiah*
In Juda, that justised the Juyne kynges; *which; ruled; Jewish*
He sete on Salamones solie, on solemne wyse, *throne; dignified*
Bot of leauté he was lat to his Lorde hende.

He used abominaciones of idolatrye, *practised*
And lette lyght bi the lawe that he was lege tylle.
Forthi oure Fader upon folde a foman hym wakned;
Nabigodenozar nuyed hym swythe.

He pursued into Palastyn with proude men mony, *advanced*
And ther he wast wyth werre the wones of thorpes;

1157–60 Daniel once described in his stories, as is also plainly shown in his prophecies, how the nobility of Israel and mighty Jerusalem was forcibly overthrown and laid low.
1162–4 Who had promised the high God to owe allegiance to Him for ever; and He set them apart as His, and helped them in their need in many great misfortunes that would be wonderful to hear about.
1172 But he was remiss in loyalty to his gracious Lord.
1174–6 And set little store by the religion that he owed allegiance to. And so our Father raised up an enemy against him on the earth; Nebuchadnezzar harassed him severely.
1178–9 And there he destroyed by warfare the sites of villages; he ravaged all Israel and took the best (it had to offer).

He heryed up alle Israel and hent of the beste,
And the gentylest of Judee in Jerusalem biseged, *noblest*

Umbewalt alle the walles wyth wyyes ful stronge, *surrounded*
At uche a dor a doghty duk, and dutte hem wythinne;
For the borgh was so bigge, baytayled alofte,
And stoffed wythinne with stout men to stalle hem theroute. *halt*

Thenne was the sege sette the ceté aboute; *laid*
Skete skarmoch skelt, much skathe lached;
At uch brugge a berfray on basteles wyse,
That seven sythe uch a day asayled the yates. *times*

Trwe tulkkes in toures teveled wythinne,
In bigge brutage of borde bulde on the walles.
Thay feght and thay fende of and fylter togeder
Til two yer overtorned, yet tok thay hit never. *went by*

At the laste, upon longe, tho ledes wythinne,
Faste fayled hem the fode, enfaminied monie;
The hote hunger wythinne hert hem wel sarre *hurt* *more severely*
Then any dunt of that douthe that dowelled theroute.

Thenne wern tho rowtes redles in tho ryche wones;
Fro that mete was myst, megre thay wexen;
And thay stoken so strayt that thay ne stray myght *(were) confined; securely*
A fote fro that forselet to forray no goudes. *fortress; forage*

1182–3 A bold chieftain at every gate, and (he) shut them inside; for the city was so mighty, battlemented above.
1186–7 Quickly skirmishing broke out, much injury was sustained; at each drawbridge was a siege-tower in the form of a bastille (turret on wheels).
1189–91 Within the city, worthy men laboured in towers, inside strong wooden hoarding built on the walls. They attacked and defended and joined battle.
1193–4 In the end, after a long time, the people inside became desperately short of food, and many starved.
1196–8 Than any blow from that army that waited outside. Then the crowds in that great city were in despair; once food was lacking, they grew thin.

Thenne the kyng of the kyth a counsayl hym takes,
Wyth the best of his burnes, a blench for to make;
Thay stel out on a stylle nyght er any steven rysed, *outcry*
And harde hurles thurgh the oste er enmies hit wyste.

Bot er thay atwappe ne moght the wach wythoute,
Highe skelt was the askry the skewes anunder.
Loude alarom upon launde lulted was thenne; *earth; sounded*
Ryche, ruthed of her rest, ran to here wedes;

Hard hattes thay hent and on hors lepes; *helmets*
Cler claryoun crak cryed on lofte. *blast; sounded*
By that was alle on a hepe hurlande swythee,
Folwande that other flote, and fonde hem bilyve, *troop; at once*

Overtok hem as tyd, tult hem of sadeles, *immediately; tipped*
Tyl uche prynce hade his per put to the grounde. *opponent*
And ther was the kyng kaght wyth Caldé prynces, *by Chaldean*
And alle hise gentyle forjusted on Jerico playnes, *nobles; unhorsed*

And presented wern as presoneres to the prynce rychest,
Nabigodenozar, noble in his chayer; *throne*
And he the faynest freke that he his fo hade, *happiest of men*
And speke spitously hem to, and spylt therafter.

The kynges sunnes in his syght he slow everuchone,
And holkked out his auen yyen heterly bothe,
And bede the burne to be broght to Babyloyn the ryche,
And there in dongoun be don, to dreye ther his wyrdes. *put; endure* *fate*

1201–2 Then the king of the country takes a decision, with the best of his men, to play a trick.
1204–6 And rushed quickly through the host before their enemies knew of it. But before they might slip past the watch outside, the alarm was raised loudly under the heavens.
1208 Noblemen, roused from their sleep, ran to their clothes.
1211 By then all were charging forward in a body with all speed.
1220 And he spoke contemptuously to them, and afterwards killed them.
1222 And savagely gouged out both his own eyes.

Now se! so the Soverayn set has his wrake.
Nas hit not for Nabugo ne his noble nauther
That other depryved was of pryde, with paynes stronge,
Bot for his beryng so badde agayn his blythe Lorde.

For hade the Fader ben his frende that hym bifore keped,
Ne never trespast to him in teche of mysseleve,
To colde wer alle Caldé and kythes of Ynde—
Yet take Torkye hem wyth, her tene hade ben little.

Yet nolde never Nabugo this ilke note leve
Er he hade tyrved this toun and torne hit to grounde. *overthrown*
He joyned unto Jerusalem a gentyle duc thenne— *despatched; noble*
His name was Nabuzardan—to noye the Jues. *Nebuzaradan; harass*

He was mayster of his men and myghty himselven, *captain*
The chef of his chevalrye his chekkes to make.
He brek the bareres as bylyve, and the burgh after,
And enteres in ful ernestly in yre of his hert. *wrathfully*

What! the maysterry was mene, the men wern away; *victory; poor*
The best bowed wyth the burne that the borgh yemed; *went; ruled*
And tho that byden wer so biten with the bale hunger
That on wyf hade ben worthe the welgest fourre.

1225–33 Now see! in this way the Sovereign has taken His revenge. It was not for Nebuchadnezzar or his nobles that the other (Zedekiah) was deprived of glory, with cruel torments, but for his bad behaviour towards his gracious Lord. For had the Father whom he once heeded been his friend, and had he never offended against Him in the sin of wrong faith, then all Chaldea and the lands of India would have been too weak (to do him any harm)—take Turkey with them as well, their hostility would have been of little account. Nebuchadnezzar still would not abandon this course of action.

1238–9 The leader of his (Nebuchadnezzar's) knights in carrying out his attacks. He breached the outworks at once, and the city afterwards.

1243–7 And those who remained were so wasted by terrible hunger that one woman would have been worth the strongest four. Nebuzaradan would not by any means spare them on that account, but ordered everyone to be put to the bare blade of the sword. They killed there the sweetest of fair ladies.

Nabizardan noght forthy nolde not spare,
Bot bede al to the bronde under bare egge.
Thay slowen of swettest semlych burdes,
Bathed barnes in blod and her brayn spylled, *children*

Prestes and prelates thay presed to dethe, *pressed*
Wyves and wenches her wombes tocorven
That her boweles outborst aboute the diches,
And al was carfully kylde that thay cach myght. *ignominiously*

And alle swypped unswolwed of the sworde kene,
Thay wer cagged and kaght on capeles al bare,
Festned fettres to her fete under fole wombes,
And brothely broght to Babyloyn ther bale to suffer,

To sytte in servage and syte that sumtyme wer gentyle.
Now ar chaunged to chorles and charged wyth *burdened*
werkkes, *labours*
Bothe to cayre at the kart and the kuy mylke, *drive; cow*
That sumtyme sete in her sale syres and burdes.

And yet Nabuzardan nyl never stynt, *pause*
Er he to the tempple tee wyth his tulkkes alle; *go; men*
Betes on the barers, brestes up the yates,
Slouen alle at a slyp that served therinne, *stroke; officiated*

Pulden prestes bi the polle and plat of her hedes, *crown; struck*
Dighten dekenes to dethe, dungen doun clerkkes,
And alle the maydenes of the munster maghtyly hokyllen
Wyth the swayf of the sworde that swolwed *sweep; devoured*
hem alle.

1250 Cut open the stomachs of women and girls.
1253–7 And all who escaped undevoured by the sharp sword were bound and tied naked on horses, with fetters fastened to their feet under the horses' bellies, and they, who had once been genteel, were brought wretchedly to Babylon to endure misery there, to live in bondage and sorrow.
1260 Those who once sat in their hall as lords and ladies.
1263 They beat on the barriers (in front of the gates), smash the gates.
1266–7 Put deacons to death, struck down clerics, and ruthlessly mowed down all the maidens of the Temple.

Thenne ran thay to the relykes as robbors wylde, *sacred objects*
And pyled alle the apparement that pented to the kyrke,
The pure pyleres of bras pourtrayd in golde, *noble pillars; decorated*
And the chef chaundeler, charged with the lyght,

That ber the lamp upon lofte that lemed evermore *held; shone*
Bifore the sancta sanctorum, ther selcouth was ofte. *Holy of Holies* *marvellous event*
Thay caght away that condelstik and the crowne als, *took; lamp-stand*
That the auter hade upon, of athel golde ryche, *on it; fine*

The gredirne and the goblotes garnyst of sylver, *gridiron; decorated with*
The bases of the bryght postes and bassynes so schyre, *pillars* *beautiful*
Dere disches of golde and dubleres fayre, *precious; platters*
The vyoles and the vesselment of vertuous stones.

Now has Nabuzardan nomen alle thyse noble thynges, *taken*
And pyled that precious place and pakked those godes; *holy*
The golde of the gazafylace, to swythe gret noumbre,
Wyth alle the urnmentes of that hous, he hamppred togeder.

Alle he spoyled spitously in a sped whyle
That Salomon so mony a sadde yer soght to make. *long*
Wyth alle the coyntyse that he cowthe clene to wyrke
Devised he the vesselment, the vestures clene;

1270 And pillaged all the furniture that belonged to the church.
1272 And the great lamp-stand, entrusted with the light.
1280 The bowls for incense and the vessels of stones of special power.
1283–5 He put in cases the gold of the Temple treasury, to a very great sum, together with all the furnishings of that house. Contemptuously, in a short while, he plundered everything.
1287–9 With all the skill in fine workmanship that he possessed he fashioned the vessels, the splendid vestments; in the cunning of his arts, to glorify his Sovereign.

Wyth slyght of his ciences, his Soverayn to love,
The hous and the anournementes he hyghtled togedere. *furnishings* *embellished*
Now has Nabuzardan nummen hit al samen, *at once*
And sythen bet doun the burgh and brend hit in askes.

Thenne wyth legiounes of ledes over londes he rydes, *men; countryside*
Heryes of Israel the hyrne aboute; *harries; hinterland*
Wyth charged chariotes the cheftayn he fyndes, *laden*
Bikennes the catel to the kyng that he caght hade, *delivers; treasure*

Presented him the presoneres in pray that thay token, *as booty*
Moni a worthly wyye whil her worlde laste,
Moni semly syre soun, and swythe rych maydenes,
The pruddest of the province, and prophetes childer, *noblest*

As Ananie and Azarie and als Mizael,
And dere Daniel also, that was devine noble, *worthy; prophet*
With moni a modey moder chylde mo then innoghe. *proud man; more*
And Nabugodenozar makes much joye,

Nou he the kyng has conquest and the kyth wunnen,
And dreped alle the doghtyest and derrest in armes,
And the lederes of her lawe layd to the grounde, *religion*
And the pryce of the profetie presoners maked. *best; prophets*

Bot the joy of the juelrye, so gentyle and ryche,
When hit was schewed hym so schene, scharp was his wonder; *bright; great*
Of such vessel avayed, that vayled so huge,
Never yet nas Nabugodenozar er thenne.

1292 And afterwards razed the city and burned it to ashes.
1298–9 Many a man of noble rank in his time, many a fair son of a lord, and very well-born maidens.
1305–6 Now that he has conquered the king and taken the country, and killed all the boldest and bravest in arms.
1309 But the beauty of the treasure, so splendid and rich.
1311–12 Never until that time had Nebuchadnezzar been shown such vessels, of such great value.

He sesed hem with solemneté, the Soverayn he praysed — *reverence*
That was athel over alle, Israel Dryghtyn;
Such god, such gounes, such gay vesselles
Comen never out of kyth to Caldee reames. — *Chaldean realms*

He trussed hem in his tresorye in a tryed place, — *packed; chosen*
Rekenly, wyth reverens, as he ryght hade;
And ther he wroght as the wyse, as ye may wyt hereafter,
For hade he let of hem lyght hym moght haf lumpen worse.

That ryche in gret rialté rengned his lyve;
As conquerour of uche a cost he cayser was hatte,
Emperour of alle the erthe, and also the saudan, — *sultan*
And als the god of the grounde was graven his name. — *as; world; inscribed*

And al thurgh dome of Daniel, fro he devised hade
That alle goudes com of God, and gef hit hym bi samples,
That he ful clanly bicnu his carp bi the laste;
And ofte hit mekned his mynde, his maysterful werkkes.

Bot al drawes to dyye with doel upon ende;
By a hathel never so hyghe, he heldes to grounde; — *be; man; falls*
And so Nabugodenozar, as he nedes moste,
For alle his empire so highe, in erthe is he graven. — *power; buried*

Bot thenn the bolde Baltazar, that was his barn aldest, — *Belshazzar* *son*
He was stalled in his stud, and stabled the rengne
In the burgh of Babiloyne, the biggest he trawed,
That nauther in heven ne on erthe hade no pere.

1314–15 Who was excellent above all others, the Lord of Israel. Such goods, such vestments, such fine vessels.

1318–22 Suitably, with reverence, as was proper for him to do; and in this he acted like a wise man, as you will see later, for had he set little store by them he might have fared worse. That mighty king reigned in great splendour for the rest of his life; as the conqueror of every land he was called master.

1325–9 And all through Daniel's advice, after he had explained that all things come from God, and made it clear to him in parables, so that in the end he fully accepted what he said; and often it softened his purpose, his imperious actions. But all come to die pitifully in the end.

1334–5 He was installed as his successor, and governed the kingdom in the city of Babylon, the mightiest (of men) as he thought.

For he bigan in alle the glori that hym the gome lafte, *man*
Nabugodenozar, that was his noble fader;
So kene a kyng in Caldee com never er thenne. *great*
Bot honoured he not hym that in heven wonies, *dwells*

Bot fals fantummes of fendes formed with handes,
Wyth tool out of harde tre, and telded on lofte,
And of stokkes and stones, he stoute goddes calls,
When thay ar gilde al with golde and gered wyth sylver. *adorned*

And there he kneles and calles and clepes after help; *asks for*
And thay reden him ryght, rewarde he hem hetes,
And if thay gruchen him his grace, to gremen his hert,
He cleches to a gret klubbe and knokkes hem to peces. *takes up*

Thus in pryde and olipraunce his empyre he haldes, *arrogance*
In lust and in lecherye and lothelych werkkes, *hateful*
And hade a wyf for to welde, a worthelych quene, *enjoy; noble*
And mony a lemman never-the-later that ladis wer called. *mistress; nevertheless*

In the clernes of his concubines and curious wedes,
In notyng of nwe metes and of nice gettes,
Al was the mynde of that man on misschapen thinges,
Til the Lorde of the lyfte liste hit abate.

Thenne this bolde Baltazar bithenkkes hym ones
To vouche on avayment of his vayneglorie;
Hit is not innogh to the nice al noghty think use,
Bot if alle the worlde wyt his wykked dedes. *unless; know of*

1341–3 But he addresses as mighty gods false images of devils made by hand, with tools out of hard wood and stocks and stones, and raised upright.

1346–7 If they will deal well with him, he promises them reward, but if they should refuse his boon, to make him angry at heart.

1353–4 In the beauty of his concubines and elegant clothes, in the appreciation of new dishes and of extravagant fashions.

1356–9 Until the Lord of the heavens was pleased to put an end to it. Then this bold Belshazzar decides on a certain occasion to give a display of his vainglory; to the wanton man it is not enough to indulge in all vile practices.

Baltazar thurgh Babiloyn his banne gart crye,
And thurgh the cuntre of Caldee his callyng *summons*
con spryng, *went out*
That alle the grete upon grounde schulde geder hem samen,
And assemble at a set day at the saudans fest.

Such a mangerie to make the man was avised
That uche a kythyn kyng schuid com thider;
Uche duk wyth his duthe, and other dere lordes, *retinue*
Schulde com to his court to kythe hym for lege,

And to reche hym reverens and his revel herkken,
To loke on his lemanes and ladis hem calle. *mistresses*
To rose hym in his rialty rych men soghtten, *praise; came*
And mony a baroun ful bolde, to Babyloyn the noble.

Ther bowed toward Babiloyn burnes so mony, *went*
Kynges, cayseres ful kene, to the court wonnen,
Mony ludisch lordes that ladies broghten, *noble*
That to neven the noumbre to much nye were. *state; trouble*

For the bourgh was so brod, and so bigge alce,
Stalled in the fayrest stud the sterres anunder,
Prudly on a plat playn, plek alther-fayrest,
Umbesweyed on uch a syde with seven grete *surrounded*
wateres; *rivers*

With a wonder wroght walle, wruxeled ful highe,
With koynt carneles above, corven ful clene,
Troched toures bitwene, twenty spere lenthe,
And thiker throwen umbethour with overthwert palle.

1361 Had his edict proclaimed.
1363 That all the great men in the world should come together.
1365–6 The man was determined to prepare a banquet such that the kings of all countries should come to it.
1368–9 To acknowledge him as sovereign, and pay him their respects and attend to his revels.
1374 Kings, mighty emperors, made their way to the court.
1377–9 For the city was so large, and so strong also, situated in the fairest place under the stars, proudly on a level plain in the very best spot.
1381–7 With a wonderfully constructed wall, built up to a great height, with skilfully-made battlements above, most excellently fashioned; pinnacled towers at intervals of twenty spear-lengths, and horizontal paling set

The place that plyed the pursaunt wythinne
Was longe and ful large, and ever ilych sware,
And uch a syde upon soyle helde seven myle,
And the saudans sete sette in the myddes. *abode*

That was a palayce of pryde, passande alle other, *noble; surpassing*
Bothe of werk and of wunder, and walled al aboute;
Heghe houses withinne, the halle to hit med;
So brod bilde, in a bay, that blonkkes myght renne.

When the terme of the tyde was towched of the feste,
Dere drowen therto and upon des metten,
And Baltazar upon bench was busked to sete;
Stepe stayred stones of his stoute throne.

Thenne was alle the halle flor hiled with knyghtes, *covered*
And barounes at the sidebordes bounet aywhere,
For non was dressed upon dece bot the dere selven,
And his clere concubynes in clothes ful bryght. *beautiful*

When alle segges were ther set, then servyse bygynnes; *seated*
Sturne trumpen strake, steven in halle;
Aywhere by the wowes wrasten krakkes,
And brode baneres therbi, blusnande of gold.

round about at closer intervals. The area that the surrounding wall enclosed was extensive in length and breadth, and square on all sides, and each side measured seven miles along the ground.

1390–6 Both elaborate and wonderful, and walled all about; high buildings inside, the hall in keeping with it; so spaciously built, in the shape of a bay, that horses might run there. When the appointed time for the feast arrived, noblemen went there and met on the dais, and Belshazzar was made ready for his place at table; the precious stones of his great throne gleamed brightly.

1398–9 And everywhere there were (present) barons at the side tables, for none was seated on the dais but the great one himself.

1402–19 (There was) a loud blast of trumpets, clamour in the hall; everywhere along the walls flourishes burst out, and (there were) great banners on the trumpets, gleaming of gold. Men (were) carrying the roast meats on large platters, that were of silver appearance, and sauces with them; high houses (as dish covers) over them, figured on the upper part, cut out of paper and painted over with gold; fearsome grotesques on top, beasts below, birds fluttering here and there in foliage, and everything

Burnes berande the bredes upon brode skeles,
That were of sylveren syght, and seves therwyth;
Lyfte logges therover and on lofte corven,
Pared out of paper and poynted of golde;

Brothe baboynes abof, besttes anunder,
Foles in foler flakerande bitwene,
And al in asure and ynde enaumayld ryche;
And al on blonkken bak bere hit on honde.

And ay the nakeryn noyse, notes of pipes;
Tymbres and tabornes tulket among,
Symbales and sonetes sware the noyse,
And bougouns busch batered so thikke.

So was served fele sythe the sale alle aboute,
With solace at the sere course, bifore the self lorde.
Ther the lede and alle his love lenged at the table,
So faste thay weghed to him wyne, hit warmed his hert, *brought*

And breythed uppe into his brayn and blemyst his mynde, *rushed; befuddled*
And al waykned his wyt, and welneghe he foles;
For he waytes on wyde, his wenches he byholdes, *looks around*
And his bolde baronage aboute bi the wowes. *barons*

Thenne a dotage ful depe drof to his hert,
And a caytif counsayl he caght bi hymselven.
Maynly his marschal the mayster upon calles,
And comaundes hym cofly coferes to lauce, *quickly; open*

richly enamelled in azure and indigo; and all (the servants) carried it in their hands on horseback. And always the noise of horns, notes of pipes; tambourines and drums sounded constantly, cymbals and bells answered the noise, and the rattle of drumsticks reverberated rapidly. So the hall was served all round many times, with delight in the various courses, in front of the lord himself. There where the prince and all his loves were seated at the table.

1422 And his reason was all enfeebled, and he became almost deranged.

1425–7 Then a most grievous folly entered his heart, and he conceived an evil plan that was all his own. Loudly the lord calls for his marshal.

And fech forth the vessel that his fader broght, *vessels*
Nabugodenozar, noble in his strenthe,
Conquerd with his knyghtes and of kyrk rafte
In Judé, in Jerusalem, in gentyle wyse: *respectful*

'Bryng hem now to my borde, of beverage hem fylles; *table; fill*
Let thise ladyes of hem lape, I luf hem in hert. *drink*
That schal I cortaysly kythe, and thay schin knawe sone,
Ther is no bounté in burne lyk Baltazar thewes.'

Thenne towched to the tresour this tale was sone,
And he with keyes uncloses kystes ful mony; *chests*
Mony burthen ful bryght was broght into halle, *many a burden*
And covered mony a cupborde with clothes ful quite.

The jueles out of Jerusalem with gemmes ful bryght *treasures*
Bi the syde of the sale were semely arayed; *attractively set out*
The athel auter of brasse was hade into place,
The gay coroun of golde gered on lofte.

That hade ben blessed bifore wyth bischopes hondes, *that which*
And wyth besten blod busily anoynted,
In the solempne sacrefyce that goud savor hade
Bifore the Lorde of the lyfte, in loving hymselven,

Now is sette for to serve Satanas the blake,
Bifore the bolde Baltazar, wyth bost and wyth pryde. *pomp ceremony*
Hoven upon this auter was athel vessel, *raised up; vessels*
That wyth so curious a crafte corven was wyly.

1431 (That he) captured with his knights and carried off from the church.
1435–7 'I shall graciously demonstrate that, and they will soon see that there is no bounty in any man like the favour of Belshazzar.' Then this matter was quickly made known to the treasurer.
1440 And many a sideboard was covered with whitest cloths.
1443–4 The noble altar of bronze was brought to its place, the bright crown of gold set on top of it.
1446–8 And zealously consecrated with the blood of animals, in the solemn sacrifice in His praise that smelt sweet to the Lord of the heavens.
1452–98 That with so subtle an art were cunningly fashioned. Solomon

Salamon sete him seven yere and a sythe more,
With alle the syence that hym sende the soverayn Lorde,
For to compas and kest to haf hem clene wroght.
For ther wer bassynes ful bryght of brende golde clere,

Enaumaylde with azer, and eweres of sute;
Covered cowpes foul clene, as casteles arayed,
Enbaned under batelment, with bantelles quoynt,
And fyled out of fygures of ferlylé schappes.

The coperounes of the covacles that on the cuppe reres
Wer fetysely formed out in fylyoles longe;
Pinacles pyght ther apert that profert bitwene,
And al bolled abof with braunches and leves,

Pyes and papejayes purtrayed withinne,
As thay prudly hade piked of pomgarnades;
For alle the blomes of the boghes were blyknande perles,
And alle the fruyt in tho formes of flaumbeande gemmes,

Ande safyres and sardiners and semely topace,
Alabaundeirynes and amarauns and amastised stones,
Casydoynes and crysolytes and clere rubies,
Penitotes and pynkardines, ay perles bitwene.

So trayled and tryfled a-traverce wer alle,
Bi uche bekyr ande bolle, the brurdes al umbe;

applied himself for seven years and more, with all the skill that the sovereign Lord sent him, to set his wits to work to have them excellently made. For there were very beautiful basins of pure bright gold, enamelled with azure, and pitchers to match; most splendid lidded cups, shaped like castles, machicolated (i.e. provided with an external gallery) under the battlements, with skilfully-made stepped corbels, and fashioned into figures of marvellous shapes. The ornamental tops of the lids that rose high on the cups were skilfully drawn out into long turrets, with pinnacles elegantly set on them, projecting at intervals, and all embossed on the surface with branches and leaves, amongst which magpies and parrots were depicted, as though splendidly partaking of pomegranates; for all the blooms on the boughs were shining pearls, and all the fruit in those designs was of brilliant gems, sapphires and sardine-stones and fair topaz, almandines and emeralds and stones of amethyst, chalcedonies and chrysolites and beautiful rubies, peridots and pinkardines, with pearls at intervals throughout. Thus all (the vessels) had trailing designs and trefoils across them, on each beaker and bowl, all round the edges; the

The gobelotes of golde graven aboute,
And fyoles fretted with flores and flees of golde.

Upon that auter was al aliche dresset;
The candelstik bi acost was cayred thider sone,
Upon the pyleres apyked that praysed hit mony,
Upon hit bases of brasse that ber up the werkes.

The boghes bryght therabof, brayden of golde,
Braunches bredande theron, and bryddes ther seten
Of mony kyndes, of fele kyn hues,
As thay with wynge upon wynde hade waged her fytheres.

Inmong the leves of the launces lampes wer graythed,
And other louflych lyght that lemed ful fayre,
As mony morteres of wax, merkked withoute
With mony a borlych best al of brende golde.

Hit was not wonte in that wone to wast no serges,
Bot in temple of the trauthe trwly to stonde,
Bifore the sancta sanctorum, ther sothefast Dryghtyn
Expouned his speche spiritually to special prophetes.

Leve thou wel that the Lorde that the lyfte yemes
Displesed much at that play in that plyt stronge,
That his jueles so gent wyth javeles wer fouled,
That presyous in his presens wer proved sumwhyle.

goblets of gold were engraved round the circumference, and the bowls for incense were inlaid with flowers and butterflies of gold. Everything was placed without distinction on the altar; the lamp-stand was quickly brought in alongside, set on the pillars so that many admired it, on its bases of bronze that supported the structure. The branches above were bright, embellished with gold, with small branches spreading out from them on which birds sat—birds of many kinds, of various colours—as if fluttering their feathers with their wings in the wind. Amongst the leaves of the branches lamps were set, and other beautiful lights that shone most excellently, such as many mortars of wax, figured on the outside with many a noble beast all of pure gold. It (the lamp-stand) was not accustomed to waste candles in that place, but to stand in the Temple of the true faith, as was proper, before the Holy of Holies, where the true God made spiritual utterance to chosen prophets. Be sure that the Lord who rules the heavens was much displeased at that sport in that alien setting, that His splendid treasures were defiled by louts, treasures which had formerly been established as holy in His presence. Some had been solemnly consecrated in sacrifice to Him, by command of the One who sits so high.

Soberly in his sacrafyce summe wer anoynted,
Thurgh the somones of himselfe that syttes so hyghe;
Now a boster on benche bibbes therof *drinks from them*
Tyl he be dronkken as the devel, and dotes ther he *drivels*
syttes.

So the worcher of this worlde wlates therwyth
That in the poynt of her play he porvayes a mynde;
Bot er harme hem he wolde in haste of his yre,
He wayned hem a warnyng that wonder hem thoght.

Nou is alle this guere geten glotounes *equipment fetched*
to serve,
Stad in a ryche stal, and stared ful bryght.
Baltazar in a brayd: 'Bede uus therof!
Weghe wyn in this won! Wassayl!' he cryes.

Swyfte swaynes ful swythe swepen thertylle,
Kyppe kowpes in honde kynges to serve;
In bryght bolles ful bayn birlen thise other,
And uche mon for his mayster machches alone.

Ther was rynging on ryght of ryche metalles
Quen renkkes in that ryche rok rennen hit to cache;
Clatering of covacles that kesten tho burdes
As sonet out of sauteray songe als myry.

Then the dotel on dece drank that he myght, *fool*
And thenne arn dressed dukes and prynces, *served*

1501–4 The Creator of the world is so disgusted on that account that at the height of their revelry He formulates a purpose; but before he would harm them in the haste of His anger, he sent them a warning which amazed them.

1506–16 Set up in a splendid place, and it shone most brightly. Belshazzar forthwith: 'Serve us (drink) from it! Bring wine in this place! Wassail!' he cries. Nimble servants quickly rush to it, grasp cups to serve the kings; eagerly they offer drink to them in bright bowls, and each servant strives for his master alone. There was ringing indeed of rich metals when men in that splendid company ran to seize it; the clattering of the lids that the women threw away rang out as merrily as music from a psaltery.

Concubines and knyghtes, bi cause of that merthe;
As uchon hade hym in helde, he haled of the cuppe.

So long likked thise lordes thise lykores swete,
And gloryed on her falce goddes and her grace calles, *ask for*
That were of stokkes and stones, stille evermore; *silent*
Never steven hem astel, so stoken is hor tonge.

Alle the goude golden goddes the gaules yet nevenen, *wretches* *call on*
Belfagor, and Belyal, and Belssabub als, *Baal-peor*
Heyred hem as hyghly as heven wer thayres; *worshipped; devoutly*
Bot hym that alle goudes gives, that God thay foryeten. *(good) things* *forgot*

For ther a ferly bifel that fele folk seyen; *marvel; many; saw*
Fyrst knew hit the kyng, and alle the cort after;
In the palays pryncipale, upon the playn wowe, *royal* *bare wall*
In contrary of the candelstik, that clerest hit schyned,

Ther apered a paume, with poyntel in fyngres, *hand; stylus*
That was grysly and gret, and grymly he wrytes; *great*
Non other forme bot a fust faylande the wryste
Pared on the parget, purtrayed lettres.

When that bolde Baltazar bluschED to that neve, *looked; fist*
Such a dasande drede dusched to his hert *numbing; came over*
That al falewed his face and fayled the chere;
The stronge strok of the stonde strayned his joyntes.

1519–21 For the sake of that sport; as each man was aged, so he drank from the cup. For a long time these lords tasted these sweet liquors.
1524 No sound ever escaped them, their tongue was so stuck fast.
1532 Opposite the lamp-stand, which shone most brightly.
1535–6 No other shape but a fist without the wrist carved on the plaster, formed letters.
1539–45 That his face grew all pale and his composure broke down; the strong impact of the blow afflicted his joints. His knees knock together and his legs double up, and he tears his cheeks by beating his fists (against them), and bellows like a frightened bull that roars for fear, continually looking at the hand till it had finished engraving, and had scratched strange sayings on the rough wall.

His cnes cachches to close and cluchches his hommes,
And he with plattyng his paumes displayes his leres,
And romyes as a rad ryth that rores for drede,
Ay biholdand the honde til hit hade al graven,
And rasped on the rogh wowe runisch saues.

When hit the scrypture hade scraped wyth a *writing*
scrof penne, *rough*
As a coltour in clay cerves tho forwes,
Thenne hit vanist verayly and voyded of syght;
Bot the lettres bileved ful large upon plaster. *remained*

Sone so the kynge for his care carping myght wynne,
He bede his burnes bow to that wer bok-lered,
To wayte the wryt that hit wolde, and wyter hym to say:
'For al hit frayes my flesche, the fyngres so grymme.'

Scoleres skelten theratte the skyl for to fynde,
Bot ther was never on so wyse couthe on worde rede,
Ne what ledisch lore ne langage nauther,
What tythyng ne tale, tokened tho draghtes.

Thenne the bolde Baltazar bred ner wode, *became almost mad*
And bede the ceté to seche segges thurghout
That wer wyse of wychecrafte, and warlawes other *sorcerers*
That con dele wyth demerlayk and devine lettres.

'Calle hem alle to my cort, tho Caldé *Chaldean*
clerkkes, *scholars*
Unfolde hem alle this ferly that is bifallen here, *make known to*

1547–8 As a ploughshare cuts furrows in clay, then it vanished completely and disappeared from sight.
1550–7 As soon as the king in his distress might find words, he commanded his learned men to approach, to examine what the writing meant, and to tell him plainly: 'For the grim fingers terrify me utterly.' At that scholars came hurrying to discover the meaning, but there was not one wise enough to make out a single word, nor what people's lore or language, what message or meaning, those characters represented.
1559 And commanded men to be sought throughout the city.
1561 Who dealt in magic arts and interpreted writings.

And calle wyth a highe cry: "He that the kyng wysses *loud* *instructs*
In expounyng of speche that spredes in thise lettres,

And makes the mater to malt my mynde wythinne, *sense; penetrate*
That I may wyterly wyt what that wryt menes, *plainly know*
He schal be gered ful gaye in gounes of porpre,
And a coler of cler golde clos umbe his throte. *fastened round*

He schal be prymate and prynce of pure clergye, *of religion*
And of my threvenest lordes the thrydde he schal,
And of my reme the rychest to ryde wyth myselven,
Outtaken bare two, and thenne he the thrydde."' *except for only*

This cry was upcaste, and ther comen mony *proclamation; uttered*
Clerkes out of Caldye that kennest wer knauen, *wisest* *known to be*
As the sage sathrapas that sorsory couthe;
Wyches and walkyries wonnen to that sale,

Devinores of demorlaykes that dremes cowthe rede,
Sorsers of exorsismus, and fele such clerkes.
And alle that loked on that letter, as lewed thay were *writing* *unenlightened*
As thay had loked in the lether of my lyft bote. *as if; left boot*

Thenne cryes the kyng and kerves his wedes; *tears*
What! he corsed his clerkes and calde hem chorles; *look!*
To henge the harlotes he heyed ful ofte; *rogues; threatened*
So was the wyye wytles he wed wel ner.

1565 In the interpretation of the language which is expressed in these writings.
1568 He shall be attired most richly in gowns of purple.
1571–2 And he shall be third amongst my noblest lords, the worthiest in my kingdom to ride with me.
1576–9 Such as learned sages who knew sorcery; wizards and enchanters made their way to that hall, practitioners of magic arts who could interpret dreams, exorcists, and many such scholars.
1585–6 The man was so distracted he was almost mad. She who was the chief queen heard him railing at the household.

Ho herde hym chyde to the chambre that was the chef quene;
When ho was wytered bi wyyes what was the cause, *informed*
Suche a chaungande chaunce in the chef halle, *fortune; great*
The lady, to lauce that los that the lorde hade, *alleviate; trouble*
Glydes doun by the grece and gos to the kyng. *stairway*

Ho kneles on the colde erthe and carpes to hymselven *speaks*
Wordes of worchyp wyth a wys speche: *respect*

'Kene kyng,' quoth the quene, 'kayser of urthe, *great*
Ever laste thy lyf in lenthe of dayes!
Why has thou rended thy robe for redles hereinne, *torn; in despair*
Thagh those ledes ben lewed lettres to rede,

And has a hathel in thy holde, as I haf herde ofte,
That has the gostes of God that gyes alle sothes?
His sawle is ful of syence sawes to schawe,
To open uch a hide thyng of aunteres uncowthe.

That is he that ful ofte has hevened thy fader
Of mony anger ful hote with his holy speche;
When Nabugodenozar was nyed in stoundes, *troubled at times*
He devysed his dremes to the dere trawthe. *explained; innermost*

He kevered hym with his counsayl of caytyf wyrdes;
Alle that he spured hym in space he expowned clene,
Thurgh the sped of the spyryt that sprad hym withinne
Of the godelest goddes that gaynes aywhere.

1594 May the days of your life last for ever!
1596–602 Though those men are unable to interpret writings, when you have a man in your kingdom, as I have heard often, who has the spiritual powers of God who commands all truths? His soul is full of wisdom to explain sayings, to reveal every hidden thing concerning strange happenings. He is the one who often raised your father out of many a hot fit of anger with his holy speech.
1605–8 He saved him by his counsel from a wretched fate; all that in course of time he asked him he expounded fully, through the power of the spirit that was present in him—the spirit of the most excellent gods (plural from Dan. v. 11) who have power everywhere.

For his depe divinité and his dere sawes, *excellent sayings*
Thy bolde fader Baltazar bede by his name,
That now is demed Danyel of derne coninges, *called; secret arts*
That caght was in the captyvidé in cuntré of Jues. *(Jewish) Captivity*

Nabuzardan hym nome, and now is he here, *captured*
A prophete of that province and pryce of the worlde. *the best in*
Sende into the cetė to seche hym bylyve,
And wynne hym with the worchyp to wayne the bote;

And thagh the mater be merk that merked is yender,
He schal declar hit also as hit on clay standes.'
That gode counseyl at the quene was cached as swythe; *from* *accepted at once*
The burne byfore Baltazar was broght in a whyle. *man*

When he com bifore the kyng and clanly had halsed, *politely* *greeted him*
Baltazar umbebrayde hym, and 'Leve sir,' he sayde, *embraced; dear*
'Hit is tolde me bi tulkes that thou trwe were *men*
Profete of that provynce that prayed my fader, *ravaged*

Ande that thou has in thy hert holy connyng, *understanding*
Of sapyence thi sawle ful, sothes to schawe;
Goddes gost is the geven that gyes alle thynges,
And thou unhyles uch hidde that heven-kyng myntes.

And here is a ferly byfallen, and I fayn wolde *marvel*
Wyt the wytte of the wryt that on the wowe clyves,
For alle Caldé clerkes han cowwardely fayled; *have miserably*
If thou with quayntyse conquere hit, I quyte the thy mede.

1610 Your bold father commanded his name to be Belteshazzar.
1615–18 Send messengers into the city to look for him at once, and prevail on him respectfully to give you assistance; and though the matter written there may be obscure, he will explain it just as it stands on the plaster.
1626–8 (You have) your soul full of wisdom, to reveal truths; the spirit of God, who rules all things, is given to you, and you uncover each hidden thing that the King of Heaven has in mind.
1630 Know the meaning of the writing that is fixed on the wall.
1632–40 If through your wisdom you succeed in deciphering it, I shall pay you your reward. Thus if you interpret it correctly and make sense of it,

For if thou redes hit by ryght and hit to resoun brynges,
Fyrst telle me the tyxte of the tede lettres,
And sythen the mater of the mode mene me therafter,
And I schal halde the the hest that I the hyght have,

Apyke the in porpre clothe, palle alther-fynest,
And the byghe of bryght golde abowte thyn nekke;
And the thryd thryvenest that thrynges me after,
Thou schal be baroun upon benche, bede I the no lasse.'

Derfly thenne Danyel deles thyse wordes: *boldly; speaks*
'Ryche kyng of this rengne, rede the oure Lorde!
Hit is surely soth, the Soverayn of heven *true*
Fylsened ever thy fader and upon folde cheryched,

Gart hym grattest to be of governores alle,
And alle the worlde in his wylle, welde as hym lykes.
Who-so wolde wel do, wel hym bityde,
And quos deth so he dezyre he dreped als fast;

Who-so hym lyked to lyft, on lofte was he sone,
And quo-so hym lyked to lay was lowed bylyve.
So was noted the note of Nabugodenozar; *famed; practice*
Styfly stabled the rengne, bi the stronge Dryghtyn.

For of the hyghest he hade a hope in his hert *Most High; belief*
That uche pouer past out of that prynce *came from*
even; *directly*

first tell me the wording of the fated letters, and then explain to me afterwards the sense of the thought, and I shall keep for you the promise that I have made to you, array you in purple cloth, the very finest material, and put the collar of bright gold round your neck; and you shall be a lord of the king's council, I promise you no less, the third most worthy who owes allegiance to me.

1642 Great king of this kingdom, may our Lord guide you!

1644–50 Always helped your father and looked after him on earth, made him the greatest of all rulers, and made all the world to be at his command, let him govern as it pleases him. Whoever he wished to be well off, good fortune befell him, and the man whose death he desired he killed immediately; whoever it pleased him to lift up was soon on high, and whoever it pleased him to lay low was quickly brought down.

1652 He governed the kingdom firmly, with the help of the mighty Lord.

And whyle that was cleght clos in his hert, *fixed firmly*
There was no mon upon molde of myght as hymselven. *earth; as powerful*

Til hit bitide on a tyme towched hym pryde, *one day*
For his lordeschyp so large and his lyf ryche; *great*
He hade so huge an insyght to his aune dedes *opinion of*
That the power of the hyghe prynce he purely foryetes. *completely*

Thenne blynnes he not of blasfemy, on to blame the Dryghtyn;
His myght mete to Goddes he made with his wordes: *equal*
"I am god of the grounde, to gye as me lykes, *world; govern*
As he that hyghe is in heven, his aungeles that weldes.

If he has formed the folde and folk therupone,
I haf bigged Babiloyne, burgh alther-rychest,
Stabled therinne uche a ston in strenkthe of myn armes;
Moght never myght bot myn make such another."

Was not this ilke worde wonnen of his mowthe
Er thenne the Soverayn sawe souned in his eres:
"Now, Nabugodenozar, innoghe has spoken. *you have said enough*
Now is alle thy pryncipalté past at ones, *sovereignty*

And thou, remued fro monnes sunes, on mor most abide,
And in wasturne walk, and wyth the wylde dowelle,
As best byte on the bent of braken and erbes,
With wrothe wolfes to won, and wyth wylde asses." *fierce; live*

1661 Then he does not refrain from blasphemy, from uttering impiety against the Lord.
1666–70 'I have built Babylon, the mightiest city of all, have placed every stone therein with my own strength; no power except mine might ever make such another.' This speech was not out of his mouth before the words of the Sovereign sounded in his ears.
1673–5 And you, banished from the sons of men, must live on the moor, and walk in the wilderness, and dwell with the wild animals, feed like a beast on pasture of bracken and grass.

Inmydde the poynt of his pryde departed he there
Fro the soly of his solempneté—his solace he leves,
And carfully is outkast to contré unknawen, *ignominiously*
Fer into a fyr fryth there frekes never comen.

His hert heldet unhole, he hoped non other
Bot a best that he be, a bol other an oxe;
He fares forth on alle faure, fogge was his mete,
And ete ay as a horce when erbes were fallen.

Thus he countes hym a kow, that was a kyng ryche,
Quyle seven sythes were overseyed someres, I trawe.
By that mony thik thyghe thryght umbe his lyre,
That alle was dubbed and dyght in the dew of heven;

Faxe fyltered and felt flosed hym umbe,
That schad fro his schulderes to his schyre-wykes,
And twenty-folde twynande hit to his tos raght,
Ther mony clyvy as clyde hit clyght togeder.

His berde ibrad alle his brest to the bare urthe,
His browes bresed as breres aboute his brode chekes;
Holwe were his yyen and under campe hores,
And al was gray as the glede, with ful grymme clawes,

That were croked and kene as the kyte paume;
Erne-hwed he was and al overbrawden,

1677–8 At the height of his glory he departed thither, from the seat of his high estate—he leaves his comforts.

1680–704 Far into a remote wilderness where men never come. His mind became unsound, he believed nothing else but that he was a beast, a bull or an ox; he went about on all fours, coarse grass was his food, and he ate hay like a horse when the grass was withered. Thus he counts himself a cow, he who had been a great king, until seven summers had passed away, as I believe. By then many a thick thigh crowded about his flesh, which was all arrayed and adorned in the dew of Heaven; tangled and matted hair fell in strands about him, coming down from his shoulders to the middle of his body, and twisting round many times it reached to his toes, where many a bur stuck it together like a poultice. His beard overspread all his breast to the bare earth, his eyebrows bristled like briars about his

Til he wyst ful wel who wroght alle myghtes,
And cowthe uche kyndam tokerve and kever when hym lyked.

Thenne he wayned hym his wyt that hade wo soffered,
That he com to knawlach and kenned hymselven.
Thenne he loved that Lorde, and leved in trawthe
Hit was non other then he that hade al in honde.

Thenne sone was he sende agayn, his sete restored; *returned; throne*
His barounes bowed hym to, blythe of his come; *went; coming*
Hagherly in his aune hwe his heved was covered,
And so yeply was yarked and yolden his state.

Bot thou, Baltazar, his barne and his bolde ayre, *son; heir*
Sey these syngnes with syght and set hem at lyttel,
Bot ay has hofen thy hert agaynes the hyghe Dryghtyn,
With bobaunce and with blasfamye bost at hym kest,

And now his vessayles avyled in vanyté unclene,
That in his hows hym to honour were hevened of fyrst;
Bifore the barouns has hom broght, and byrled therinne
Wale wyne to thy wenches in waryed stoundes.

Bifore thy borde has thou broght beverage in thede *vessels*
That blythely were fyrst blest with bischopes hondes, *zealously*
Lovande theron lese goddes that lyf haden never, *praising with them; false*
Made of stokkes and stones that never styry moght. *stir*

broad cheeks; his eyes were hollow and under rough lashes, and he was all grey as the kite, with most grim claws, that were curved and sharp like the kite's talon; he was coloured like an eagle and all covered over (with plumage), until he understood fully who created all powers, and could destroy each kingdom and restore it when it pleased Him. Then He sent him his reason, the man who had endured adversity, so that he came to his senses and knew himself. Then he praised the Lord, and believed truly that it was none other than He who ruled all things.

1707–8 He was properly restored to his own shape, and thus his high estate was quickly re-established.

1710–16 Saw these miraculous events and thought little of them, but you have always raised up your heart against the great Lord, have hurled defiance at Him with arrogance and blasphemy, and now with foul presumption you have defiled His vessels, which in the beginning were raised up in His house to honour Him; you have brought them before the barons, and in them you have served choice wine to your women in accursed times.

And for that frothande fylthe, the Fader of heven *festering*
Has sende into this sale thise syghtes uncowthe, *hall; strange*
The fyste with the fyngeres that flayed thi hert, *dismayed*
That rasped renyschly the wowe with the rogh penne. *harshly*

Thise ar the wordes here wryten, withoute werk more, *ado*
By uch fygure as I fynde, as oure Fader lykes:
Mane, Techal, Phares, merked in thrynne,
That thretes the of thyn unthryfte upon thre wyse.

Now expowne the this speche spedly I thenk:
Mane menes als much as maynful Gode *almighty*
Has counted thy kyndam bi a clene noumbre,
And fulfylled hit in fayth to the fyrre ende.

To teche the of Techal, that terme thus menes:
Thy wale rengne is walt in weghtes to heng,
And is funde ful fewe of hit fayth dedes;
And Phares folwes for those fawtes, to frayst the trawthe.

In Phares fynde I for sothe thise felle sawes:
Departed is thy pryncipalté, depryved thou worthes;
Thy rengne rafte is the fro and raght is the Perses;
The Medes schal be maysteres here, and thou of menske
schowved.'

The kyng comaunded anon to clethe that *be clothed*
wyse *wise man*
In frokkes of fyn cloth, as forward hit *garments; agreement*
asked;
Thenne sone was Danyel dubbed in ful dere porpor, *dressed*
And a coler of cler golde kest umbe his swyre. *placed; neck*

1726–9 Character by character as I understand them, as our Father permits: Mane, Tekel, Peres, written as three words, which threaten you on account of your folly in three ways. Now I intend to explain these words to you without delay.

1731–40 Has assessed your kingdom in a full reckoning, and brought it indeed to its final end. To instruct you concerning Tekel, that word means as follows: your noble reign is marked out to be weighed in the balance, and is found to be greatly lacking in honest works; and Peres comes next on account of those offences, to tell the truth. In Peres I find indeed these grim sayings: your principality is divided, you are deposed; your kingdom is taken away from you and given to the Persians; the Medes shall be masters here, and you shall be driven from your noble estate.

Then was demed a decré bi the duk selven; *proclaimed*
Bolde Baltazar bed that hym bowe schulde
The comynes al of Caldé that to the kyng longed,
As to the prynce pryvyest preved the thrydde,

Heghest of alle other, saf onelych tweyne, *worthiest; only*
To bow after Baltazar in borghe and in felde.
Thys was cryed and knawen in cort als fast,
And alle the folk therof fayn that folwed hym tylle.

Bot how-so Danyel was dyght, that day overyede;
Nyght neghed ryght now with nyes fol mony;
For dawed never another day that ilk derk after, *dawned; night*
Er dalt were that ilk dome that Danyel devysed.

The solace of the solempneté in that sale dured,
Of that farand fest, tyl fayled the sunne. *pleasant; set*
Thenne blykned the ble of the bryght skwes, *faded; colour; skies*
Mourkenes the mery weder, and the myst dryves;

Thorgh the lyst of the lyfte, bi the low medoes,
Uche hathel to his home hyyes ful fast,
Seten at her soper and songen therafter; *(they) sat*
Then foundes uch a felawschyp fyrre at forth naghtes.

Baltazar to his bedd with blysse was caryed; *ceremony; brought*
Reche the rest as hym lyst, he ros never therafter;
For his foes in the felde, in flokkes ful grete, *in battle; armies*
That longe hade layted that lede, his londes to strye,

1746–8 Bold Belshazzar ordered that all the people of Chaldea who were subject to the king should owe allegiance to him, as to the prince recognized as third most important.
1750–4 To pay homage to Belshazzar in town and country. This was immediately proclaimed and made known in the court, and all the people who owed allegiance to him were glad of it. But however Daniel was dealt with, that day passed away; night approached swiftly with many troubles.
1756–7 Before the doom that Daniel described was dealt out. The joy of the festivity continued in that hall.
1760–2 The clear air darkens, and the mist drives in; through the edge of the clear air, along the low meadows, each man (i.e. the ordinary people of the town, not Belshazzar's guests) hastens to his home.
1764 Then later on in the night each party of guests departs.
1766 Let him take rest as it pleases him, he never rose afterwards.
1768 Who had long sought that prince, to destroy his lands.

Now are thay sodenly assembled at the self tyme; *very*
Of hem wyst no wyye that in that won dowelled.
Hit was the dere Daryus, the duk of thise Medes, *noble*
The prowde prynce of Perce, and Porros of Ynde, *Persia; Porus*

With mony a legioun ful large, with ledes of armes, *men at arms*
That now has spyed a space to spoyle Caldees.
Thay throngen theder in the thester on thrawen hepes,
Asscaped over the skyre watteres and scaled the walles,

Lyfte laddres ful longe and upon lofte wonen,
Stelen stylly the toun er any steven rysed.
Withinne an oure of the niyght an entré thay hade, *nightfall*
Yet afrayed thay no freke—fyrre thay passen, *alarmed; further*

And to the palays pryncipal thay aproched *royal*
ful stylle. *quietly*
Thenne ran thay in on a res, on rowtes ful grete; *rush; crowds*
Blastes out of bryght brasse brestes so hyghe,
Ascry scarred on the scue, that scomfyted mony.

Segges slepande were slayne er thay slyppe myght; *men; escape*
Uche hous heyred was withinne a *ransacked*
hondewhyle. *short time*
Baltazar in his bed was beten to dethe,
That bothe his blod and his brayn blende on the *mingled*
clothes.

The kyng in his cortyn was kaght bi the heles, *bedcurtain*
Feryed out bi the fete and fowle dispysed, *brought; maltreated*
That was so doghty that day and drank of the vessayl; *bold*
Now is a dogge also dere that in a dych lygges. *as precious; lies*

1770 No man who lived in that city was aware of them.
1774–8 Who had now spied an opportunity to ravage the Chaldeans. They rushed thither in the darkness in close-packed battalions, slipped over the bright rivers and scaled the walls, lifted up long ladders and made their way aloft, quietly took the town before any outcry arose.
1783–4 Blasts burst out loudly from bright brass trumpets, clamour flew up to the sky, throwing many into confusion.

For the mayster of thyse Medes on the morne ryses,
Dere Daryous that day, dyght upon trone; *placed*
That ceté seses ful sounde, and saghtlyng makes
Wyth alle the barouns theraboute, that bowed hym after.

And thus was that londe lost for the lordes synne,
And the fylthe of the freke that defowled hade *defiled*
The ornementes of Goddes hous that holy were maked.
He was corsed for his unclannes and cached therinne, *overtaken in it*

Done doun of his dyngneté for dedes unfayre, *struck; unseemly*
And of thyse worldes worchyp wrast out for ever, *honour; cast*
And yet of lykynges on lofte letted, I trowe;
To loke on oure lofly Lorde late bitydes.

Thus upon thrynne wyses I haf yow thro schewed
That unclannes tocleves in corage dere *sticks; heart; noble*
Of that wynnelych Lorde that wonyes in heven, *gracious; dwells*
Entyses hym to be tene, telled up his wrake.

Ande clannes is his comfort, and coyntyse he lovyes,
And those that seme arn and swete schyn se his face.
That we gon gay in oure gere that grace he uus sende,
That we may serve in his syght ther solace never blynnes.
Amen.

1795–6 Takes secure possession of that city, and makes peace with all the barons round about, who paid homage to him.
1799 The sanctified ornaments of God's house.
1803–5 And also deprived of delights in Heaven, as I believe; looking on our gracious Lord will be long deferred (for him). Thus in three ways I have shown you clearly.
1808–12 Incites Him to be angry, His hostility aroused. But cleanness is His delight, and He loves refinement, and those that are seemly and pleasant shall see His face. May He send us the grace to be well dressed, so that we may serve in His sight where bliss never ends.

PATIENCE

PROLOGUE

Pacience is a poynt, thagh hit displese ofte. *virtue*
When hevy herttes ben hurt wyth hethyng other elles,
Suffraunce may aswagen hem and the swelme lethe,
For ho quelles uche a qued and quenches malyce.

For quo-so suffer cowthe syt, sele wolde folwe,
And quo for thro may noght thole, the thikker he sufferes.
Then is better to abyde the bur umbestoundes
Then ay throw forth my thro, thagh me thynk ylle.

I herde on a halyday, at a hyghe masse, *holy day*
How Mathew melede that his mayster his *said*
meyny con teche; *taught his followers*
Aght happes he hem hyght, and ucheon a mede
Sunderlupes for hit dissert upon a ser wyse.

Thay arn happen that han in hert poverté, *blessed; have*
For hores is the hevenryche to holde for ever.
Thay ar happen also that haunte mekenesse, *practise*
For thay schall welde this worlde and alle her wylle *possess*
have.

Thay ar happen also that for her harme wepes, *sin*
For thay schal comfort encroche in kythes *obtain; lands*
ful mony.
Thay ar happen also that hungeres after ryght,
For thay schal frely be refete ful of alle gode. *fed*

2–8 When heavy hearts are hurt by scorn or anything else, patience may soothe them and lessen the bitterness, for it subdues every evil and extinguishes malice. Prosperity follows for the man who is able to put up with misfortune, but he who may not endure, on account of his impatience, suffers the more. And so it is better for me to accept the blow when it falls than to be always giving vent to my impatience, though I may not like it.

11–12 Eight blessed states He decreed to them, and a reward for each in turn according to its merit.

14 For theirs is the kingdom of Heaven to have for ever.

Thay ar happen also that han in hert rauthe, *pity*
For mercy in alle maneres her mede schal *forms; reward*
worthe. *be*
Thay ar happen also that arn of hert clene,
For thay her Savyour in sete schal se with her yyen. *throne; eyes*

Thay ar happen also that halden her pese, *are peaceful*
For thay the gracious Godes sunes schal godly be *fittingly*
called.
Thay ar happen also that con her hert stere, *govern*
For hores is the hevenryche, as I er sayde. *before*

These arn the happes alle aght that uus bihyght weren, *promised*
If we thyse ladyes wolde lof in lyknyng of thewes:
Dame Povert, dame Pitee, dame Penaunce the thrydde,
Dame Mekenesse, dame Mercy and miry Clannesse, *fair*

And thenne dame Pes and Pacyence put in therafter;
He were happen that hade one, alle were the better.
Bot syn I am put to a poynt that poverté hatte, *state; is called*
I schal me porvay pacyence and play me with bothe.

For in the tyxte there thyse two arn in teme layde,
Hit arn fettled in on forme, the forme and the laste,
And by quest of her quoyntyse enquylen on mede;
And als, in myn upynyoun, hit arn of on kynde, *they*

For ther as povert hir proferes ho nyl be put utter,
Bot lenge wheresoever hir lyst, lyke other greme;
And there as povert enpresses, thagh mon pyne thynk,
Much, maugré his mun, he mot nede suffer.

30 If we would love these ladies by copying their virtues.

36–9 I shall take patience upon myself and cultivate both. For in the text (i.e. Matt. v. 3–10) where these two are spoken of, they are arranged first and last in a series, and by the judgement of their Lord they receive one reward.

41–4 For where poverty presents herself she will not be put outside, but shall stay wherever she pleases, like it or not; and where poverty is oppressive a man must suffer much, in spite of his resistance, though he thinks it hard.

Thus poverté and pacyence arn nedes *necessarily*
playferes; *playfellows*
Sythen I am sette with hem samen, suffer me byhoves.
Thenne is me lyghtloker hit lyke and her lotes prayse
Thenne wyther wyth and be wroth and the wers have. *resist*

Yif me be dyght a destyné due to have, *ordained; appointed*
What dowes me the dedayn other dispit make?
Other yif my lege lorde lyst on lyve me to bidde
Other to ryde other to renne to Rome in his ernde,

What graythed me the grychchyng bot grame more seche?
Much yif he me ne made, maugref my chekes,
And thenne thrat moste I thole and unthonk to mede,
The had bowed to his bode bongré my hyure.

Did not Jonas in Judé suche jape sumwhyle? *Judea; folly; once*
To sette hym to sewrté, unsounde he hym feches.
Wyl ye tary a lyttel tyne and tent me a whyle, *moment; attend to*
I schal wysse yow therwyth as Holy Wryt telles. *tell; about it*

I

Hit bitydde sumtyme in the termes of Judé *happened; boundaries*
Jonas joyned was therinne jentyle prophete.
Goddes glam to hym glod that hym unglad made, *speech; came*
With a roghlych rurd rowned in his ere:

46–7 Since I am beset by them together, I must endure them. Then it is better for me to make the best of it and praise their ways.
50–6 Of what use is indignation to me, or defiance? Or if my liege lord pleased to command me to go to Rome on his errand, what would grumbling do for me except to invite more trouble? It would be too good to be true if he did not compel me (to go), in spite of my objections, and then I must endure misery and displeasure for a reward, I who ought to have bowed to his bidding according to the terms of my hire.
58 In trying to achieve safety, he brings disaster upon himself.
62 That there Jonah was appointed prophet to the gentiles.
64 Breathed in his ear with a harsh sound.

'Rys radly,' he says, 'and rayke forth even; *quickly; go; at once*
Nym the way to Nynyve wythouten other speche, *take; further*
And in that cetë my sawes soghe alle aboute *sayings; spread*
That in that place, at the poynt, I put in thi hert. *when the time comes*

For iwysse hit arn so wykke that in that won dowelles, *indeed; city*
And her malys is so much, I may not abide, *endure it*
Bot venge me on her vilanye and venym bilyve.
Now sweye me thider swyftly and say me this arende.'

When that steven was stynt that stowned his mynde,
Al he wrathed in his wyt and wytherly he thoght:
'If I bowe to his bode and bryng hem this tale, *bidding; message*
And I be nummen in Nunive, my nyes begynes. *arrested; troubles*

He telles me those traytoures arn typped schrewes; *consummate villains*
I com wyth those tythynges, thay ta me bylyve, *tidings; take at once*
Pynes me in a prysoun, put me in stokkes, *confine*
Wrythe me in a warlok, wrast out myn yyen.

This is a mervayl message a man for to preche *marvellous*
Amonge enmyes so mony and mansed fendes, *accursed evildoers*
Bot if my gaynlych God such gref to me wolde,
For desert of sum sake, that I slayn were.

71–4 'But must revenge myself at once on their villainy and venom. Now go there quickly and proclaim this message for me.' When that voice, which stunned his senses, was silent, he became very angry in himself and thought rebelliously.

80 Torture me in a foot-shackle, tear out my eyes.

83–4 Unless my gracious God wished such harm to me as to want me killed, in punishment for some offence or other.

At alle peryles,' quoth the prophete, 'I aproche hit *risks*
no nerre; *nearer*
I wyl me sum other waye that he ne *will go*
wayte after. *watches over*
I schal tee into Tarce and tary there a whyle, *go; Tarshish*
And lyghtly when I am lest he letes me alone.' *perhaps; gone*

Thenne he ryses radly and raykes bilyve, *quickly; goes*
Jonas toward port Japh, ay janglande for *Jaffa; grumbling*
tene *indignation*
That he nolde thole for no thyng non of those *endure*
pynes, *afflictions*
Thagh the Fader that hym formed were fale of his hele.

'Oure Syre syttes,' he says, 'on sege so hyghe, *throne*
In his glowande glorye, and gloumbes ful lyttel *worries*
Thagh I be nummen in Nunnive and naked dispoyled, *stripped*
On rode rwly torent with rybaudes mony.'

Thus he passes to that port his passage to seche,
Fyndes he a fayr schyp to the fare redy, *for the voyage*
Maches hym with the maryneres, makes her paye
For to towe hym into Tarce as tyd as thay myght. *take; quickly*

Then he tron on tho tres and thay her tramme ruchen,
Cachen up the crossayl, cables thay fasten,
Wight at the wyndas weyen her ankres,
Spynde spak to the sprete the spare bawelyne,

Gederen to the gyde-ropes—the grete cloth falles.
Thay layden in on laddeborde and the lofe wynnes;

92 Were unconcerned about his welfare.
96 Pitifully torn to pieces on a cross by many evil men.
99 Settles with the mariners, gives them payment.
101–8 Then he goes aboard (lit. stepped on the boards) and they get the gear ready, hoist the square-sail, fasten cables, swiftly weigh the anchors at the windlass, smartly fasten the bowline, carried in reserve, to the bowsprit, tug at the guy-ropes—the mainsail comes down (i.e. as it unfurls). They lay in oars on the port side and gain the luff (i.e. a position more or

The blythe brethe at her bak the bosum he fyndes,
He swenges me thys swete schip swefte fro the haven.

Was never so joyful a Jue as Jonas was thenne,
That the daunger of Dryghtyn so derfly ascaped.
He wende wel that that wyy that al the world planted
Hade no maght in that mere no man for to greve.

Lo, the wytles wrechche, for he wolde noght suffer, *because*
Now has he put hym in plyt of peril wel more. *state; greater*
Hit was a wenyng unwar that welt in his mynde,
Thagh he were soght fro Samarye, that God sey no fyrre.

Yise, he blusched ful brode, that burde hym by sure;
That ofte kyd hym the carpe that kyng sayde,
Dyngne David on des that demed this speche
In a psalme that he set the Sauter withinne: *Psalter*

'O foles in folk, feles otherwhyle,
And understondes umbestounde, thagh ye be stape fole.
Hope ye that he heres not that eres alle made? *think*
Hit may not be that he is blynde that bigged uche yye.' *created*

Bot he dredes no dynt that dotes for elde,
For he was fer in the flod foundande to Tarce. *ocean; hurrying*
Bot I trow ful tyd overtan that he were, *believe; overtaken*
So that schomely to schort he schote of his ame.

less against the wind in which the sail becomes effective); the merry wind at their back finds the belly of the sail (i.e. as the ship turns), and swings this sweet ship swiftly from the harbour.

110–12 Who had so boldly escaped the power of the Lord. He knew well that the One who had created all the world had no power in that sea to harm any man.

115–19 It was a foolish thought that turned in his mind, that though he were gone from Samaria, God looked no further. Yes, He looked with wide-open eyes, he should have been certain of that; he had been told that often in the words which the king spoke, noble David on his throne who uttered this speech.

121–2 O fools amongst the people, be sensible now and then, and show understanding occasionally, though you are quite mad.

125 But he, foolish in his old age, fears no blow.

128–33 So that he shot shamefully too short of his mark. For the Lord of

For the welder of wyt that wot alle thynges,
That ay wakes and waytes, at wylle has he slyghtes.
He calde on that ilk crafte he carf with his hondes;
Thay wakened wel the wrotheloker for wrothely he cleped:

'Ewrus and Aquiloun that on est sittes,
Blowes bothe at my bode upon blo watteres.' *dark*
Thenne was no tom ther bytwene his tale and her dede, *delay; words*
So bayn wer thay bothe two his bone for to wyrk.

Anon out of the north-est the noys bigynes,
When bothe brethes con blowe upon blo watteres. *winds blew*
Rogh rakkes ther ros, with rudnyng anunder;
The see soughed ful sore, gret selly to here.

The wyndes on the wonne water so wrastel togeder
That the wawes ful wode waltered so highe,
And efte busched to the abyme, that breed fysches
Durst nowhere for rogh arest at the bothem.

When the breth and the brok and the bote metten, *sea*
Hit was a joyles gyn that Jonas was inne, *craft*
For hit reled on roun upon the roghe ythes; *around; waves*
The bur ber to hit baft, that braste alle her gere.

Then hurled on a hepe the helme and the sterne;
Furst tomurte mony rop, and the mast after; *broke*
The sayl sweyed on the see; thenne suppe bihoved *collapsed; sup*
The coge of the colde water, and thenne the cry ryses. *ship*

wisdom who knows all things, who always wakes and watches, has means at His command. He called on those powers He had made with His hands; they wakened the more angrily in that angrily He called: 'Eurus (an easterly wind) and Aquilon (a north-easterly wind) who sit in the East.'

136 So eager were they both to carry out His command.

139–44 Ragged clouds came up, with red light under them; the sea roared most dreadfully, awesome to hear. The winds so wrestled together on the dark water that the waves in their anger rolled so high, and so plunged back into the abyss, that nowhere were the terrified fish able to remain quiet at the bottom, on account of the upheaval.

148–9 The gale took it abaft, so that all the gear was shattered. Then the tiller and the stern crashed in a heap.

Yet corven thay the cordes and kest al theroute; *cut; threw*
Mony ladde ther forth lep to lave and to kest, *leapt; bale* *cast out*
Scopen out the scathel water that fayn scape wolde,
For be monnes lode never so luther, the lyf is ay swete. *burden; heavy*

Ther was busy overborde bale to kest, *eagerness; packages*
Her bagges and her fether-beddes and her bryght wedes, *clothes*
Her kysttes and her coferes, her caraldes alle, *chests; casks*
And al to lyghten that lome, yif lethe wolde schape.

Bot ever was ilyche loud the lot of the wyndes, *just as; noise*
And ever wrother the water and wodder the stremes. *angrier; wilder* *seas*
Then tho wery forwroght wyst no bote,
Bot uchon glewed on his god that gayned hym beste. *called; helped*

Summe to Vernagu ther vouched avowes solemne,
Summe to Diana devout and derf Neptune, *holy; mighty*
To Mahoun and to Mergot, the mone and the sunne, *Mahomet; Magog*
And uche lede as he loved and layde had his hert.

Thenne bispeke the spakest, dispayred wel nere: *wisest*
'I leve here be sum losynger, sum lawles wrech, *think; traitor*
That has greved his god and gos here amonge uus. *offended*
Lo, al synkes in his synne and for his sake marres. *perishes*

I louve that we lay lotes on ledes uchone,
And who-so lympes the losse, lay hym theroute;
And quen the gulty is gon, what may gome trawe, *man; believe*
Bot he that rules the rak may rwe on those other?'

155 Scooped out the threatening water, desiring to save their lives.
160 And all to lighten that vessel, to see if relief would come.
163 Then those men, worn out with work, saw no remedy.
165 Some there made solemn vows to Vernagu (a Saracen god).
168 Each man as he had faith and had committed his heart.
173–4 I suggest that we cast lots amongst all the men, and whoever loses, throw him overboard.
176 But that He who rules the storm may pity the rest?

This was sette in asent, and sembled thay were, *agreed; assembled*
Heryed out of uche hyrne to hent that falles;
A lodesmon lyghtly lep under hachches
For to layte mo ledes and hem to lote bryng.

Bot hym fayled no freke that he fynde myght,
Saf Jonas the Jwe, that jowked in derne;
He was flowen, for ferde of the flode lotes,
Into the bothem of the bot, and on a brede lyggede,

Onhelde by the hurrok, for the heven wrache,
Slypped upon a sloumbe-selepe, and sloberande he routes.
The freke hym frunt with his fot and bede hym ferk up; *kicked* *get*
Ther Ragnel in his rakentes hym rere of his dremes!

Bi the hasp-hede he hentes hym thenne,
And broght hym up by the brest and upon borde sette, *deck*
Arayned hym ful runyschly what raysoun he hade *questioned; roughly*
In such slaghtes of sorwe to slepe so faste. *desperate straits*

Sone haf thay her sortes sette and serelych deled,
And ay the lote upon laste lymped on Jonas.
Thenne ascryed thay hym sckete and asked ful loude: *berated; quickly*
'What the devel has thou don, doted wrech? *stupid*

178–86 Routed out of every corner to take what should befall; a steersman quickly leapt below deck to look for more men and bring them to the casting of lots. But no man was missing whom he might expect to find except Jonah the Jew, who was sleeping in a hidden place; he had fled, for fear of the roaring of the sea, into the bottom of the boat, and was lying on a plank, huddled up by the rudder-band, to escape Heaven's vengeance, sunk in a deep sleep, and slobbering as he snored.

188–9 So may Ragnel (a devil) in his chains rouse him from his dreams! He seizes him then by the clasp (of his garment).

193–4 Soon they have prepared their lots and dealt them out in turn, and always the lot finally fell to Jonah.

What seches thou on see, synful schrewe,
With thy lastes so luther to lose uus uchone?
Has thou, gome, no governour ne god on to calle, *fellow; master*
That thou thus slydes on slepe when thou slayn worthes? *are about to be*

Of what londe art thou lent, what laytes thou here, *come; seek*
Whyder in worlde that thou wylt, and what is thyn arnde?
Lo, thy dom is the dyght, for thy dedes ille;
Do gyf glory to thy godde, er thou glyde hens.' *go hence*

'I am an Ebru,' quoth he, 'of Israyl borne;
That wyye I worchyp, iwysse, that wroght alle thynges, *One*
Alle the worlde with the welkyn, the wynde and the sternes, *sky* *stars*
And alle that wones ther withinne, at a worde one. *lives; single*

Alle this meschef for me is made at thys tyme, *trouble*
For I haf greved my God and gulty am founden;
Forthy beres me to the borde and bathes me theroute;
Er gete ye no happe, I hope forsothe.'

He ossed hym by unnynges that thay undernomen
That he was flawen fro the face of frelych Dryghtyn.
Thenne such a ferde on hem fel and flayed hem withinne
That thay ruyt hym to rowwe, and letten the rynk one.

Hatheles hyyed in haste with ores ful longe, *men hurried*
Syn her sayl was hem aslypped, on sydes to rowe,
Hef and hale upon hyght to helpen hymselven.
Bot al was nedles note, that nolde not bityde;

197–8 Why are you trying to destroy us all on the sea with your foul crimes, you evil wretch?

202–3 Where in the world are you going, and what is your errand? See, your fate is decided, for your evil deeds.

211–16 'And so carry me to the side and throw me overboard; you will get no good fortune before then, I am certain.' He showed them by signs which they understood that he had fled from the face of the most high Lord. Then such a fear fell on them and dismayed their hearts that they bestirred themselves to row, and left the man alone.

218–20 Since their sail had escaped them, to row at the sides, to heave and pull with all their might to help themselves. But all their effort was useless, it was not to be.

In bluber of the blo flod bursten her ores. *turbulence*
Thenne hade thay noght in her honde that hem help myght;
Thenne nas no coumfort to kever, ne counsel non other
Bot Jonas into his juis jugge bylyve.

Fyrst thay prayen to the prynce that prophetes serven
That he gef hem the grace to greven hym never
That thay in baleles blod ther blenden her handes,
Thagh that hathel wer his that thay here quelled.

Tyd by top and bi to thay token hym synne,
Into that lodlych loghe thay luche hym sone.
He was no tytter outtulde that tempest ne sessed;
The se saghtled therwith as sone as ho moght.

Thenne thagh her takel were torne that totered on ythes,
Styffe stremes and streght hem strayned a whyle,
That drof hem dryylych adoun the depe to serve,
Tyl a swetter ful swythe hem sweyed to bonk.

Ther was lovyng on lofte, when thay the londe wonnen,
To oure mercyable God, on Moyses wyse,
With sacrafyse upset and solempne vowes, *raised up*
And graunted hym on to be God, and graythly non other.

Thagh thay be jolef for joye, Jonas yet dredes; *light-hearted*
Thagh he nolde suffer no sore, his seele is on anter;
For what-so worthed of that wyye fro he in water dipped,
Hit were a wonder to wene, yif Holy Wryt nere.

223–4 Then there was no comfort to be had, nor any other counsel except to consign Jonah to his doom at once.
226–38 That He should give them the grace never to offend Him by (their) steeping their hands in innocent blood, even if the man they killed there were His. Quickly then they took him by top and toe, pitched him at once into that fearsome sea. No sooner was he thrown out than the tempest stopped; with that the sea became calm as soon as it might. Then though the tackle of that ship, which tottered on the waves, was torn to pieces, strong and compelling currents took charge of them for a while, driving them along relentlessly in the power of the deep, until a more favourable one sped them swiftly to land. Praise was raised on high, when they reached land, to our merciful God, after the manner of Moses.
240 And they acknowledged that He alone was God, and truly no other.
242–4 Though he would not suffer hardship, his welfare is in doubt; for what became of that man after he plunged into the water would be difficult to believe, if it were not for Holy Writ.

II

Now is Jonas the Jwe jugged to drowne; *doomed*
Of that schended schyp men schowved hym sone. *wrecked*
A wylde walterande whal, as wyrde then schaped,
That was beten fro the abyme, bi that bot flotte,

And was war of that wyye that the water soghte, *aware*
And swyftely swenged hym to swepe and his swolw opened.
The folk yet haldande his fete, the fysch hym tyd hentes;
Withouten towche of any tothe he tult in his throte. *tumbled*

Thenne he swenges and swayves to the se bothem, *swings; sweeps*
Bi mony rokkes ful roghe and rydelande *swirling*
strondes, *currents*
Wyth the mon in his mawe malskred in drede— *dazed*
As lyttel wonder hit was, yif he wo dreyed, *was in distress*

For nade the hyghe heven-kyng, thurgh his *had not*
honde myght, *power*
Warded this wrech man in warlowes guttes, *guarded; monster's*
What lede moght lyve, bi lawe of any kynde,
That any lyf myght be lent so longe hym withinne?

Bot he was sokored by that Syre that syttes so highe, *succoured*
Thagh were wanles of wele in wombe of that fissche,
And also dryven thurgh the depe, and in derk walteres.
Lorde, colde was his cumfort, and his care huge! *trouble*

For he knew uche a cace and kark that hym lymped,
How fro the bot into the blober was with a best lachched,

247–8 A wild wallowing whale, as fate then brought it about, that was driven from the depths, was floating near the boat.
250–1 And swiftly swooped and opened its gullet. With the people still holding his feet, the fish quickly seizes him.
259–60 What man could believe that he might, by any natural law, be granted life for such a long time inside (the whale)?
262–3 Though he was without hope of well-being in the belly of that fish, and driven through the deep besides, and though he rolled about in the darkness.
265–8 For he was aware of every misfortune and trouble that had befallen him, how he was seized by a monster out of the boat into the seething water, and how he sped in through its throat without more ado, like a mote in at a cathedral door, so great were its jaws.

And thrwe in at hit throte withouten thret more,
As mote in at a munster dor, so mukel wern his chawles.

He glydes in by the giles thurgh glaymande glette, *slimy filth*
Relande in by a rop, a rode that hym thoght,
Ay hele over hed hourlande aboute, *tumbling*
Til he blunt in a blok as brod as a halle. *stopped; cavern*

And ther he festnes the fete and fathmes aboute,
And stod up in his stomak that stank as the devel.
Ther in saym and in sorwe that savoured as helle,
Ther was bylded his bour that wyl no bale suffer.

And thenne he lurkkes and laytes where was le best
In uche a nok of his navel, bot nowhere he fyndes
No rest ne recoverer bot ramel ande myre,
In wych gut so-ever he gos—bot ever is God swete.

And ther he lenged at the last and to the lede called: *halted; Lord*
'Now, prynce, of thy prophete pité thou have.
Thagh I be fol and fykel and falce of my hert, *foolish*
Dewoyde now thy vengaunce, thurgh vertu of rauthe.

Thagh I be gulty of gyle, as gaule of prophetes, *scum*
Thou art God, and alle gowdes ar graythely thyn owen; *things; truly*
Haf now mercy of thy man and his mysdedes,
And preve the lyghtly a lorde in londe and in water.' *readily*

With that he hitte to a hyrne and helde hym therinne,
Ther no defoule of no fylthe was fest hym abute.
Ther he sete also sounde, saf for merk one,
As in the bulk of the bote ther he byfore sleped. *hold*

270 Reeling in along a gut, that seemed to him a road.
273 And there he gets his footing and gropes about.
275–9 There in grease and filth that stank as Hell, there was made the bower of the man who would suffer no hardship. And then he creeps and looks for the best shelter in every corner of its guts, but nowhere does he find any rest or safety, only muck and mire.
284 Forego your vengeance now, through the power of your pity.
289–91 With that he came upon a nook and installed himself in it, where no foulness of filth was near him. There he remained as secure, save only for darkness.

So in a bouel of that best he bides on lyve, *lives on*
Thre dayes and thre nyght, ay thenkande on Dryghtyn,
His myght and his merci, his mesure thenne; *moderation*
Now he knawes hym in care that couthe not in sele.

Ande ever walteres this whal bi wyldren depe,
Thurgh mony a regioun ful roghe,
  thurgh ronk of his wylle; *in the pride*
For that mote in his mawe mad hym, I trowe, *made*
Thagh hit lyttel were hym wyth, to wamel at his hert.

Ande as sayled the segge, ay sykerly he herde
The bygge borne on his bak and bete on his sydes.
Then a prayer ful prest the prophete ther maked; *quickly*
On this wyse, as I wene, his wordes were mony: *believe*

III

'Lorde, to the haf I cleped in cares ful stronge; *called*
Out of the hole thou me herde of hellen wombe; *of Hell*
I calde, and thou knew myn uncler steven. *voice*
Thou diptes me of the depe se into the dymme hert;

The grete flem of thy flod folded me umbe; *flow; around*
Alle the gotes of thy guferes and groundeles powles,
And thy stryvande stremes of stryndes so mony,
In on daschande dam dryves me over.

296–7 Now in trouble he acknowledges Him, he who did not know how to do so in prosperity. And still the whale wallows through the angry deep.
300–2 (Made it) feel sick at heart, though it were tiny by comparison. And as the man sailed on, he heard, always in safety, the mighty ocean on its back and beating on its sides.
308 You plunged me into the dim heart of the deep sea.
310–12 All the surges of your whirlpools and bottomless deeps, and your restless seas of many currents, drive over me in one overwhelming flood.

And yet I sayde, as I seet in the se bothem: *sat*
"Careful am I, kest out fro thy cler yyen, *distressed; eyes*
And desevered fro thy syght; yet surely I hope *cut off*
Efte to trede on thy temple and teme to thyselven."

I am wrapped in water to my wo stoundes;
The abyme byndes the body that I byde inne;
The pure poplande hourle playes on my heved;
To laste mere of uche a mount, man, am I fallen.

The barres of uche a bonk ful bigly me haldes,
That I may lachche no lont, and thou my lyf weldes;
Thou schal releve me, renk, whil thy ryght slepes,
Thurgh myght of thy mercy that mukel is to tryste.

For when th'acces of anguych was hid in my sawle, *pang*
Thenne I remembred me ryght of my rych Lorde, *duly; noble*
Prayande him for peté his prophete to here,
That into his holy hous myn orisoun moght entre. *prayer*

I haf meled with thy maystres mony longe day,
Bot now I wot wyterly that those unwyse ledes,
That affyen hym in vanyté and in vayne thynges, *trust in*
For think that mountes to noght her mercy forsaken.

Bot I dewoutly awowe, that verray bes halden,
Soberly to do the sacrafyse when I schal save worthe,
And offer the for my hele a ful hol gyfte, *safety; proper*
And halde goud that thou me hetes, haf here my trauthe.'

316–24 'To walk in your temple and be yours again.' I am wrapped in water to my pangs of woe (Jonah ii. 6: to the soul); the abyss binds the body that I inhabit; the boiling sea-surge itself plays on my head; I am fallen, Sir, to the last boundary of every mountain (Jonah ii. 7: to the bottoms of the mountains). The bars of every land hold me strongly, so that I may not reach the shore, and you rule my life; you must succour me, Sir, while your justice sleeps, through the power of your mercy that one may readily rely on.

329–30 I have spoken with your men of learning for many a long day, but I now know for certain that those unwise men.

332–4 Give up the mercy that would be theirs for things that amount to nothing. But I solemnly promise, I who am considered truthful, to make sacrifice to you with propriety when I am saved.

336 And accept what you command me, you have my word here.

Thenne oure Fader to the fysch ferslych biddes — *sternly; commands*
That he hym sput spakly upon spare drye.
The whal wendes at his wylle and a warthe fyndes,
And ther he brakes up the buyrne as bede hym oure Lorde.

Thenne he swepe to the sonde in sluchched clothes;
Hit may wel be that mester were his mantyle to wasche.
The bonk that he blosched to and bode hym bisyde
Wern of the regiounes ryght that he renayed hade.

Thenne a wynde of Goddes worde efte the wyye bruxles:
'Nylt thou never to Nunive bi no kynnes wayes?'
'Yisse, Lorde,' quoth the lede, 'lene me thy grace — *give*
For to go at thi gre; me gaynes non other.'

'Ris, aproche then to prech, lo, the place here!
Lo, my lore is in the loke, lauce hit therinne!'
Thenne the renk radly ros as he myght, — *quickly*
And to Ninive that naght he neghed ful even.

Hit was a ceté ful syde and selly of brede;
On to threnge therthurghe was thre dayes dede.
That on journay ful joynt Jonas hym yede,
Er ever he warpped any worde to wyye that he mette, — *spoke*

And thenne he cryed so cler that kenne myght alle; — *understand*
The trwe tenor of his teme he tolde on this wyse: — *purport; message*

338–46 That it should quickly spit him out upon dry land. The whale goes at His will and finds a shore, and there it spews up the man as our Lord commanded. Then he swept to the shore in filthy clothes; it may well be that there was need for him to wash his mantle. The land that met his gaze, lying around him, belonged to the very country which he had renounced. Then a breath of God's word again upbraids the man: 'Will you still not go to Nineveh, not by any route?'

348–50 'To go as you desire; no other course will profit me.' 'Rise, then approach this place here, look, to preach to it! Look, my teaching is locked inside you, release it in that place!'

352–5 And he came very near to Nineveh that night. It was a most extensive city and of wondrous breadth; to press on through it took three days. Jonah travelled very quickly for one day's journey.

'Yet schal forty dayes fully fare to an ende,
And thenne schal Ninive be nomen and to noght worthe.

Truly this ilk toun schal tylte to grounde; *fall*
Up so doun schal ye dumpe depe to the abyme, *pell-mell; dive*
To be swolwed swyftly wyth the swart erthe, *by; black*
And alle that lyvyes hereinne lose the swete.' *life-blood*

This speche sprang in that space and spradde alle aboute *went out; place*
To borges and to bacheleres that in that burgh lenged.
Such a hidor hem hent and a hatel drede
That al chaunged her chere and chylled at the hert.

The segge sesed not yet, bot sayde ever ilyche:
'The verray vengaunce of God schal voyde this place.' *destroy*
Thenne the peple pitosly pleyned ful stylle, *lamented; continually*
And for the drede of Dryghtyn doured in hert. *were troubled*

Heter hayres thay hent that asperly bited,
And those thay bounden to her bak and to her bare sydes,
Dropped dust on her hede, and dymly bisoghten *feebly*
That that penaunce plesed him that playnes on her wronge. *complains of*

And ay he cryes in that kyth tyl the kyng herde; *still; place*
And he radly upros and ran fro his chayer. *promptly; throne*
His ryche robe he torof of his rigge naked, *ripped from; back*
And of a hep of askes he hitte in the myddes.

359–60 From this time shall forty days pass away, and then Nineveh shall be taken and destroyed.
366–9 To the burgesses and the young men who lived in that town. Such fright and cruel fear seized them that all were transformed and were chilled at heart. Still the man did not cease, but said again and again.
373 They took rough hair-shirts that bit sharply.
380–2 And he set himself in the middle of a heap of ashes. Urgently he

He askes heterly a hayre and hasped hym umbe,
Sewed a sekke therabof, and syked ful colde.
Ther he dased in that duste, with droppande teres, *lay stunned*
Wepande ful wonderly alle his wrange dedes.

Thenne sayde he to his serjauntes: 'Samnes yow bilyve;
Do dryve out a decré, demed of myselven,
That alle the bodyes that ben withinne this borgh quyk,
Bothe burnes and bestes, burdes and childer,

Uch prynce, uche prest, and prelates alle,
Alle faste frely for her falce werkes. *shall fast willingly*
Seses childer of her sok, soghe hem so never,
Ne best bite on no brom, ne no bent nauther,

Passe to no pasture, ne pike non erbes,
Ne non oxe to no hay, ne no horse to water.
Al schal crye, forclemmed, with alle oure clere strenthe;
The rurd schal ryse to hym that rawthe schal have; *noise; pity*

What wote other wyte may yif the wyye lykes,
That is hende in the hyght of his gentryse?
I wot his myght is so much, thagh he be myssepayed, *displeased*
That in his mylde amesyng he mercy may fynde. *gentleness*

And if we leven the layk of oure layth synnes, *practice; foul*
And stylle steppen in the styye he styghtles hymselven,
He wyl wende of his wodschip, and his wrath leve, *turn from; fury*
And forgif uus this gult, yif we hym God leven.' *believe*

asked for a hair-shirt and clasped it round him, sewed a piece of sackcloth on it and sighed most woefully.

384–8 Weeping prodigiously for all his evil deeds. Then he said to his servants: 'Assemble at once; proclaim a decree, ordained by myself, that all living creatures in this town, men and animals, women and children.'

391–3 Take children from the breast, no matter how much it may distress them, nor shall any beast feed on broom, or grass either, go to pasture, or crop plants.

395 Pinched with hunger, we must all cry out with all our full strength.

397–8 Who knows or may know whether God, who is gracious in the excellence of His nobility, will not be pleased?

402 And walk quietly in the path that He Himself marks out.

Thenne al leved on his lawe and laften her synnes,
Parformed alle the penaunce that the prynce radde. *imposed*
And God thurgh his godnesse forgef as he sayde;
Thagh he other bihyght, withhelde his vengaunce.

IV

Muche sorwe thenne satteled upon segge Jonas;
He wex as wroth as the wynde towarde oure Lorde. *became*
So has anger onhit his hert, he calles *entered*
A prayer to the hyghe prynce, for pyne, on thys wyse: *anguish*

'I biseche the, Syre, now thou self jugge,
Was not this ilk my worde that worthen is nouthe,
That I kest in my cuntré, when thou thy carp sendes
That I schulde tee to thys toun thi talent to preche?

Wel knew I thi cortaysye, thy quoynt soffraunce, *wise patience*
Thy bounté of debonerté, and thy bene grace,
Thy longe abydyng wyth lur, thy late vengaunce;
And ay thy mercy is mete, be mysse never so huge. *sufficient; wrong*

I wyst wel, when I hade worded quat-so-ever I cowthe *knew could*
To manace alle thise mody men that in this mote dowelles,
Wyth a prayer and a pyne thay myght her pese gete, *penance make*
And therfore I wolde haf flowen fer into Tarce. *fled; far*

405 Then all accepted his edict and abandoned their sins.
407–8 And God in His goodness forgave them, as the king had said He would; although He had promised otherwise, God withheld His vengeance.
414–16 Was not this that has now happened the very thing I said would happen, (back) in my own country, when you sent word that I should go to this town to preach your purpose?
418–19 The bounty of your kindness, and your good grace, your long endurance of injury, your tardy vengeance.
422 To threaten all these insolent men who live in this city.

Now, Lorde, lach out my lyf, hit lastes to longe; *take away; too*
Bed me bilyve my bale stour and bryng me on ende;
For me were swetter to swelt as swythe, as me thynk,
Then lede lenger thi lore, that thus me les makes.'

The soun of oure Soverayn then swey in his ere, *voice; sounded*
That upbraydes this burne upon a breme wyse: *man; stern*
'Herk, renk, is this ryght so ronkly to wrath *sir; haughtily*
For any dede that I haf don other demed the yet?' *ordained for you*

Jonas al joyles and janglande upryses, *grumbling*
And haldes out on est half of the hyghe place,
And farandely on a felde he fetteles hym to bide,
For to wayte on that won what schulde worthe after.

Ther he busked hym a bour, the best that he myght, *made himself*
Of hay and of everferne and erbes a fewe, *ditch-fern*
For hit was playn in that place for plyande greves,
For to schylde fro the schene other any schade keste. *bright sun*

He bowed under his lyttel bothe, his bak to the sunne, *sat: arbour*
And ther he swowed and slept sadly al nyght, *fell asleep; soundly*
The whyle God of his grace ded growe of that soyle *did*
The fayrest bynde hym abof that ever burne wyste. *vine; saw*

When the dawande day Dryghtyn con sende, *dawning; did*
Thenne wakened the wyy under wodbynde, *woodbine*
Loked alofte on the lef that lylled grene. *leaves; shimmered*
Such a lefsel of lof never lede hade,

426–8 Give me my death-throes quickly and bring me to my end; for I would rather die at once, I think, than have anything more to do with your counsel, you who thus make me untruthful.
434–6 And goes out on the east side of the city, and he prepares to wait in comfort in a field, in order to watch what would happen in that city later on.
439 For that spot was bare of swaying groves.
448 Never did a man have such a fine bower.

For hit was brod at the bothem, boghted on lofte, *vaulted above*
Happed upon ayther half, a hous as hit were, *closed in; all sides*
A nos on the north syde and nowhere non elles,
Bot al schet in a schawe that schaded ful cole.

The gome glyght on the grene graciouse leves,
That ever wayved a wynde so wythe and so cole.
The schyre sunne hit umbeschon, thagh no schafte myght
The mountaunce of a lyttel mote upon that man schyne.

Thenne was the gome so glad of his gay logge, *fine arbour*
Lys loltrande therinne lokande to toune; *lies lounging*
So blythe of his wodbynde he balteres therunder *capers*
That of no diete that day—the devel haf!—he roght.

And ever he laghed as he loked the loge alle aboute,
And wysched hit were in his kyth ther he wony schulde,
On heghe upon Effraym other Ermonnes hilles.
'Iwysse, a worthloker won to welde I never keped.'

And quen hit neghed to naght nappe hym bihoved;
He slydes on a sloumbe-slep sloghe under leves,
Whil God wayned a worme that wrot upe the rote, *sent; dug*
And wyddered was the wodbynde bi that the wyye wakned. *withered; when*

And sythen he warnes the west to waken ful softe,
And sayes unto Zeferus that he syfle warme,
That ther quikken no cloude bifore the cler sunne,
And ho schal busch up ful brode and brenne as a candel.

451–6 A doorway on the north side and none anywhere else, but all enclosed in a thicket that cast cool shade. The man looked at the lovely green leaves, that a wind, so mild and cool, continually agitated. The bright sun shone round it, though no ray, not so much as a speck, might shine on that man.

460 That he takes no thought for food that day—to the devil with it!

462–6 And wished it were in his land where he must live, high up on Mount Ephraim or the hills of Mount Hermon. 'Indeed, I never wished to own a better dwelling.' But when night approached he had to sleep; he slipped tiredly into a deep sleep under the leaves.

469–72 And then He asks the west wind to waken quietly, and tells Zephyr (the west wind) to blow warm, so that no cloud should form in front of the bright sun, which was to rise unobscured and burn like a candle.

Then wakened the wyye of his wyl dremes, *pleasant*
And bluschęd to his wodbynde that brothely was marred.
Al welwed and wasted tho worthelych leves;
The schyre sunne hade hem schent er ever the schalk wyst.

And then hef up the hete and heterly brenned;
The warm wynde of the weste wertes he *plants*
swythes. *scorches*
The man marred on the molde that moght hym not hyde;
His wodbynde was away, he weped for sorwe.

With hatel anger and hot heterly he calles: *bitter*
'A, thou maker of man, what maystery the thynkes
Thus thy freke to forfare forbi alle other?
With alle meschef that thou may, never thou me spares.

I kevered me a cumfort that now is caght fro me, *acquired; taken*
My wodbynde so wlonk that wered my heved. *fine; protected*
Bot now I se thou art sette my solace to reve;
Why ne dyghttes thou me to diye? I dure to longe.'

Yet oure Lorde to the lede laused a speche: *uttered*
'Is this ryghtwys, thou renk, alle thy ronk *right; rebellious*
noyse,
So wroth for a wodbynde to wax so sone? *grow*
Why art thou so waymot, wyye, for so lyttel?' *irate*

'Hit is not lyttel,' quoth the lede, 'bot lykker to ryght;
I wolde I were of this worlde, wrapped in moldes.'
'Thenne bythenk the, mon, if the forthynk sore,
If I wolde help my hondewerk, haf thou no wonder.

474–7 And looked at his woodbine which was suddenly ruined. The splendid leaves were all shrivelled and wasted; the bright sun had destroyed them before the man knew it. And then the heat mounted and burned fiercely.

479 The man grieved on the earth that offered him no shelter.

482–4 Ah, you maker of man, what kind of achievement does it seem to you thus to ruin your man before all others? You never stop attacking me with all possible mischief.

487–8 But now I see you are determined to rob me of my pleasure; why do you not pronounce my death? I live too long.

493–5 'But rather a matter of justice; I wish I were away from this world, buried in my grave.' 'Then consider, sir, if you are sorely displeased.'

Thou art waxen so wroth for thy wodbynde,
And travayledes never to tent hit the tyme of an howre,
Bot at a wap hit here wax and away at an other;
And yet lykes the so luther, thi lyf woldes thou tyne.

Thenne wyte not me for the werk, that I hit wolde help,
And rwe on tho redles that remen for synne.
Fyrst I made hem myself of materes myn one,
And sythen I loked hem ful longe and hem on lode hade.

And if I my travayl schulde tyne, of termes so longe,
And type doun yonder toun when hit turned were, *bring; repented*
The sor of such a swete place burde synk to my hert, *pain; must*
So mony malicious mon as mournes therinne.

And of that soumme yet arn summe, such sottes formadde,
As lyttel barnes on barme that never bale wroght,
And wymmen unwytte, that wale ne couthe
That on hande fro that other for alle this hyghe worlde.

[Bitwene the stele and the stayre disserne noght cunen,
What rule renes in roun bitwene the ryght hande
And his lyfte, thagh her lyf schulde lost be therfor.]

498–505 And yet you never put in an hour's work to tend it, but it sprang up here at one stroke and was gone at another; and yet you take it so badly you wish to do away with your life. Then do not blame me for wanting to help my handiwork and take pity on those desperate people who cry out for their sins. First I made them out of primal matter, by myself alone, and then I looked after them for a long time and had them under my guidance. And if I should lose my labour, of such long duration.

508–15 There being so many sinful men who lament their sins there. And of that number there are some who are utter simpletons, such as little children at the breast who never did harm, and foolish women, unable to tell one hand from the other for all this great world. They cannot distinguish between the side of the ladder and the step, nor can they see what rule mysteriously divides the right hand from the left, though they should lose their lives thereby. (The poet may have intended to cancel lines 513–515.)

And als ther ben doumbe bestes in the burgh mony, *also; town*
That may not synne in no syt hemselven to greve.
Why schulde I wrath wyth hem, sythen wyyes wyl torne, *since*
And cum and cnawe me for kyng, and my carpe leve?

Wer I as hastif as thou, heere, were harme lumpen;
Couthe I not thole bot as thou, ther thryved ful fewe.
I may not be so malicious and mylde be halden,
For malyse is nogh to mayntyne boute mercy withinne.'

Be noght so gryndel, godman, bot go forth thy wayes, *angry; good sir*
Be prevé and be pacient in payne and in joye; *quiet*
For he that is to rakel to renden his clothes
Mot efte sitte with more unsounde to sewe hem togeder.

Forthy when poverté me enpreces and paynes innoghe,
Ful softly with suffraunce saghttel me bihoves.
Forthy penaunce and payne topreve hit in syght
That pacience is a nobel poynt, thagh hit displese ofte. *virtue*
Amen.

517 That may not commit any sin to harm themselves.
519–23 And come and acknowledge me as king, and accept what I say? Were I as hasty as you, sir, it would be unfortunate; if I could endure only as you do, few would prosper. I may not be so severe and still be considered gentle, for severity is not to be practised without mercy in one's heart.
526–30 For he who is too hasty in tearing his clothes must afterwards put up with further annoyance in sewing them together. And so when poverty oppresses me and many sorrows, I must quietly make my peace with patience. And so suffering and sorrow prove it for all to see.

SIR GAWAIN AND THE GREEN KNIGHT

I

Sithen the sege and the assaut was sesed at Troye, *after; ceased*
The borgh brittened and brent to brondes and askes,
The tulk that the trammes of tresoun ther wroght
Was tried for his tricherie, the trewest on erthe.
Hit was Ennias the athel and his highe kynde *noble; kindred*
That sithen depreced provinces, and patrounes bicome *subdued; lords*
Welneghe of al the wele in the West Iles: *wellnigh; wealth*
Fro riche Romulus to Rome ricchis hym swythe,
With gret bobbaunce that burghe he biges upon fyrst,
And nevenes hit his aune nome, as hit now hat;
Ticius to Tuskan, and teldes bigynnes; *(goes to) Tuscany; dwellings*
Langaberde in Lumbardie lyftes up homes;
And fer over the French flod Felix Brutus
On mony bonkkes ful brode Bretayn he settes *slopes; founds*
    wyth wynne, *joy*
  Where werre and wrake and wonder
  Bi sythes has wont therinne,
  And oft bothe blysse and blunder
  Ful skete has skyfted synne.

Ande quen this Bretayn was bigged bi this burn rych,
Bolde bredden therinne, baret that lofden,
In mony turned tyme tene that wroghten.

2 The city destroyed and burnt to brands and ashes.
3–4 The man who had planned treasonable plots was tried for his treachery, the most certain on earth.
8–10 When noble Romulus makes his way swiftly to Rome, first he builds that city with great pride and gives it his own name, by which it is now called.
13 *French flod,* i.e. English Channel; *Brutus,* the great-grandson of Aeneas and the legendary founder of Britain.
16–19 Where war and vengeance and atrocities have at times existed, and where joy and trouble have quickly alternated ever since.
20–2 And when Britain was founded by this noblc warrior, in it were bred bold men who loved fighting, who made mischief in many a troubled time.

Mo ferlyes on this folde han fallen here oft
Then in any other that I wot, syn that ilk tyme. *know; since*
Bot of alle that here bult of Bretaygne kynges *dwelt; Britain's*
Ay was Arthur the hendest, as I haf herde telle. *noblest*
Forthi an aunter in erde I attle to schawe,
That a selly in sight summe men hit holden,
And an outtrage awenture of Arthures wonderes.
If ye wyl lysten this laye bot on littel quile, *a . . . while*
I schal telle hit astit, as I in toun herde, *at once*
with tonge;
As hit is stad and stoken *set down*
In stori stif and stronge, *brave*
With lel letteres loken,
In londe so has ben longe.

This kyng lay at Camylot upon Krystmasse
With mony luflych lorde, ledes of the best, *gracious; men*
Rekenly of the Rounde Table alle tho rich brether,
With rych revel oryght and rechles merthes.
Ther tournayed tulkes by tymes ful mony, *knights*
Justed ful jolilé thise gentyle knightes, *Jousted; gallantly*
Sythen kayred to the court, caroles to make.
For ther the fest was ilyche ful fiften dayes, *festival; the same*
With alle the mete and the mirthe that men couthe avyse: *food; devise*
Such glaum ande gle glorious to here, *noise; merriment*
Dere dyn upon day, daunsyng on nyghtes; *pleasant; noise*
Al was hap upon heghe in halles and chambres *happiness; to a high degree*
With lordes and ladies, as levest him thoght.

23 More marvels have often happened in this land.

27–9 And so I mean to show an actual adventure, which some men will consider a wonderful thing to see, and an extraordinary adventure among all the marvellous tales about Arthur.

35 Linked with true letters. (A reference to alliteration.)

36 In accordance with the ancient tradition of this land.

39–40 All the noble and courteous brethren of the Round Table, with revels of befitting splendour and with carefree pleasure.

43 Then they rode to court to sing and dance carols. (The 'carol' was a combination of ring-dance and song.)

49 Among the lords and ladies, who did whatever pleased them best.

With all the wele of the worlde thay woned ther samen,
The most kyd knyghtes under Krystes selven, — *renowned; Christ Himself*
And the lovelokkest ladies that ever lif haden, — *loveliest*
And he the comlokest kyng that the court haldes. — *handsomest; rules*
For al was this fayre folk in her first age — *in their prime*
on sille, — *in the hall*
The hapnest under heven, — *most fortunate*
Kyng hyghest mon of wylle; — *noblest; in temper (of mind)*
Hit were now gret nye to neven
So hardy a here on hille. — *bold; company*

Wyle Nw Yer was so yep that hit was nwe cummen,
That day doubble on the dece was the douth served,
Fro the kyng was cummen with knyghtes into the halle, — *after*
The chauntré of the chapel cheved to an ende.
Loude crye was ther kest of clerkes and other,
Nowel nayted onewe, nevened ful ofte;
And sythen riche forth runnen to reche hondeselle,
Yeyed yeres yiftes on high, yelde hem bi hond,
Debated busyly aboute tho giftes.
Ladies laghed ful loude, thogh thay lost haden,
And he that wan was not wrothe, that may ye wel trawe.
Alle this mirthe thay maden to the mete tyme. — *meal*
When thay had waschen worthyly thay wenten to sete,
The best burne ay abof, as hit best semed; — *man; in a higher seat*

50 With all the joy in the world they lived there together.

58 It would be very hard to mention.

60–1 On New Year's Day, while the year was still young, the company on the dais was served with double portions (of food).

63 The singing (of mass) in the chapel having come to an end.

64–5 Loud cries were then raised by clerics and others, Noel celebrated anew, named very often. ('Noel' was used as a greeting during the Christmas season.)

66–70 And then noble knights ran forward to give presents, announced aloud their New Year's gifts, offered them by hand and busily argued about them. Ladies laughed loudly, even though they had lost, and a person who won was not angry, you can be sure of that. (These lines refer to some kind of guessing game like Handy-dandy.)

72 When they had washed (their hands) becomingly, they went to their seats.

Whene Guenore, ful gay, graythed in the myddes,
Dressed on the dere des, dubbed al aboute—
Smal sendal bisides, a selure hir over
Of tryed Tolouse, of Tars tapites innoghe,
That were enbrawded and beten wyth the best gemmes *embroidered; set*
That myght be preved of prys wyth penyes to bye
in daye.
The comlokest to discrye *fairest; behold*
Ther glent with yyen gray; *glanced; eyes*
A semloker that ever he syye, *one more fair; saw*
Soth moght no mon say. *truly; could*

Bot Arthure wolde not ete til al were served,
He was so joly of his joyfnes, and sumquat childgered:
His lif liked hym lyght, he lovied the lasse
Auther to longe lye or to longe sitte, *either*
So bisied him his yonge blod and his brayn wylde.
And also another maner meved him eke, *custom; influenced*
That he thurgh nobelay had nomen he wolde never ete
Upon such a dere day, er hym devised were
Of sum aventurus thyng an uncouthe tale, *strange*
Of sum mayn mervayle, that he myght trawe, *great; believe*
Of alderes, of armes, of other aventurus; *ancestors*
Other sum segg hym bisoght of sum siker knyght
To joyne wyth hym in justyng, in jopardé to lay,
Lede lif for lyf, leve uchon other,
As fortune wolde fulsun hom, the fayrer to have.

74–7 Queen Guinevere, as gay as could be, placed in the midst of them, seated on the noble dais, with adornments all round her—fine silk curtains by her side, a canopy over her of costly Toulouse silk and of ample hangings from Turkestan.

79–80 That ever money could buy.

86–7 He was so youthfully gay and somewhat boyish: he liked an active life.

89 His young blood and restless brain stirred him so much.

91–2 That he had nobly taken on himself never to eat on such a great festival until he had been told.

96–9 Or (until) someone had begged him for a trusty knight to joust with, to set all at hazard, risk life for life, each to allow the other the advantage, according as fortune favoured them.

This was kynges countenaunce where he in court were, *custom*
At uch farand fest among his fre meny
in halle.
Therfore of face so fere *proud*
He stightles stif in stalle;
Ful yep in that Nw Yere, *active*
Much mirthe he mas with alle. *makes merry*

Thus ther stondes in stale the stif kyng hisselven,
Talkkande bifore the hyghe table of trifles ful hende. *courtly*
There gode Gawan was graythed Gwenore bisyde,
And Agravayn a la dure mayn on that other syde sittes,
Bothe the kynges sister sunes and ful siker knightes; *nephews; trusty*
Bischop Bawdewyn abof bigines the table,
And Ywan, Uryn son, ette with hymselven.
Thise were dight on the des and derworthly served, *seated; honourably*
And sithen mony siker segge at the sidbordes. *side-tables*
Then the first cors come with crakkyng of trumpes, *course; flourish*
Wyth mony baner ful bryght that therbi henged; *from them; hung*
Nwe nakryn noyse with the noble pipes,
Wylde werbles and wyght wakned lote,
That mony hert ful highe hef at her towches.
Dayntés dryven therwyth of ful dere metes,
Foysoun of the fresche, and on so fele disches
That pine to fynde the place the peple biforne
For to sette the sylveren that sere sewes halden
on clothe.

101 At every splendid feast among his noble company.
104 He stands fearlessly.
107 And so the bold king stays standing there.
109 There the good Gawain was seated beside Guinevere.
112–13 Bishop Baldwin sits in the place of honour (i.e. on the right of Arthur, whose seat was in the middle of the high table), and Iwain, Urien's son, ate with him. (Each pair of guests had dishes in common; see line 128.)
118–20 A new noise of kettledrums and noble pipes, whose wild, vigorous notes woke the echoes, making many a heart thrill to their music.
121–5 Then were brought in dainty and costly foods, an abundance of fresh meats, and on so many dishes that it was difficult to find room on the table to set down before the guests the silver (things) that held the various pottages.

Iche lede as he loved hymselve
Ther laght withouten lothe;
Ay two had disches twelve, *each*
Good ber and bryght wyn bothe.

Now wyl I of hor servise say yow no more, *service (at table)*
For uch wyye may wel wit no wont that ther were
An other noyse ful newe neghed bilive,
That the lude myght haf leve liflode to cach.
For unethe was the noyce not a whyle sesed, *hardly; noise*
And the fyrst cource in the court kyndely served, *duly*
Ther hales in at the halle dor an aghlich mayster,
On the most on the molde on mesure hyghe,
Fro the swyre to the swange so sware and so thik,
And his lyndes and his lymes so longe and so grete, *loins*
Half etayn in erde I hope that he were;
Bot mon most I algate mynn hym to bene,
And that the myriest in his muckel that myght ride,
For of bak and of brest al were his bodi *although*
sturne, *strong*
Both his wombe and his wast were worthily smale,
And alle his fetures folwande in forme that he hade,
ful clene.
For wonder of his hwe men hade, *colour*
Set in his semblaunt sene;
He ferde as freke were fade,
And overal enker grene.

126–7 Each man took what (food) he wanted, and no one grudged him it.

131 For everyone can be sure there was no lack of anything.

132–3 Another noise, a quite new one, quickly drew near, which was to give the King permission to eat (i.e. it was the beginning of the adventure that Arthur insisted on having before he sat down to dinner on New Year's Day).

134 For the noise (of the music) had hardly died away.

136–8 (When) there rushed in at the hall door a terrible man, the very biggest on earth, thickset and squarely built from the neck to the waist.

140–2 I think he may have been half-giant; but at any rate I declare he was the biggest of men and the handsomest knight on horseback.

144–6 Both his belly and his waist were fittingly slender, and all his features wholly in keeping with his shape.

147–50 They were astounded at his colour, so plainly to be seen. He behaved like an elvish man, and was a vivid green all over.

Ande al graythed in grene this gome and his wedes:
A strayt cote ful streght that stek on his sides,
A mere mantile abof, mensked withinne
With pelure pured apert, the pane ful clene
With blythe blaunner ful bryght, and his hod bothe,
That was laght fro his lokkes and layde on his schulderes; *thrown back from*
Heme, wel-haled hose of that same grene,
That spenet on his sparlyr, and clene spures under
Of bryght golde, upon silk bordes barred ful ryche,
And scholes under schankes there the schalk rides.
And alle his vesture verayly was clene verdure, *clothing*; *bright green*
Bothe the barres of his belt and other blythe stones, *brilliant*
That were richely rayled in his aray clene *set*
Aboutte hymself and his sadel, upon silk werkes, *embroidery*
That were to tor for to telle of tryfles the halve
That were enbrauded abof, wyth bryddes and flyyes,
With gay gaudi of grene, the golde ay inmyddes.
The pendauntes of his payttrure, the proude cropure,
His molaynes and alle the metail anamayld was thenne;
The steropes that he stod on stayned of the same,
And his arsouns al after and his athel skurtes,
That ever glemered and glent al of grene stones. *gleamed; glinted*
The fole that he ferkkes on fyn of that ilke,
        sertayn: *certainly*

151–5 And this man and his clothes were all covered in green: a tight, straight coat that fitted closely at the waist, and above it a splendid mantle, adorned on the inside with a closely trimmed fur for all to see, the cloth resplendent with trimming of bright ermine, and his hood as well.

157–60 Neat, tightly drawn hose of the same green colour, that clung to his calves, and bright golden spurs below, fastened over richly barred socks of embroidered silk, and no shoes on his feet where the man rides (with his feet in the stirrups).

165–7 That it would be hard to tell half the details—the birds and the butterflies—that were embroidered on it in bright green mingled with gold.

168–71 The pendants of his horse's breast-harness, the splendid crupper, the ornamental studs on the bridle and all the other metal (fittings) were enamelled green; the stirrups he stood on were of the same colour, and so too were his saddle-bows and noble saddle-skirts.

173 The horse that he rides on was completely of the same colour.

A grene hors gret and thikke,
A stede ful stif to strayne, — *strong; curb*
In brawden brydel quik— — *embroidered; restive*
To the gome he was ful gayn. — *man; useful*

Wel gay was this gome gered in grene, — *attired*
And the here of his hed of his hors swete.
Fayre fannand fax umbefoldes his schulderes;
A much berd as a busk over his brest henges,
That wyth his highlich here that of his hed reches
Was evesed al umbetorne abof his elbowes,
That half his armes therunder were halched in the wyse
Of a kynges capados that closes his swyre.
The mane of that mayn hors much to hit lyke, — *mighty*
Wel cresped and cemmed, wyth knottes ful mony — *curled; combed*
Folden in wyth fildore aboute the fayre grene,
Ay a herle of the here, an other of golde.
The tayl and his toppyng twynnen of a sute,
And bounden bothe wyth a bande of a bryght grene,
Dubbed wyth ful dere stones, as the dok lasted;
Sythen thrawen wyth a thwong, a thwarle-knot alofte,
Ther mony belles ful bryght of brende golde rungen. — *burnished*
Such a fole upon folde, ne freke that hym rydes,
Was never sene in that sale wyth syght er that tyme,
with yye.
He loked as layt so lyght, — *lightning; bright*
So sayd al that hym syye; — *saw*
Hit semed as no mon myght
Under his dynttes dryye. — *blows; survive*

180–6 And the hair of his head matched that of his horse. Fair, waving hair enfolds his shoulders. Over his breast hangs a great beard, like a bush, which together with the splendid hair hanging from his head was clipped all round just above his elbows, so that his arms were half hidden underneath in the manner of a king's cape that fits closely round the neck (and covers the shoulders).

188–94 Well curled and combed, with many ornamental knots of gold thread and green hair plaited, one strand of hair and one of gold. The tail and forelock match exactly, and both were bound with a band of bright green, adorned with precious stones, for their whole length; then tied with a tightly knotted thong.

196–8 Such a horse and rider had never been seen before in that hall by mortal eye.

Whether hade he no helme ne hawbergh nauther,
Ne no pysan, ne no plate that pented to armes,
Ne no schafte, ne no schelde, to schwve ne to smyte, *spear; thrust*
Bot in his on honde he hade a holyn bobbe, *one; holly branch*
That is grattest in grene when greves ar bare, *woods*
And an ax in his other, a hoge and unmete, *huge; monstrous*
A spetos sparthe to expoun in spelle, quo-so myght.
The hede of an elnyerde the large lenkthe hade, *ell-rod; great length*
The grayn al of grene stele and of golde hewen, *spike*
The bit burnyst bryght, with a brod egge *blade; edge*
As wel schapen to schere as scharp rasores. *cut*
The stele of a stif staf the sturne hit bi grypte,
That was wounden wyth yrn to the wandes ende,
And al bigraven with grene in gracios werkes; *engraved; designs*
A lace lapped aboute, that louked at the hede, *folded; was fastened*
And so after the halme halched ful ofte,
Wyth tryed tasseles therto tacched innoghe
On botouns of the bryght grene brayden ful ryche.
This hathel heldes hym in and the halle entres, *knight; goes in*
Drivande to the heghe dece, dut he no wothe.
Haylsed he never one, bot heghe he over loked. *greeted*
The fyrst word that he warp: 'Wher is,' he sayd, *spoke*
'The governour of this gyng? Gladly I wolde *ruler; company*
Se that segg in syght, and with hymself speke raysoun.'
To knyghtes he kest his yye, *cast; eye*
And reled hym up and doun.
He stemmed and con studie
Quo walt ther most renoun.

203–4 Yet he had no helm nor hauberk either, no protection for chest or neck, no steel plate forming part of a knight's armour.
209 A terrible battle-axe for anyone to describe in words, whoever it might be.
214–15 The handle the grim knight gripped it by was a strong staff bound with iron up to the end.
218–20 And looped round and round the handle, with many fine tassels fastened to it on buttons of richly embroidered bright green.
222–3 Making his way to the high dais, he feared no danger. He greeted no one, but looked high over their heads.
226–7 Set eyes on that man, and have words with him.
229–31 And rolled them (i.e. his eyes) to and fro. He stopped and looked carefully to see who enjoyed the greatest renown there.

Ther was lokyng on lenthe, the lude to beholde, *for a long time; man*
For uch mon had mervayle quat hit mene myght *each*
That a hathel and a horse myght such a hwe lach
As growe grene as the gres and grener hit semed, *(to) grow; grass*
Then grene aumayl on golde glowande bryghter.
Al studied that ther stod, and stalked hym nerre,
Wyth al the wonder of the worlde what he worch schulde. *do*
For fele sellyes had thay sen, bot such never are; *many marvels before*
Forthi for fantoum and fayryye the folk there hit demed.
Therfore to answare was arwe mony athel freke,
And al stouned at his steven and stonstil seten
In a swoghe sylence thurgh the sale riche:
As al were slypped upon slepe so slaked hor lotes
in hyye.
I deme hit not al for doute, *think; fear*
Bot sum for cortaysye; *courtesy*
Bot let hym that al schulde loute
Cast unto that wyye.

Thenn Arthour bifore the high dece that aventure byholdes, *high dais*
And rekenly hym reverenced, for rad was he never,
And sayde: 'Wyye, welcum iwys to this place, *sir: indeed*
The hede of this ostel Arthour I hat.
Light luflych adoun and lenge, I the praye,
And quat-so thy wylle is we schal wyt after.' *whatever; learn*

234 That a knight and his horse could get such a colour.
236 Glowing brighter than green enamel on gold.
237 All who were standing there watched intently, and walked cautiously up to him.
240–5 And so the people there thought it must be illusion and magic. Many a noble knight, therefore, was afraid to answer, and they were all amazed at his voice and sat stock-still in dead silence throughout the splendid hall: their noise suddenly stopped as if they had all fallen asleep.
248–9 They let him (i.e. Arthur) whom all should reverence speak (first) to the man.
251 And greeted him courteously, for he was by no means afraid.
253–4 I am the master of this house, and I am called Arthur. Be so good as to dismount and stay (with us), I pray you.

'Nay, as help me,' quoth the hathel, 'he that on hyghe syttes, *man* *dwells*
To wone any quyle in this won, hit was not myn ernde.
Bot for the los of the, lede, is lyft up so hyghe,
And thy burgh and thy burnes best ar holden, *men; considered*
Stifest under stel-gere on stedes to ryde,
The wyghtest and the worthyest of the worldes kynde,
Preve for to play wyth in other pure laykes,
And here is kydde cortaysye, as I haf herd carp, *shown; tell*
And that has wayned me hider, iwyis, at this tyme. *brought; indeed*
Ye may be seker bi this braunch that I bere here *sure*
That I passe as in pes, and no plyght seche. *peace; peril*
For had I founded in fere, in feghtyng wyse,
I have a hauberghe at home and a helme bothe, *hauberk*
A schelde and a scharp spere, schinande bryght,
Ande other weppenes to welde, I wene wel, als;
Bot for I wolde no were, my wedes ar softer.
Bot if thou be so bold as alle burnes tellen,
Thou wyl grant me godly the gomen that I ask bi ryght.' *graciously; sport*
Arthour con onsware, *answered*
And sayd: 'Sir cortays knyght,
If thou crave batayl bare,
Here fayles thou not to fyght.'

'Nay, frayst I no fyght, in fayth I the telle. *seek*
Hit arn aboute on this bench bot berdles chylder;
If I were hasped in armes on a heghe stede, *buckled*
Here is no mon me to mach, for myghtes so wayke.
Forthy I crave in this court a Crystemas gomen, *game*
For hit is Yol and Nwe Yer, and here ar yep mony. *Yule* *young (men)*

257–8 To stay any length of time in this dwelling was not (part of) my mission. But because your renown, my lord, is praised so highly.
260–2 The strongest of armoured knights on horseback, the bravest and worthiest of men, valiant to contend with in noble sports.
267 For if I had come in (martial) array, in warlike fashion.
270–1 And well I know that I have other weapons I can handle, too; but since I don't want war, my clothes are of softer make.
277–8 If you're asking for single combat, you won't fail to get a fight.
280 There are none but beardless children sitting round on this bench.
282 Here is no man to match me, his strength is so weak.

If any so hardy in this hous holdes hymselven, *considers himself*
Be so bolde in his blod, brayn in hys hede,
That dar stifly strike a strok for an other, *dare; boldly*
I schal gif hym of my gyft thys giserne ryche, *battle-axe*
This ax, that is hevé innogh, to hondele as hym lykes, *heavy; handle*
And I schal bide the fyrst bur, as bare as I sitte. *blow; unarmed*
If any freke be so felle to fonde that I telle,
Lepe lyghtly me to, and lach this weppen—
I quit-clayme hit for ever, kepe hit as his auen.
And I schal stonde hym a strok, stif on this flet,
Elles thou wyl dight me the dom to dele hym an other,
barlay;
And yet gif hym respite *(I) give*
A twelmonyth and a day.
Now hyye, and let se tite
Dar any herinne oght say.'

If he hem stowned upon fyrst, stiller were thanne *astonished; at first*
Alle the heredmen in halle, the hygh and the lowe. *retainers*
The renk on his rouncé hym ruched in his sadel,
And runischly his rede yyen he reled aboute,
Bende his bresed browes, blycande grene,
Wayved his berde for to wayte quo-so wolde ryse.
When non wolde kepe hym with carp he coghed ful hyghe,
Ande rimed hym ful richly, and ryght hym to speke:
'What, is this Arthures hous,' quoth the hathel thenne, *knight*
'That al the rous rennes of thurgh ryalmes so mony? *fame; realms*

286 Or is of such bold mettle, so hot-headed.
291–3 If any man is fierce enough to try what I suggest, let him run quickly up to me and grasp this weapon—I renounce it for ever, let him keep it as his own.
294–5 And I shall stand and take his stroke on this floor without flinching, so long as you grant me the right to deal him another (in return).
296 *barlay* seems to mean 'I lay claim (to the first blow)'.
299–300 Now hurry, and show me quickly if anyone here dares speak at all.
303–8 The man on his horse turned in his saddle and fiercely rolled his eyes around, knitted his bristling brows of a shining green, and swept his beard this way and that as he looked to see who would rise (from his seat). When (he found that) no one would speak with him he coughed very loudly, cleared his throat in lordly style, and proceeded to say.

Where is now your sourquydrye and your conquestes, *pride*
Your gryndellayk and your greme and your grete wordes? *fierceness; anger*
Now is the revel and the renoun of the Rounde Table *revelry*
Overwalt wyth a worde of on wyyes speche, *overthrown; one man's*
For al dares for drede withoute dynt schewed!'
Wyth this he laghes so loude that the lorde greved;
The blod schot for scham into his schyre face and lere. *shame; fair cheek*
He wex as wroth as wynde; *grew*
So did alle that ther were.
The kyng, as kene bi kynde, *bold; nature*
Then stod that stif mon nere. *strong*

Ande sayde: 'Hathel, by heven thyn askyng is nys, *knight foolish*
And as thou foly has frayst, fynde the behoves.
I know no gome that is gast of thy grete wordes. *man; afraid*
Gif me now thy geserne, upon Godes halve,
And I schal baythen thy bone that thou boden habbes.'
Lyghtly lepes he hym to, and laght at his honde; *caught hold of*
Then feersly that other freke upon fote lyghtis.
Now has Arthure his axe, and the halme grypes, *handle*
And sturnely stures hit aboute, that stryke wyth hit thoght.
The stif mon hym bifore stod upon hyght, *to his full height*
Herre then ani in the hous by the hede and more. *taller*
Wyth sturne schere ther he stod he stroked his berde, *face; where*
And wyth a countenaunce dryye he drow doun his cote, *unmoved; drew*
No more mate ne dismayd for hys mayn dintes
Then any burne upon bench hade broght hym to drynk of wyne. *man*

315–16 'For all (of you) cower with fear without a blow being struck!' With this he laughed so loudly that the lord (i.e. Arthur) was annoyed.
324 And as you ask for a foolish thing, I must find it for you.
326–7 Now give me your battle-axe, in God's name, and I will grant you the request you have made.
329 Then the other man fiercely dismounted.
331 And grimly brandishes it, as if he intended to strike with it.
336 No more daunted or dismayed by the mighty blows (which threatened him).

Gawan, that sate bi the quene, *sat*
To the kyng he can enclyne: *bowed*
'I beseche now with sawes sene *in plain words*
This melly mot be myne.'

'Wolde ye, worthilych lorde,' quoth Wawan to the kyng, *honoured*
'Bid me bowe fro this benche and stonde by yow there, *go*
That I wythoute vylanye myght voyde this table, *discourtesy; leave*
And that my legge lady lyked not ille,
I wolde com to your counseyl bifore your cort ryche. *to advise you* *noble*
For me think hit not semly, as hit is soth knawen,
Ther such an askyng is hevened so hyghe in your sale,
Thagh ye yourself be talenttyf, to take hit to yourselven,
Whil mony so bolde yow aboute upon bench sytten,
That under heven, I hope, non hagherer of wylle,
Ne better bodyes on bent ther baret is rered.
I am the wakkest, I wot, and of wyt feblest, *weakest; know*
And lest lur of my lyf, quo laytes the sothe.
Bot for as much as ye ar myn em, I am only to prayse:
No bounté bot your blod I in my bodé knowe. *virtue*
And sythen this note is so nys that noght hit yow falles,
And I have frayned hit at yow fyrst, foldes hit to me; *asked; grant it*
And if I carp not comlyly, let alle this cort rych
bout blame.'

342 That this combat may be mine.

346 And if it did not displease my liege lady.

348–53 For, in truth, it does not seem right to me, when a request like this is made so arrogantly in your court, that you should deal with it yourself, even though you desire to do so, while on the bench all round you sit so many bold men, who, I believe, are as warlike in temper and as strong of body as any on earth, when fighting begins on the field (of battle).

355–6 And the loss of my life (would be) of least account, if the truth were known (lit. whoever wishes to know the truth). But I am only to be praised because you are my uncle.

358 And since this business is so foolish that it is unsuitable for you.

360–1 And if I do not speak fittingly, let all this noble court be free of blame.

Ryche togeder con roun, *nobles; whispered*
And sythen thay redden alle same *advised; together*
To ryd the kyng wyth croun,
And gif Gawan the game.

Then comaunded the kyng the knyght for to ryse,
And he ful radly up ros and ruchched hym fayre,
Kneled doun bifore the kyng, and caches that weppen;
And he luflyly hit hym laft, and lyfte up his honde
And gef hym Goddes blessyng, and gladly hym biddes
That his hert and his honde schulde hardi be bothe. *bold*
'Kepe the, cosyn,' quoth the kyng, 'that thou on kyrf sette,
And if thou redes hym ryght, redly I trowe
That thou schal byden the bur that he schal bede after.'
Gawan gos to the gome, with giserne in honde, *man; battle-axe*
And he baldly hym bydes, he bayst never the helder.
Then carppes to Sir Gawan the knyght in the grene: *speaks*
'Refourme we oure forwardes, er we fyrre passe.
Fyrst I ethe the, hathel, how that thou hattes, *entreat; are called*
That thou me telle truly, as I tryst may.' *believe*
'In god fayth,' quoth the goode knyght, 'Gawan
I hatte, *am called*
That bede the this buffet, quat-so bifalles after,
And at this tyme twelmonyth take at the another *take from you*
Wyth what weppen so thou wylt, and wyth no wyy elles
on lyve.'
That other onswares agayn: *replies*
'Sir Gawan, so mot I thryve, *may; prosper*
As I am ferly fayn *wondrously; glad*
This dint that thou schal dryve.' *blow; strike*

364 To relieve their crowned king of the combat.
367 And he promptly arose and courteously made ready.
369 And he graciously handed it over to him, and lifted up his hand.
372–4 'Take care, cousin,' said the king, 'how you set about the blow, and if you strike him just right, I fully believe you'll survive the blow he gives you afterwards.'
376 And he boldly waits for him, none the more dismayed.
378 Let us restate our agreement before we go any further.
382 Who offer you this blow, whatever happens after.
384–5 And with no one else alive (to help you).

'Bi gog,' quoth the grene knyght, 'Sir Gawan, me lykes
That I schal fange at thy fust that I haf frayst here.
And thou has redily rehersed, bi resoun ful trwe, *in words*
Clanly al the covenaunt that I the kynge asked, *wholly*
Saf that thou schal siker me, segge, bi thi trawthe,
That thou schal seche me thiself, where-so thou hopes *think*
I mȧy be funde upon folde, and foch the such wages *earth; receive*
As thou deles me to-day bifore this douthe ryche.' *company*
'Where schulde I wale the,' quoth Gauan, 'where is thy place? *seek*
I wot never where thou wonyes, bi hym that me wroght, *know*
Ne I know not the, knyght, thy cort ne thi name.
Bot teche me truly therto, and telle me howe thou hattes,
And I schal ware alle my wyt to wynne me theder;
And that I swere the for sothe, and by my seker traweth.'
'That is innogh in Nwe Yer, hit nedes no more,'
Quoth the gome in the grene to Gawan the hende:
'Yif I the telle trwly, quen I the tape have
And thou me smothely has smyten, smartly I the teche
Of my hous and my home and myn owen nome. *name*
Then may thou frayst my fare, and forwardes holde;
And if I spende no speche, thenne spedes thou the better,
For thou may leng in thy londe and layt no fyrre— *stay; seek*
bot slokes! *enough!*
Ta now thy grymme tole to the, *take; weapon*
And let se how thou cnokes.' *strike*
'Gladly, sir, for sothe,'
Quoth Gawan; his ax he strokes.

390–1 By God, . . . I like the idea of receiving from your hand what I have asked for here.

394 Except that you must give me your word.

399 I know nothing about where you live, by Him who made me.

401–3 But tell me how to get there and what you are called, and I will use all my wits to find my way there; and this I swear truly, upon my word of honour.

404–10 'It's enough for one New Year, no more is needed,' said the man in green to the courteous Gawain, 'if I tell you truly that when I have received the blow, and you have duly struck me, I will promptly inform you of my home and my name. Then you can inquire after my welfare and keep your agreement; and if I say nothing, then it will be all the better for you.'

The grene knyght upon grounde graythely hym dresses:
A littel lut with the hede, the lere he discoveres;
His longe lovelych lokkes he layd over his croun, *lovely*
Let the naked nec to the note schewe.
Gauan gripped to his ax and gederes hit on hyght, *lifts; high*
The kay fot on the folde he before sette, *left foot; ground*
Let hit doun lyghtly lyght on the naked,
That the scharp of the schalk schyndered the bones,
And schrank thurgh the schyire grece, and scade hit in
twynne,
That the bit of the broun stel bot on the grounde.
The fayre hede fro the halce hit to the erthe, *neck*
That fele hit foyned wyth her fete, there hit forth *many; kicked*
roled;
The blod brayd fro the body, that blykked on *spurted; shone*
the grene.
And nawther faltered ne fel the freke never the *man*
helder, *more*
Bot stythly he start forth upon styf schonkes,
And runyschly he raght out, there as renkkes stoden,
Laght to his lufly hed, and lyft hit up sone; *seized*
And sythen bowes to his blonk, the brydel he *goes; horse*
cachches,
Steppes into stel-bawe and strydes alofte, *stirrup*
And his hede by the here in his honde haldes.
And as sadly the segge hym in his sadel sette *steadily*
As non unhap had hym ayled, thagh hedles nowe *mishap*
in stedde. *there*
He brayde his bluk aboute, *twisted; trunk*
That ugly bodi that bledde;
Moni on of hym had doute, *a one; fear*
Bi that his resouns were redde.

417–18 The green knight at once takes his stand: bending his head forward a little he exposes the flesh.

420 And let his neck show bare for that business.

423–6 And brought it swiftly down on the bare flesh, so that the sharp blade shattered the man's bones and sank into the fair flesh, severing it in two, and the bright steel blade bit the ground.

431–2 But stoutly strode forward on legs that were still firm, and fiercely reached out to where the knights were standing.

443 By the time he had finished speaking.

For the hede in his honde he haldes up even, *straight*
Toward the derrest on the dece he dresses the face;
And hit lyfte up the yye-lyddes, and loked ful brode, *with a broad stare*
And meled thus much with his muthe, as ye may now here:
'Loke, Gawan, thou be graythe to go as thou hettes, *ready* *promised*
And layte as lelly til thou me, lude, fynde,
As thou has hette in this halle, herande thise knyghtes. *in the hearing of*
To the grene chapel thou chose, I charge the, to fotte *go* *receive*
Such a dunt as thou has dalt—disserved thou habbes— *blow; dealt*
To be yederly yolden on Nw Yeres morn. *promptly; given*
The knyght of the grene chapel men knowen me mony;
Forthi me for to fynde, if thou fraystes, fayles thou never.
Therfore com, other recreaunt be calde the behoveus.'
With a runisch rout the raynes he tornes, *violent jerk; reins*
Halled out at the hal-dor, his hed in his hande, *rushed*
That the fyr of the flynt flawe fro fole hoves.
To quat kyth he becom knwe non there, *land; came*
Never more then thay wyste fram quethen he was wonnen.
What thenne?
The kyng and Gawen thare *there*
At that grene thay laghe and grenne;
Yet breved was hit ful bare
A mervayl among tho menne.

Thagh Arther the hende kyng at hert hade wonder, *heart*
He let no semblaunt be sene, bot sayde ful hyghe *sign; loudly*
To the comlych quene, wyth cortays speche: *comely; courteous*

445 He turns the face towards the noblest lady on the dais (cf. lines 2459–2462).
447 And spoke with its mouth to this effect, as you may now hear.
449 And look for me faithfully, sir, until you find me.
455–6 And so, if you ask, you cannot fail to find me. Come, therefore, or be called a coward.
459 And the sparks flew up from the stones under his horse's hooves.
461 Any more than they knew where he had come from.
464–6 Laugh and grin at the green man, and yet it was openly spoken of as a marvel by them.

'Dere dame, to-day demay yow never; *don't be dismayed*
Wel bycommes such craft upon Cristmasse,
Laykyng of enterludes, to laghe and to syng
Among thise kynde caroles of knyghtes and ladyes.
Never-the-lece to my mete I may me wel dres, *meal; proceed*
For I haf sen a selly, I may not forsake.' *marvel; deny*
He glent upon Sir Gawen and gaynly he sayde: *glanced; courteously*
'Now sir, heng up thyn ax, that has innogh hewen.' *hang; enough*
And hit was don abof the dece, on doser to henge,
Ther alle men for mervayl myght on hit loke, *as a marvel*
And bi trwe tytel therof to telle the wonder. *right*
Thenne thay bowed to a borde thise burnes togeder, *went; men*
The kyng and the gode knyght, and kene men hem served *bold*
Of alle dayntyes double, as derrest myght falle,
Wyth alle maner of mete and mynstralcie bothe. *kinds of food*
Wyth wele walt thay that day, til worthed an ende in londe.
Now thenk wel, Sir Gawan,
For wothe that thou ne wonde *peril; hesitate*
This aventure for to frayn, *to seek out*
That thou has tan on honde. *undertaken*

II

This hanselle has Arthur of aventurus on fyrst *gift*
In yonge yer, for he yerned yelpyng to here.
Thagh hym wordes were wane when thay to sete wenten, *lacking*
Now ar thay stoken of sturne werk, stafful her hond.

471–3 Such occupations are proper at Christmas time, like the playing of interludes and the laughter and singing during the courtly carols of knights and ladies.

478 And it was placed above the dais, and hung against an ornamental backcloth.

483 A double portion of every delicacy, in the noblest manner possible.

485 They passed the time joyfully until the day drew to an end.

492 For he longed to hear of some bold exploit.

494 Now they are occupied with serious business, their hands quite full.

Gawan was glad to begynne those gomnes in halle, *games*
Bot thagh the ende be hevy, haf ye no wonder;
For thagh men ben mery in mynde quen thay han mayn *strong*
drynk,
A yere yernes ful yerne, and yeldes never lyke;
The forme to the fynisment foldes ful selden.
Forthi this Yol overyede, and the yere after, *passed by*
And uche sesoun serlepes sued after other:
After Crystenmasse com the crabbed Lentoun, *Lent*
That fraystes flesch wyth the fysche and fode more *tries*
symple.
Bot thenne the weder of the worlde wyth wynter hit *weather*
threpes, *contends*
Colde clenges adoun, cloudes uplyften, *shrinks*
Schyre schedes the rayn in schowres ful warme, *brightly; falls*
Falles upon fayre flat, flowres there schewen. *meadow; appear*
Bothe groundes and the greves grene ar her wedes,
Bryddes busken to bylde, and bremlych syngen *prepare; loudly*
For solace of the softe somer that sues therafter *joy; follows*
bi bonk; *on every slope*
And blossumes bolne to blowe *swell; bloom*
Bi rawes rych and ronk, *hedgerows; luxuriant*
Then notes noble innoghe *many*
Ar herde in wod so wlonk. *glorious*

After, the sesoun of somer wyth the soft wyndes, *afterwards*
Quen Zeferus syfles hymself on sedes and erbes;
Wela wynne is the wort that waxes theroute,
When the donkande dewe dropes of the leves, *moistening*
To bide a blysful blusch of the bryght sunne. *wait for; gleam*
Bot then hyyes hervest, and hardenes hym sone,
Warnes hym for the wynter to wax ful rype;
He dryves wyth droght the dust for to ryse, *drought*
Fro the face of the folde to flyye ful hyghe; *earth; fly*

498–9 A year passes swiftly, and events never repeat themselves; the beginning is very seldom like the end.
501 And the seasons followed each other in turn.
508 Both the fields and the woods are dressed in green.
517 When Zephyrus (the West wind) blows on seeds and plants.
518 Very joyful is the plant that grows out of doors.
521–2 But then autumn comes hurrying along, and soon grows severe, warning it to grow ripe for fear of winter.

Wrothe wynde of the welkyn wrasteles with the sunne,
The leves laucen fro the lynde and lyghten on the grounde, *fall; lime-tree*
And al grayes the gres that grene was ere; *grows grey; before*
Thenne al rypes and rotes that ros upon fyrst. *rose*
And thus yirnes the yere in yisterdayes mony,
And wynter wyndes ayayn, as the worlde askes,
no fage, *in truth*
Til Meghelmas mone
Was cumen wyth wynter wage. *challenge*
Then thenkkes Gawan ful sone
Of his anious vyage. *wearisome journey*

Yet quyl Al-hal-day with Arther he lenges,
And he made a fare on that fest, for the frekes sake,
With much revel and ryche of the Rounde Table. *revelry*
Knyghtes ful cortays and comlych ladies, *courteous; fair*
Al for luf of that lede in longynge thay were;
Bot never-the-lece ne the later thay nevened bot merthe,
Mony joyles for that jentyle japes ther maden.
For aftter mete with mournyng he meles to his eme,
And spekes of his passage, and pertly he sayde: *openly*
'Now, lege lorde of my lyf, leve I yow ask. *leave*
Ye knowe the cost of this cace, kepe I no more
To telle yow tenes therof, never bot trifel;
Bot I am boun to the bur barely to-morne,
To sech the gome of the grene, as God wyl me wysse.' *seek* *guide*
Thenne the best of the burgh bowed togeder, *castle; went*
Aywan and Errik and other ful mony, *Iwain*

525 An angry wind from the heavens wrestles with the sun.
529–30 And so the year wears itself out in many yesterdays, and winter comes again, as the way of the world is.
532 Till the Michaelmas moon (i.e. harvest moon).
536–7 Yet till All Saints' Day (Nov. 1) he stays with Arthur, and he (i.e. Arthur) held a feast on that day for the knight's sake.
540–3 They were full of grief, all for love of that knight; but nevertheless they talked only of pleasant things, and many made jokes who felt joyless for that gentle knight's sake. For after dinner he spoke sorrowfully to his uncle.
546–8 You know the nature of this business, and I don't wish to say anything at all about the difficulties; but I'm bound to set off without fail tomorrow morning to receive the blow.

Sir Doddinaval de Savage, the duk of Clarence,
Launcelot and Lyonel and Lucan the gode,
Sir Boos and Sir Bydver, big men bothe, *Bors; Bedivere*
And mony other menskful, with Mador de la Port. *honourable*
Alle this compayny of court com the kyng nerre, *near*
For to counseyl the knyght, with care at her hert.
There was much derne doel driven in the sale,
That so worthé as Wawan schulde wende on that ernde, *go* *mission*
To dryye a delful dynt, and dele no more *endure; grievous*
wyth bronde. *sword*
The knyght mad ay god chere,
And sayde: 'Quat schuld I wonde? *why; hesitate*
Of destinés derf and dere *harsh; gentle*
What may mon do bot fonde?' *make trial*

He dowelles ther al that day, and dresses on the morn, *stays*
Askes erly hys armes, and alle were thay broght.
Fyrst a tulé tapit, tyght over the flet,
And miche was the gyld gere that glent ther alofte.
The stif mon steppes theron, and the stel hondeles, *strong; steel*
Dubbed in a dublet of a dere tars, *clad; silk of Turkestan*
And sythen a crafty capados, closed aloft,
That wyth a bryght blaunner was bounden withinne. *white fur; trimmed*
Thenne set thay the sabatouns upon the segge fotes, *steel shoes* *man's feet*
His leges lapped in stel with luflych greves, *greaves*
With polaynes piched therto, policed ful clene,
Aboute his knes knaged wyth knotes of golde; *fastened*
Queme quyssewes then, that coyntlych closed
His thik thrawen thyghes, with thwonges to tachched;

558 There was much secret sorrow suffered in that hall.
562 The knight remained cheerful.
568–9 First a carpet of red silk was spread over the floor, and much gilded armour lay gleaming on it.
572 And then (in) a skilfully made hood, fastened at the neck.
576 With knee-pieces attached to them, polished clean.
578–9 Then fine thigh-pieces, which cunningly enclosed his thick muscular thighs, secured with thongs.

And sythen the brawden bryné of bryght stel rynges — *linked; coat of mail*
Vmbeweved that wyy, upon wlonk stuffe;
And wel bornyst brace upon his bothe armes, — *burnished; arm-pieces*
With gode cowters and gay, and gloves of plate, — *elbow-pieces (steel) plate*
And alle the godlych gere that hym gayn schulde that tyde; — *goodly; benefit time*
Wyth ryche cote-armure,
His gold spores spend with pryde, — *fastened*
Gurde wyth a bront ful sure — *girt; sword*
With silk sayn umbe his syde. — *girdle; at*

When he was hasped in armes, his harnays was ryche; — *buckled; armour*
The lest lachet other loupe lemed of golde.
So harnayst as he was he herknes his masse, — *hears*
Offred and honoured at the heghe auter. — *celebrated*
Sythen he comes to the kyng and to his cort-feres, — *companions at court*
Laches lufly his leve at lordes and ladyes; — *takes; courteously*
And thay hym kyst and conveyed, bikende hym to Kryst. — *escorted commending*
Bi that was Gryngolet grayth, and gurde with a sadel
That glemed ful gayly with mony golde frenges, — *fringes*
Ayquere naylet ful nwe, for that note ryched;
The brydel barred aboute, with bryght golde bounden;
The apparayl of the payttrure and of the proude skyrtes,
The cropore and the covertor, acorded wyth the arsounes;
And al was rayled on red ryche golde nayles, — *adorned with*
That al glytered and glent as glem of the sunne. — *glinted*

581 Enveloped the warrior, over a tunic made of splendid material.

586 *cote-armure*, coat-armour, a surcoat embroidered with heraldic devices.

591 The smallest lace or loop gleamed with gold.

597 By this time Gryngolet (i.e. Gawain's horse) was ready.

599–602 Newly studded all over with ornamental rivets, made for the occasion; the bridle adorned with bars and bound with bright gold; the furnishings of the breast-harness and splendid skirts, the crupper and caparison, matched those of the saddle-bows.

Thenne hentes he the helme, and hastily hit kysses, *takes; helmet*
That was stapled stifly, and stoffed wythinne.
Hit was hyghe on his hede, hasped bihynde, *fastened*
Wyth a lyghtly urysoun over the aventayle,
Enbrawden and bounden wyth the best gemmes
On brode sylkyn borde, and bryddes on semes,
As papjayes paynted pernyng bitwene,
Tortors and trulofes entayled so thyk
As mony burde theraboute had ben seven wynter
in toune.
The cercle was more o prys *circlet; more precious*
That umbeclypped hys croun, *ringed; head*
Of diamauntes a devys *diamonds; perfect*
That bothe were bryght and broun. *dusky*

Then thay schewed hym the schelde, that was of schyr goules, *bright gules*
Wyth the pentangel depaynt of pure golde hwes.
He braydes hit by the bauderyk, aboute the hals kestes,
That bisemed the segge semlyly fayre.
And quy the pentangel apendes to that prynce noble *why; belongs*
I am intent yow to telle, thof tary hyt me schulde. *though; delay*
Hit is a syngne that Salamon set sumquyle
In bytoknyng of trawthe, bi tytle that hit habbes,
For hit is a figure that haldes fyve poyntes,
And uche lyne umbelappes and loukes in other, *overlaps; locks*
And ayquere hit is endeles, and Englych hit callen *everywhere*
Overal, as I here, the endeles knot.

606 That was strongly stapled, and padded inside.
608–14 With a light covering over the visor, embroidered and adorned with gems on a broad silken hem, with figures of birds stitched along the seams, such as preening parrots depicted at intervals, and with turtle-doves and true-love knots portrayed as thickly as if many a lady had been working seven years on it at court.
620–2 With the pentangle (i.e. five-pointed star) painted on it in pure gold colours. He takes the shield by the baldric and slings it round his neck, and it suited the knight very well.
625–6 It is a symbol that Solomon once devised as a token of fidelity, which it has a right to be.

Forthy hit acordes to this knyght and to his cler armes, *befits; bright*
For ay faythful in fyve and sere fyve sythes,
Gawan was for gode knawen and, as golde pured,
Voyded of uche vylany, wyth vertues ennourned
in mote.
Forthy the pentangel nwe
He ber in schelde and cote,
As tulk of tale most trwe *man; word*
And gentylest knyght of lote. *bearing*

Fyrst he was funden fautles in his fyve wyttes, *senses*
And efte fayled never the freke in his fyve fyngres, *again; man*
And alle his afyaunce upon folde was in the fyve woundes *trust; earth*
That Cryst kaght on the croys, as the crede telles. *received*
And quere-so-ever thys mon in melly was stad,
His thro thoght was in that, thurgh alle other thynges,
That alle his forsnes he fong at the fyve joyes
That the hende heven quene had of hir chylde; *gracious*
At this cause the knyght comlyche hade
In the inore half of his schelde hir ymage depaynted,
That quen he blusched therto his belde never payred.
The fyft fyve that I finde that the frek used *fifth group of five*
Was fraunchyse and felawschyp forbe al thyng; *liberality; above*
His clannes and his cortaysye croked were never, *purity*
And pité, that passes alle poyntes—thyse pure fyve
Were harder happed on that hathel then on any other.
Now alle these fyve sythes, for sothe, were fetled on this knyght, *multiples conjoined in*
And uchone halched in other, that non ende hade, *was joined to*

632–5 For ever faithful in five ways and five times in each way, Gawain was known as a good knight and, like refined gold, free from every imperfection, and adorned with the chivalric virtues.

644–6 And wherever this man was hard-pressed in battle, his most steadfast thought, above all else, was that he derived all his courage from the five joys.

648–50 For this reason the knight appropriately had her image painted on the inside of his shield, so that when he looked at it his courage never failed.

654–5 And compassion, that surpasses all other qualities—these perfect five were more firmly implanted in that knight than in any other.

And fyched upon fyve poyntes that fayld never, *fixed*
Ne samned never in no syde, ne sundred nouther,
Withouten ende at any noke noquere, I fynde, *angle; anywhere*
Where-ever the gomen bygan or glod to an ende.
Therfore on his schene schelde schapen was *bright; fashioned*
the knot
Ryally wyth red golde upon rede gowles, *royally; gules*
That is the pure pentaungel wyth the peple called
with lore. *learning*
Now graythed is Gawan gay, *made ready*
And laght his launce ryght thore, *took; there*
And gef hem alle goud day—
He wende for ever more. *thought*

He sperred the sted with the spures, and sprong on *spurred*
his way
So stif that the ston-fyr stroke out therafter.
Al that sey that semly syked in hert,
And sayde sothly al same segges til other,
Carande for that comly: 'Bi Kryst, hit is scathe *grieving; a pity*
That thou, leude, schal be lost, that art of lyf noble! *sir*
To fynde hys fere upon folde, in fayth, is not ethe. *equal; easy*
Warloker to haf wroght had more wyt bene,
And haf dyght yonder dere a duk to have worthed.
A lowande leder of ledes in londe hym wel semes,
And so had better haf ben then britned to noght,
Hadet wyth an alvisch mon, for angardes pryde.
Who knew ever any kyng such counsel to take
As knyghtes in cavelaciouns on Crystmasse gomnes?'
Wel much was the warme water that waltered of *flowed*
yyen, *eyes*

659 And they neither came together nor parted company.
661 Wherever the device began or ended.
671–3 So strongly that sparks were struck out of the stones. All who saw the noble knight sighed in their hearts, and the whole company said with truth to one another.
677–83 It would have been wiser to behave with more caution and give that noble knight a dukedom. He would have made a magnificent leader of men, and in this role would have been better off than he will be if he is utterly destroyed, beheaded by an elvish knight, merely to satisfy our vanity and pride. Whoever heard of a king taking such counsel as knights give in the frivolous arguments of Christmas games?

When that semly syre soght fro *went from*
tho wones *that dwelling*
thad daye. *that*
He made non abode, *delay*
Bot wyghtly went hys way; *quickly*
Mony wylsum way he rode, *devious*
The bok as I herde say.

Now rides this renk thurgh the ryalme of Logres, *knight; realm*
Sir Gauan, on Godes halve, thagh hym no gomen thoght.
Oft leudles alone he lenges on nyghtes, *companionless; rests*
Ther he fonde noght hym byfore the fare that he lyked.
Hade he no fere bot his fole bi frythes and dounes,
Ne no gome bot God bi gate wyth to karp,
Til that he neghed ful neghe into the Northe Wales.
Alle the iles of Anglesay on lyft half he haldes, *left*
And fares over the fordes by the forlondes, *crosses*
Over at the Holy Hede, til he hade eft bonk
In the wyldrenesse of Wyrale—wonde ther bot lyte
That auther God other gome wyth goud hert lovied.
And ay he frayned, as he ferde, at frekes that he met,
If thay hade herde any karp of a knyght grene, *mention*
In any grounde theraboute, of the grene chapel; *region*
And al nykked hym wyth nay, that never in her lyve
Thay seye never no segge that was of suche hwes *saw; man*
of grene.
The knyght tok gates straunge *ways*
In mony a bonk unbene; *hill-side; dreary*
His cher ful oft con chaunge,
That chapel er he myght sene. *see*

690 As I have heard the story say. (The 'book' is the poet's alleged source; cf. line 2523.)

692 Sir Gawain, in God's name, though it seemed no game to him. (*gomen* harks back to *gomnes* 683.)

694–7 Where he found no food that he liked set before him. He had no companion but his horse in the woods and hills, and no one but God to talk to on the way, until he drew very close to North Wales.

700–3 Till he reached the shore again in the wilderness of Wirral—few lived there who were loved by God or good-hearted men. And always, as he went on, he asked the people he met.

706 And they all said no, that never in their lives.

Mony klyf he overclambe in contrayes straunge, *climbed over*
Fer floten fro his frendes fremedly he rydes.
At uche warthe other water ther the wyye passed
He fonde a foo hym byfore, bot ferly hit were,
And that so foule and so felle that feght hym byhode.
So mony mervayl bi mount ther the mon fyndes, *among the hills*
Hit were to tore for to telle of the tenthe dole. *hard; part*
Sumwhyle wyth wormes he werres, and with *dragons*
wolves als, *also*
Sumwhyle wyth wodwos that woned in the knarres,
Bothe wyth bulles and beres, and bores *boars*
otherquyle, *at other times*
And etaynes that hym anelede of the heghe felle. *giants; pursued*
Nade he ben dughty and dryye, and Dryghtyn had
served,
Douteles he hade ben ded and dreped ful ofte, *killed*
For werre wrathed hym not so much, that *fighting; troubled*
wynter was wors,
When the colde cler water fro the cloudes schadde, *fell*
And fres er hit falle myght to the fale erthe. *froze; pale*
Ner slayn wyth the slete he sleped in his yrnes *sleet; armour*
Mo nyghtes then innoghe in naked rokkes,
Ther as claterande fro the crest the colde borne *dashing; stream*
rennes,
And henged heghe over his hede in hard ysse-ikkles. *hung*
Thus in peryl and payne and plytes ful harde *hardships*
Bi contray caryes this knyght tyl Krystmasse *over the land; rides*
even,
al one. *alone*
The knyght wel that tyde
To Mary made his mone, *complaint*
That ho hym red to ryde,
And wysse hym to sum wone.

714–17 Far removed from his friends he rode through country where he was a stranger. On the bank of every river and lake that he crossed it was strange if he did not find a foe waiting for him, and one so foul and fierce that he had to fight him.

721 Sometimes with wild men of the woods who lived among the crags.

724 If he had not been brave and enduring, and had not served God.

738–9 That she would show him where to ride, and guide him to some dwelling.

Bi a mounte on the morne meryly he rydes *hill*
Into a forest ful dep, that ferly was wylde,
Highe hilles on uche a halve, and holtwodes under
Of hore okes ful hoge a hundreth togeder. *grey; hundred*
The hasel and the hawthorne were
harled al samen, *tangled together*
With roghe raged mosse rayled aywhere,
With mony bryddes unblythe upon bare twyges, *unhappy*
That pitosly ther piped for pyne of the colde. *piteously; pain*
The gome upon Gryngolet glydes hem under *man*
Thurgh mony misy and myre, mon al hym one,
Carande for his costes, lest he ne kever schulde
To se the servyse of that syre, that on that self nyght
Of a burde was borne, oure baret to quelle.
And therfore sykyng he sayde: 'I beseche the, Lorde, *sighing*
And Mary, that is myldest moder so dere,
Of sum herber ther heghly I myght here masse *haven; devoutly*
Ande thy matynes to-morne, mekely I ask,
And therto prestly I pray my pater and ave *promptly*
and crede.'
He rode in his prayere,
And cryed for his mysdede;
He sayned hym in sythes sere
And sayde: 'Cros Kryst me spede!'

Nade he sayned hymself, segge, bot thrye,
Er he was war in the wod of a won in a mote, *dwelling*
Abof a launde, on a lawe, loken under boghes
Of mony borelych bole aboute bi the diches:

741 Into a deep forest, that was wonderfully wild, with high hills on every side and woods below.
745 With rough shaggy moss growing everywhere.
749–52 Through many a bog and mire, a man all alone, and uneasy about his religious observances, lest he should be unable to see the service of the Lord, who on that very night was born of a maiden, to end our sorrow.
757–8 And to this end I promptly say my Paternoster, Ave (Maria), and Creed.
761–2 He crossed himself several times and said: 'May Christ's cross help me!'
763 The knight had not crossed himself more than three times.
765–6 Rising out of an open space, on a mound, and shut in by the boughs of many massive trees that grew near the moat.

A castel the comlokest that ever knyght aghte, *fairest; owned*
Pyched on a prayere, a park al aboute, *erected; meadow*
With a pyked palays, pyned ful thik,
That umbeteye mony tre mo then two myle.
That holde on that on syde the hathel avysed,
As hit schemered and schon thurgh the schyre okes. *shimmered*
Thenne has he hendly of his helme, and heghly he thonkes
Jesus and sayn Gilyan, that gentyle ar bothe, *St Julian*
That cortaysly hade hym kydde and his cry herkened.
'Now bone hostel,' cothe the burne, 'I beseche yow yette!'
Thenne gerdes he to Gryngolet with the gilt heles, *spurs on*
And he ful chauncely has chosen to the chef gate,
That broght bremly the burne to the bryge ende
        in haste.
    The bryge was breme upbrayde, *stoutly; drawn up*
    The yates wer stoken faste, *shut*
    The walles were wel arayed— *built*
    Hit dut no wyndes blaste. *feared*

The burne bode on bonk, that on blonk hoved,
Of the depe double dich that drof to the place. *enclosed*
The walle wod in the water wonderly depe, *stood*
Ande eft a ful huge heght hit haled upon lofte,
Of harde hewen ston up to the tables,
Enbaned under the abataylment in the best lawe;
And sythen garytes ful gaye gered bitwene,
Wyth mony luflych loupe that louked ful clene:
A better barbican that burne blusched upon never. *beheld*
And innermore he behelde that halle ful hyghe, *further in*

769–71 With a spiked palisade of palings, closely fastened together, that encircled many trees in its two-mile circumference. The knight gazed at this stronghold from one side.

773 Then he reverently removed his helmet and humbly thanked.

775–6 Who had shown him courtesy and listened to his cry (for help). 'Now good lodging,' said the knight, 'I beseech you to grant.'

778 And by mere chance he chose the main road.

785 The knight halted his steed on the edge.

788–92 And rose to a huge height above it, made of hard hewn stone up to the cornices, with battlements fortified in the best style; and there were handsome turrets built at intervals (along the walls), with many loopholes joined by ornamental work.

Towres telded bytwene, trochet ful thik,
Fayre fylyoles that fyyed, and ferlyly long,
With corvon coprounes craftyly sleye.
Chalkwhyt chymnees ther ches he innoghe, *descried; many*
Upon bastel roves that blenked ful quyte.
So mony pynakle payntet was poudred ayquere
Among the castel carneles, clambred so thik,
That pared out of papure purely hit semed.
The fre freke on the fole hit fayre innoghe thoght, *noble knight; horse*
If he myght kever to com the cloyster wythinne, *manage; enclosure*
To herber in that hostel whyl halyday lested, *lodge; dwelling*
        avinant. *pleasantly*
    He calde, and sone ther com
    A porter pure plesaunt.
    On the wal his ernd he nome, *message; received*
    And haylsed the knyght erraunt. *greeted*

'Gode sir,' quoth Gawan, 'woldes thou go myn ernde *errand*
To the hegh lorde of this hous, herber to crave?' *noble; lodging*
'Ye, Peter,' quoth the porter, 'and purely I trowee *believe*
That ye be, wyye, welcum to won quyle yow lykes.' *stay*
Then yede the wyye ayayn swythe, *went; quickly*
And folke frely hym wyth, to fonge the knyght. *readily; receive*
Thay let doun the grete draght and derely out yeden,
And kneled doun on her knes upon the colde erthe
To welcum this ilk wyy, as worthy hom thoght.
Thay yolden hym the brode yate, yarked up wyde,
And he hem raysed rekenly and rod over the brygge. *graciously*

795–7 Towers regularly spaced and thickly battlemented, handsome pinnacles that were deftly joined and wonderfully tall, with carved tops cunningly worked.

799–802 On the roofs of towers that gleamed all whitely. So many painted pinnacles were scattered everywhere among the embrasures of the castle, and clustered so thickly, that it looked like a table decoration cut out of paper.

817 Then they let down the great drawbridge and courteously went out.

819–20 To welcome this knight in the way they thought most fitting. They allowed him to pass through the broad gate, which was opened wide.

Sere segges hym sesed by sadel, quel he lyght,
And sythen stabeled his stede stif men innoghe.
Knyghtes and swyeres comen doun thenne *squires*
For to bryng this buurne wyth blys into halle. *knight*
Quen he hef up his helme, ther hiyed innoghe *lifted; hastened*
For to hent hit at his honde, the hende to *take; noble man*
serven;
His bronde and his blasoun bothe thay token. *sword; shield*
Then haylsed he ful hendly tho hatheles uchone,
And mony proud mon ther presed, that *pressed (forward)*
prynce to honour.
Alle hasped in his hegh wede to halle thay hym wonnen,
Ther fayre fyre upon flet fersly brenned. *hearth; fiercely burned*
Thenne the lorde of the lede loutes fro his chambre
For to mete wyth menske the mon on the flor. *honour*
He sayde: 'Ye ar welcum to wone as yow lykes.
That here is, al is yowre awen, to have at yowre wylle
and welde.'
'Graunt mercy,' quoth Gawayn,
'Ther Kryst hit yow foryelde.' *reward*
As frekes that semed fayn *men; glad*
Ayther other in armes con felde. *each; embraced*

Gawayn glyght on the gome that godly hym *looked at*
gret, *greeted*
And thught hit a bolde burne that the burgh *castle*
aghte, *owned*
A hoge hathel for the nones, and of hyghe eldee;
Brode, bryght was his berde, and al bever-hwed, *beaver-coloured*
Sturne, stif on the stryththe on stalworth schonkes,
Felle face as the fyre, and fre of hys speche; *fierce; noble*

822–3 Several men held his saddle while he dismounted, and then many strong men led his steed to the stable.

829 Then courteously he greeted each of those knights.

831 They brought him, all buckled in his noble armour, into the hall.

833 Then the prince of those people comes from his chamber.

835–7 You are welcome to stay as long as you please. All that is here is yours, to do with as you like.

844 A huge man indeed, and in the prime of life.

846 Stern-looking, striding firmly along on stalwart legs.

And wel hym semed for sothe, as the segge thught,
To lede a lortschyp in lee of leudes ful gode.
The lorde hym charred to a chambre, and *turned aside*
chefly cumaundes *quickly*
To delyver hym a leude, hym lowly to serve;
And there were boun at his bode burnes *ready; command*
innoghe
That broght hym to a bryght boure, ther beddying *chamber*
was noble
Of cortynes of clene sylk wyth cler golde hemmes, *curtains*
And covertores ful curious with comlych panes,
Of bryght blaunmer above enbrawded bisydes,
Rudeles rennande on ropes, red golde rynges,
Tapytes tyght to the wowe, of Tuly and Tars,
And under fete, on the flet, of folwande sute.
Ther he was dispoyled, wyth speches of myerthe, *relieved; merry*
The burn of his bruny and of his bryght *coat of mail*
wedes. *raiment*
Ryche robes ful rad renkkes hym broghten, *promptly*
For to charge and to chaunge and chose *put on; change (into)*
of the best.
Sone as he on hent, and happed therinne,
That sete on hym semly, wyth saylande skyrtes,
The ver by his visage verayly hit semed
Welnegh to uche hathel, alle on hwes,
Lowande and lufly, alle his lymmes under,
That a comloker knyght never Kryst made, *more handsome*
hem thoght.
Whethen in worlde he were, *from wherever*
Hit semed as he moght *might*
Be prynce withouten pere *peer*
In felde ther felle men foght. *fierce; fought*

848–9 And it well suited him, so the knight (i.e. Gawain) thought, to hold lordship over brave men in a castle.
851 That a man should be assigned to him, to serve him humbly.
855–9 Coverlets skilfully made with lovely panels of white fur and embroidered at the sides, curtains running on cords through rings of red gold, silks of Toulouse and Turkestan hanging on the walls, and others that matched them spread on the floor.
864–8 As soon as he had taken one with flowing skirts that fitted him well, and was wrapped in it, his appearance reminded everyone of the spring-time because of all the colours, glowing and lovely, which covered his limbs.

A cheyer byfore the chemné, ther charcole brenned, *chair; fireplace*
Was graythed for Sir Gawan graythely with clothes,
Whyssynes upon queldepoyntes that koynt wer bothe.
And thenne a mere mantyle was on that mon cast *splendid*
Of a broun bleeaunt, enbrauded ful ryche, *silk; embroidered*
And fayre furred wythinne with felles of the best—
Alle of ermyn in erde—his hode of the same.
And he sete in that settel semlych ryche, *sat; seat*
And achaufed hym chefly, and thenne his cher mended.
Sone was telded up a tabil on trestes ful fayre,
Clad wyth a clene clothe that cler quyt schewed,
Sanap and salure and sylverin spones.
The wyye wesche at his wylle, and went to his mete. *washed*
Segges hym served semly innoghe *men; becomingly*
Wyth sere sewes and sete, sesounde of the best,
Double-felde, as hit falles, and fele kyn fisches,
Summe baken in bred, summe brad on the gledes,
Summe sothen, summe in sewe savered with spyces,
And ay sawses so sleye that the segge lyked.
The freke calde hit a fest ful frely and ofte
Ful hendely, quen alle the hatheles rehayted hym at ones
as hende:
'This penaunce now ye take,
And eft hit schal amende.' *afterwards; improve*
That mon much merthe con make, *made merry*
For wyn in his hed that wende. *went to*

876–7 Was at once prepared for Sir Gawain with coverings and quilted cushions, both cunningly made.

880–1 And beautifully lined with fur—the best ermine on earth—with a hood to match.

883–4 And warmed himself quickly, and then his spirits rose. Straightway a table was set up on trestles.

886 Napkin and salt-cellar and silver spoons.

889–93 With several fine soups seasoned in the best manner, and a double quantity of them, as was fitting, and many different kinds of fish, some baked in bread, some grilled on the embers, some boiled, some stewed and flavoured with spices, and all subtly sauced so as to please the knight.

894–6 The knight called it a feast readily and often and most politely, whereupon all the men at once encouraged him with equal politeness.

Thenne was spyed and spured upon spare wyse
Bi prevé poyntes of that prynce, put to hymselven,
That he beknew cortaysly of the court that he were,
That athel Arthure the hende haldes hym one,
That is the ryche ryal kyng of the Rounde Table;
And hit was Wawen hymself that in that won syttes, *house*
Comen to that Krystmasse, as case hym then lymped.
When the lorde hade lerned that he the leude hade, *prince*
Loude laghed he therat, so lef hit hym thoght, *laughed; delightful*
And alle the men in that mote maden much joye *castle*
To apere in his presense prestly that tyme, *promptly*
That alle prys and prowes and pured thewes
Apendes to hys persoun, and praysed is ever;
Byfore alle men upon molde his mensk is the most. *earth; honour*
Uch segge ful softly sayde to his fere: *companion*
'Now schal we semlych se sleghtes of thewes
And the teccheles termes of talkyng noble.
Wich spede is in speche, unspurd may we lerne,
Syn we haf fonged that fyne fader of nurture.
God has geven uus his grace godly for sothe,
That such a gest as Gawan grauntes uus to have,
When burnes blythe of his burthe schal sitte *His birth*
and synge.
In menyng of maneres mere *understanding; noble*
This burne now schal uus bryng.
I hope that may hym here
Schal lerne of luf-talkyng.' *lovers' conversation*

Bi that the diner was done and the dere up,
Hit was negh at the niyght neghed the tyme.

901–4 Then in a tactful manner they asked him discreet questions about himself, until he courteously acknowledged that he came from the court presided over by the noble Arthur.
907 Having come there that Christmas, as chance decided.
912–13 To whose person belong all excellence, prowess and noble manners, and who is praised at all times.
916–19 Now we shall have the pleasure of seeing a skilful display of courteous manners and of hearing the faultless phrases of noble conversation. We shall learn without asking what profitable speech is, since we are entertaining the father of good breeding.
926 I believe that anyone who hears him.
928–9 By the time dinner was finished and the noble company risen, night had drawn near.

Chaplaynes to the chapeles chosen the gate, *made their way*
Rungen ful rychely, ryght as thay schulden, *rang*
To the hersum evensong of the hyghe tyde. *devout; festive*
The lorde loutes therto, and the lady als; *goes; also*
Into a cumly closet coyntly ho entres.
Gawan glydes ful gay and gos theder sone;
The lorde laches hym by the lappe and ledes hym to sytte, *catches; fold (of gown)*
And couthly hym knowes and calles hym his nome,
And sayde he was the welcomest wyye of the worlde; *man*
And he hym thonkked throly, and ayther halched other,
And seten soberly samen the servise-quyle.
Thenne lyst the lady to loke on the knyght; *desired*
Thenne com ho of hir closet with mony cler burdes. *fair ladies*
Ho was the fayrest in felle, of flesche and of lyre,
And of compas and colour and costes, of alle other,
And wener then Wenore, as the wyye thoght.
He ches thurgh the chaunsel, to cheryche that hende.
An other lady hir lad bi the lyft honde, *left*
That was alder then ho, an auncian hit semed, *older; aged*
And heghly honowred with hatheles aboute. *highly; men*
Bot unlyke on to loke tho ladyes were,
For if the yonge was yep, yolwe was that other: *fresh; withered*
Riche red on that on rayled ayquere,
Rugh ronkled chekes that other on rolled.
Kerchofes of that on, wyth mony cler perles,
Hir brest and hir bryght throte bare displayed
Schon schyrer then snawe that schedes on hilles; *more brightly; falls*

934–5 She gracefully enters her private pew. Gawain gladly makes haste to go there (i.e. to the chapel).

937 And greets him familiarly and calls him by his name.

939–40 And he thanked him heartily, and they embraced each other, and sat quietly together while the service lasted.

943–6 She was the fairest of them all in skin, in flesh and complexion, in form and colouring and manners—even fairer than Guinevere, Sir Gawain thought. He went through the chancel to greet her courteously.

952–4 A rich red colouring distinguished the one, and rough wrinkled cheeks hung loosely on the other. Kerchiefs, with many lustrous pearls, covered the one.

That other wyth a gorger was gered over the swyre,
Chymbled over hir blake chyn with chalk-quyte vayles,
Hir frount folden in sylk, enfoubled ayquere,
Toret and treleted with tryfles aboute,
That noght was bare of that burde bot the blake browes, *lady*
The tweyne yyen and the nase, the naked lyppes, *eyes; nose*
And those were soure to se and sellyly blered— *marvellously*
A mensk lady on molde mon may hir calle, *honourable; earth*
        for Gode! *by*
    Hir body was schort and thik,
    Hir buttokes bay and brode; *round*
    More lykkerwys on to lyk *sweeter to the taste*
    Was that scho hade on lode. *with her*

When Gawayn glyght on that gay that graciously loked, *gazed*
Wyth leve laght of the lorde he went hem ayaynes.
The alder he haylses, heldande ful lowe;
The loveloker he lappes a lyttel in armes,
He kysses hir comlyly and knyghtly he *courteously*
  meles. *speaks*
Thay kallen hym of aquoyntaunce, and he hit quyk askes *beg*
To be her servaunt sothly, if hemself lyked. *if it pleased them*
Thay tan hym bytwene hem, wyth talkyng hym leden *take*
To chambre, to chemné, and chefly thay *fireplace; particularly*
  asken
Spyces, that unsparely men speded hom to bryng, *unstintingly*
And the wynnelych wyne therwith uche tyme. *cheerful*
The lorde luflych aloft lepes ful ofte,
Mynned merthe to be made upon mony sythes,
Hent heghly of his hode, and on a spere henged,
And wayned hom to wynne the worchip therof *directed; honour*
That most myrthe myght meve that Crystenmas whyle. *devise*

957–60 The other was swathed in a gorget that hid her neck, her swarthy chin was wrapped in chalk-white veils, her forehead enveloped in silk, and she was muffled up everywhere, trellised around with trefoils and rings.

971–3 He got the lord's permission to go and meet them. He greets the older woman, bowing very low, and lightly embraces the fairer.

981–3 Often the lord sprang up joyfully, urged them many a time to amuse themselves, gaily took off his hood, and hung it on a spear.

'And I schal fonde, bi my fayth, to fylter wyth the best
Er me wont the wede, with help of my frendes.'
Thus wyth laghande lotes the lorde hit tayt makes,
For to glade Sir Gawayn with gomnes in halle *gladden; games*
that nyght,
Til that hit was tyme
The lorde comaundet lyght. *lights*
Sir Gawen his leve con nyme *took*
And to his bed hym dight. *went*

On the morne, as uch mon mynes that tyme *remembers*
That Dryghtyn for oure destyné to deye was borne, *the Lord; die*
Wele waxes in uche a won in worlde for his sake.
So did hit there on that day thurgh dayntés mony:
Bothe at mes and at mele messes ful quaynt
Derf men upon dece drest of the best.
The olde auncian wyf heghest ho syttes;
The lorde lufly her by lent, as I trowe.
Gawan and the gay burde togeder thay seten *lady; sat*
Even inmyddes, as the messe metely come;
And sythen thurgh al the sale, as hem best semed,
Bi uche grome at his degré graythely was served.
Ther was mete, ther was myrthe, ther was much joye, *food*
That for to telle therof hit me tene were, *trouble*
And to poynte hit yet I pyned me paraventure.
Bot yet I wot that Wawen and the wale burde *know; fair lady*
Such comfort of her compaynye caghten togeder *got*
Thurgh her dere dalyaunce of her derne wordes,
Wyth clene cortays carp closed fro fylthe,

986–8 'And I shall try, on my honour, to strive with the best before I lose this garment, with the help of my friends.' And so with laughing words the lord makes merry.
997 Joy springs up in every dwelling on earth for His sake.
999–1000 Both at dinner and less formal meals stalwart men on the dais served cunningly made dishes in the best manner.
1002 The lord courteously sat beside her, I believe.
1004–6 Exactly in the middle, as the company duly assembled; and then throughout the hall each man was promptly served according to his degree, as they thought best.
1009 If perhaps I made the effort to describe it in detail.
1012–15 In the private exchange of courtly conversation, with pure and gracious talk free from defilement, that their playful words surpassed every princely game, in truth.

That hor play was passande uche prynce gomen,
in vayres.
Trumpes and nakerys, *trumpets; kettledrums*
Much pypyng ther repayres; *is present*
Uche mon tented hys, *minded his business*
And thay two tented thayres.

Much dut was ther dryven that day and that other, *mirth; made*
And the thryd as thro thronge in therafter;
The joye of sayn Jones day was gentyle to here,
And was the last of the layk, leudes ther thoghten. *holiday; people*
Ther wer gestes to go upon the gray morne,
Forthy wonderly thay woke, and the wyn dronken,
Daunsed ful dreyly wyth dere caroles. *continuously*
At the last, when hit was late, thay lachen her leve, *take*
Uchon to wende on his way that was wyye strange.
Gawan gef hym god day, the godmon hym *master of the house*
lachches, *takes*
Ledes hym to his awen chambre, the
chymné bysyde, *beside the fireplace*
And there he drawes hym on dryye, and derely hym thonkkes
Of the wynne worschip that he hym *fine honour*
wayved hade, *shown*
As to honour his hous on that hyghe tyde, *solemn season*
And enbelyse his burgh with his bele chere.
'Iwysse, sir, quyl I leve, me worthes the better
That Gawayn has ben my gest at Goddes awen fest.'
'Grant merci, sir,' quoth Gawayn, 'in god fayth hit is yowres,
Al the honour is your awen—the heghe kyng yow *High King*
yelde! *reward*
And I am, wyye, at your wylle, to worch youre hest, *sir; bidding*
As I am halden therto, in hyghe and in lowe,
bi right.'

1021 And the third (day), just as closely packed with pleasure, quickly followed.
1022 *sayn Jones day*, St John's Day (Dec. 27).
1025 And so they passed the night in wonderful style.
1028 Everyone going on his way who did not belong to the place.
1031 And there he holds him back, and courteously thanks him.
1034 And adorn his castle with his gracious company.
1035 Indeed, sir, as long as I live, I shall be the better for it.
1040–1 As I am rightly bound to do, in great things and small.

The lorde fast can hym payne *tried hard*
To holde lenger the knyght;
To hym answres Gawayn
Bi non way that he myght.

Then frayned the freke ful fayre at himselven
Quat derve dede had hym dryven at that dere tyme
So kenly fro the kynges kourt to kayre al his one,
Er the halidayes holly were halet out of toun.
'For sothe, sir,' quoth the segge, 'ye sayn bot the trawthe, *knight; speak*
A heghe ernde and a hasty me hade fro tho wones,
For I am sumned myselfe to sech to a place,
I ne wot in worlde whederwarde to wende hit to fynde.
I nolde bot if I hit negh myght on Nw Yeres morne
For alle the londe inwyth Logres, so me oure Lorde help! *in*
Forthy, sir, this enquest I require yow here, *question; ask*
That ye me telle with trawthe if ever ye tale herde *mention*
Of the grene chapel, quere hit on grounde stondes,
And of the knyght that hit kepes, of colour of grene.
Ther was stabled bi statut a steven uus bytwene
To mete that mon at that mere, yif I myght last; *landmark; live*
And of that ilk Nw Yere bot neked now wontes,
And I wolde loke on that lede, if God me let wolde, *man*
Gladloker, bi Goddes Sun, then any god welde.
Forthi, iwysse, bi yowre wylle, wende me bihoves.
Naf I now to busy bot bare thre dayes,
And me als fayn to falle feye as fayly of myyn ernde.'
Thenne laghande quoth the lorde: 'Now leng the byhoves, *laughing; stay* *you must*
For I schal teche yow to that terme bi the tymes ende. *appointed place*

1045 That he could not possibly do so.
1046–9 Then the man politely asked him what grim exploit had driven him at that festive season to ride out on his own so boldly from the King's court before the holy-days were over.
1051–4 A great and urgent mission took me from that dwelling, for I am summoned to look for a certain place, and I haven't the least idea where to go to find it. I wouldn't care not to reach it on New Year's morning.
1060 An appointment was fixed by a solemn agreement between us.
1062 And there is but little time left till the New Year.
1064–7 More gladly, by God's Son, than possess any good thing. And so, indeed, by your leave, I'm bound to go. I've barely three days in which to do my business, and I'd rather drop dead than fail in my mission.

The grene chapayle upon grounde greve yow no more; *let it trouble*
Bot ye schal be in yowre bed, burne, at thyn ese, *sir*
Quyle forth dayes, and ferk on the fyrst of the yere,
And cum to that merk at mydmorn, to make quat yow likes *appointed place*
        in spenne. *there*
    Dowelles whyle New Yeres daye, *stay until*
    And rys and raykes thenne. *depart*
    Mon schal yow sette in waye;
    Hit is not two myle henne.' *hence*

Thenne was Gawan ful glad, and gomenly he laghed: *merrily* *laughed*
'Now I thonk yow thryvandely thurgh alle other thynge; *heartily; beyond*
Now acheved is my chaunce, I schal at your wylle *accomplished; adventure*
Dowelle, and elles do quat ye demen.' *think fit*
Thenne sesed hym the syre and set hym bysyde, *took hold of*
Let the ladies be fette, to lyke hem the better. *brought; please*
Ther was seme solace by hemself stille.
The lorde let for luf lotes so myry,
As wyy that wolde of his wyte, ne wyst quat he myght.
Thenne he carped to the knyght, criande loude: *said*
'Ye han demed to do the dede that I bidde. *decided*
Wyl ye halde this hes here at thys ones?'
'Ye, sir, for sothe,' sayd the segge trwe, *knight*
'Whyl I byde in yowre borghe, be bayn to yowre hest.'
'For ye haf travayled,' quoth the tulk, 'towen fro ferre,
And sythen waked me wyth, ye arn not wel waryst
Nauther of sostnaunce ne of slepe, sothly I knowe.

1072 Until late in the morning, and leave on the first day of the year.
1085–7 They had a delightful time all by themselves. The lord, for friendship's sake, made such merry noises, like someone who was about to take leave of his senses, not knowing what he did.
1090 Will you keep your promise here and now?
1092 While I stay in your castle, I shall be obedient to your command.
1093–5 'As you have had a hard journey,' said the man, 'and come from afar, and afterwards stayed awake all night with me, you haven't properly made up your food or your sleep, I know for certain.'

Ye schal lenge in your lofte and lyye in your ese *stay; room*
To-morn quyle the messe-quyle, and to mete wende *until*
When ye wyl, wyth my wyf, that wyth yow schal sitte
And comfort yow with compayny, til I to cort torne. *return*
Ye lende, *stay*
And I schal erly ryse;
On huntyng wyl I wende.'
Gauayn grantes alle thyse,
Hym heldande, as the hende.

'Yet firre,' quoth the freke, 'a forwarde we make:
Quat-so-ever I wynne in the wod, hit worthes to youres; *shall become*
And quat chek so ye acheve, chaunge me therforne.
Swete, swap we so—sware with trawthe—
Quether, leude, so lymp lere other better.'
'Bi God,' quoth Gawayn the gode, 'I grant thertylle,
And that yow lyst for to layke, lef hit me thynkes.'
'Who brynges uus this beverage, this bargayn is maked,'
So sayde the lorde of that lede. Thay laghed uchone,
Thay dronken and daylyeden and dalten untyghtel,
Thise lordes and ladyes, quyle that hem lyked;
And sythen with frenkysch fare and fele fayre lotes
Thay stoden and stemed and stylly speken, *stopped; softly*
Kysten ful comlyly and kaghten her leve. *took*
With mony leude ful lyght and lemande torches,
Uche burne to his bed was broght at the laste
ful softe.
To bed yet er thay yede, *before; went*
Recorded covenauntes ofte; *repeated*
The olde lorde of that leude
Cowthe wel halde layk alofte.

1104 Bowing to him, as a courteous man should.
1105 'Moreover,' said the man, 'let's make an agreement.'
1107–9 And whatever advantage you gain, give it me in exchange. Good sir, let's strike this bargain—swear to keep it truly—whether, sir, we gain or lose.
1111 And I'm delighted that you wish to play (this game).
1112 If someone will bring us a drink, the bargain is made. (The reference is to drinking to seal a bargain.)
1114 They drank and chatted and exchanged pleasantries.
1116 And then with elaborate courtesy and many polite words.
1119 With many a brisk serving-man to hold gleaming torches.
1125 Could keep a game going splendidly.

III

Ful erly bifore the day the folk up rysen;
Gestes that go wolde hor gromes thay calden, *grooms*
And thay busken up bilyve blonkkes to sadel,
Tyffen her takles, trussen her males.
Richen hem the rychest, to ryde alle arayde,
Lepen up lyghtly, lachen her brydeles, *take hold of*
Uche wyye on his way ther hym wel lyked. *man; pleased*
The leve lorde of the londe was not the last *beloved*
Arayed for the rydyng, with renkkes ful mony; *men*
Ete a sop hastyly, when he hade herde masse, *(he) ate; light meal*
With bugle to bent-felde he buskes bylyve. *open field; hastens*
By that any daylyght lemed upon erthe, *by (the time that); shone*
He with his hatheles on hyghe horsses weren. *men*
Thenne thise cacheres that couthe cowpled hor houndes,
Unclosed the kenel dore and calde hem theroute,
Blwe bygly in bugles thre bare motes; *strongly; single notes*
Braches bayed therfore and breme noyse maked, *hounds; loud*
And thay chastysed and charred on chasyng that went,
A hundreth of hunteres, as I haf herde telle,
    of the best.
  To trystors vewters yod,
  Couples huntes of kest;
  Ther ros for blastes gode
  Gret rurd in that forest. *noise*

At the fyrst quethe of the quest quaked the wylde;
Der drof in the dale, doted for drede, *fled; went mad*
Hiyed to the hyghe, bot heterly thay were
Restayed with the stablye, that stoutly ascryed.

1128–30 And they hurry to saddle their horses, put their gear in order, and pack their bags. The guests of highest rank dress in readiness to ride.
1139 Then huntsmen who knew their job coupled the hounds (i.e. leashed them together in pairs).
1143 And they whipped and turned back those who went chasing off.
1146–7 The keepers of the deer-hounds went to their hunting stations, the huntsmen threw off the leashes.
1150 At the first sound of the baying of the hounds the wild creatures trembled.
1152–3 Quickly made for the high ground, but were promptly checked by the beaters, who shouted loudly.

Thay let the herttes haf the gate, with the hyghe hedes, *pass freely*
The breme bukkes also with hor brode paumes; *fierce; antlers*
For the fre lorde hade defende in fermysoun tyme
That ther schulde no mon meve to the male dere.
The hindes were halden in with 'hay!' and 'war!'
The does dryven with gret dyn to the depe slades. *valleys*
Ther myght mon se, as thay slypte, slentyng of arwes; *were loosed; glancing*
At uche wende under wande wapped a flone,
That bigly bote on the broun with ful brode hedes.
What! thay brayen and bleden, bi bonkkes thay deyen, *scream* *die*
And ay rachches in a res radly hem folwes,
Hunteres wyth hyghe horne hasted hem after, *loud*
Wyth such a crakkande kry as klyffes haden brusten.
What wylde so atwaped wyyes that schotten
Was al toraced and rent at the resayt,
Bi thay were tened at the hyghe and taysed to the wattres.
The ledes were so lerned at the lowe trysteres,
And the grehoundes so grete, that geten hem bylyve
And hem tofylched as fast as frekes myght loke,
ther ryght.
The lorde for blys abloy *transported*
Ful oft con launce and lyght, *galloped; dismounted*
And drof that day wyth joy *passed*
Thus to the derk nyght. *till*

Thus laykes this lorde by lynde-wodes eves,
And Gawayn the god mon in gay bed lyges, *lies*

1156–8 For the noble lord had forbidden any interference with the male deer during the close season. The hinds were held in with cries of 'hey!' and 'ware!'

1161–2 At each turn in the wood an arrow flew and strongly pierced the brown hides with its broad head.

1164 And all the time the hounds rush headlong after them.

1166–73 With such a resounding noise that it seemed as though the cliffs had split in two. Any of the wild beasts that escaped the bowmen were pulled down and killed at the stations where men were posted with fresh hounds, after being harassed from the high ground and driven to the water. The men at the low-lying stations were so expert, and their greyhounds so big, that they quickly caught and pulled them down on the spot, as fast as the eye could see.

1178 Thus the lord enjoys his sport along the edge of the forest.

Lurkkes quyl the daylyght lemed on the wowes,
Under covertour ful clere, cortyned aboute. *canopy*
And as in slomeryng he slode, sleyly he herde
A littel dyn at his dor, and derfly upon;
And he heves up his hed out of the clothes, *lifts*
A corner of the cortyn he caght up a lyttel, *raised*
And waytes warly thiderwarde quat hit be myght.
Hit was the ladi, loflyest to beholde, *loveliest*
That drow the dor after hir ful dernly and stylle, *drew; silently*
And bowed towarde the bed; and the burne *moved*
schamed, *was embarrassed*
And layde hym doun lystyly and let as he slepte. *artfully; pretended*
And ho stepped stilly and stel to his bedde, *softly; stole*
Kest up the cortyn and creped withinne,
And set hir ful softly on the bed-syde
And lenged there selly longe, to loke quen he *stayed; very*
wakened.
The lede lay lurked a ful longe quyle, *low*
Compast in his concience to quat that cace myght
Meve other amount, to mervayle hym thoght.
Bot yet he sayde in hymself: 'More semly hit were
To aspye wyth my spelle in space quat ho wolde.'
Then he wakenede and wroth and to-hir-warde *stretched himself*
torned,
And unlouked his yye-lyddes and let as hym wondered,
And sayned hym, as bi his sawe the saver to worthe,
with hande.
Wyth chynne and cheke ful swete,
Bothe quit and red in blande, *together*
Ful lufly con ho lete,
Wyth lyppes smal laghande. *laughing*

1180 Lies snug until the light of day gleamed on the walls.
1182–3 And as he lay dozing, he heard a small, stealthy sound at his door, and then heard it quickly open.
1186 And looks warily in that direction to see what it could be.
1196–7 Turned over in his mind what this incident could mean or what its outcome would be, for it seemed a marvel to him.
1199 To find out in the course of conversation what she wants.
1201–3 And opened his eyelids and pretended to be surprised, and crossed himself, as if to make himself the safer by prayer.
1206 She behaved most graciously.

'God moroun, Sir Gawayn,' sayde that gay lady, *morning*
'Ye ar a sleper unslyye, that mon may slyde hider. *careless; slip*
Now ar ye tan astyt, bot true uus may schape,
I schal bynde yow in your bedde, that be ye trayst.' *be sure of that*
Al laghande the lady lauced tho bourdes. *made; those jests*
'Goud moroun, gay,' quoth Gawayn the blythe, *joyful*
'Me schal worthe at your wille, and that me wel lykes,
For I yelde me yederly and yeye after grace;
And that is the best, be my dome, for me byhoves nede.'
And thus he bourded ayayn with mony a blythe laghter. *jested; in return*
'Bot wolde ye, lady lovely, then leve me grante, *leave*
And deprece your prysoun and pray hym to ryse, *release; prisoner*
I wolde bowe of this bed and busk me better, *leave; dress*
I schulde kever the more comfort to karp yow wyth.'
'Nay, for sothe, beau sir,' sayd that swete,
'Ye schal not rise of your bedde. I rych yow better:
I schal happe yow here that other half als,
And sythen karp wyth my knyght that I kaght have; *talk; caught*
For I wene wel, iwysse, Sir Wowen ye are, *know well; indeed*
That alle the worlde worchipes, quere-so ye ride.
Your honour, your hendelayk is hendely praysed *courtesy; nobly*
With lordes, wyth ladyes, with alle that lyf bere. *by*
And now ye ar here, iwysse, and we bot oure one; *by ourselves*
My lorde and his ledes ar on lenthe faren, *men; gone far away*
Other burnes in her bedde, and my burdes als, *knights; ladies too*
The dor drawen and dit with a derf haspe. *fastened; strong*
And sythen I have in this hous hym that al lykes,
I schal ware my whyle wel, quyl hit lastes,
with tale.

1210 Now you are captured in a moment, and unless we can make a truce.

1214–16 You shall do with me as you like, and I am well pleased, for I quickly surrender and cry for mercy; and that is the best I can do, in my opinion, for I can't help myself.

1221 I should get all the more pleasure from talking to you.

1223–4 I have something better for you to do: I shall tuck you up on this other side as well.

1234–6 And since I have in this house the man whom everyone loves, I shall spend my time well, while it lasts, in conversation with him.

Ye ar welcum to my cors, *body*
Yowre awen won to wale; *pleasure; take*
Me behoves of fyne force *sheer necessity*
Your servaunt be, and schale.' *and I will be*

'In god fayth,' quoth Gawayn, 'gayn hit me thynkkes, *an advantage*
Thagh I be not now he that ye of speken;
To reche to such reverence as ye reherce here *attain; describe*
I am wyye unworthy, I wot wel myselven. *person; know*
Bi God, I were glad and yow god thoght
At sawe other at servyce that I sette myght
To the plesaunce of your prys—hit were a pure joye.'
'In god fayth, Sir Gawayn,' quoth the gay lady,
'The prys and the prowes that pleses al other, *excellence*
If I hit lakked other set at lyght, hit were littel dayntė;
Bot hit ar ladyes innoghe that lever wer nowthe
Haf the, hende, in hor holde, as I the habbe here,
To daly with derely your dayntė wordes,
Kever hem comfort and colen her cares,
Then much of the garysoun other golde that thay haven.
Bot I louve that ilk lorde that the lyfte haldes,
I haf hit holly in my honde that al desyres, *wholly*
thurghe grace.'
Scho made hym so gret chere,
That was so fayr of face;
The knyght with speches skere *pure*
Answared to uche a cace. *everything she said*

'Madame,' quoth the myry mon, 'Mary yow yelde, *reward*
For I haf founden, in god fayth, yowre fraunchis nobele. *generosity*

1237 *to my cors* means literally 'to my body', but in this context it may not mean more than 'to me'.
1242 Though I am not the sort of man you speak of.
1245–7 I should be glad if you thought fit to let me devote myself, in word or deed, to the pleasure of serving you.
1250–6 If I disparaged or thought light of it, such action would show little courtesy. There are many ladies who would rather have you, dear knight, in their power, as I have you here, to exchange delightful words most lovingly, to find comfort for themselves and relieve their sorrow, than possess any amount of treasure or gold. But praise the Lord who rules the heavens.
1259 She behaved thus graciously to him.

And other ful much of other folk fongen hor dedes,
Bot the daynté that thay delen for my disert nysen.
Hit is the worchyp of yourself that noght bot wel connes.'
'Bi Mary,' quoth the menskful, 'me thynk hit another; *noble lady* *otherwise*
For were I worth al the wone of wymmen alyve, *multitude*
And al the wele of the worlde were in my honde, *wealth*
And I schulde chepen and chose to cheve me a lorde,
For the costes that I haf knowen upon the, knyght, here, *qualities*
Of bewté and debonerté and blythe semblaunt,
And that I haf er herkkened and halde hit here trwee,
Ther schulde no freke upon folde bifore yow be chosen.'
'Iwysse, worthy,' quoth the wyye, 'ye haf waled wel better;
Bot I am proude of the prys that ye put on me, *value*
And, soberly your servaunt, my soverayn I holde yow,
And yowre knyght I becom, and Kryst yow foryelde!' *reward*
Thus thay meled of muchquat til mydmorn paste, *talked; many things*
And ay the lady let lyk a hym loved mych;
The freke ferde with defence, and feted ful fayre.
'Thagh I were burde bryghtest,' the burde in mynde hade, *fairest lady*
'The lasse luf in his lode'—for lur that he soght
boute hone,
The dunte that schulde hym deve, *blow; strike down*
And nedes hit most be done.
The lady thenn spek of leve, *leaving*
He granted hir ful sone. *immediately*

1265–7 And others receive very much (praise) from other people for their deeds, but the respect shown to me is not for any merit of my own. It reflects honour upon yourself that you treat me so courteously.
1271 If I could strike a bargain and choose my own husband.
1273–5 Of beauty, courtesy and gay demeanour, which I have heard of before and now know to be true, there is no man on earth I would choose before you.
1276 'Indeed, noble lady,' said the knight, 'you have chosen much better.'
1278 And, your servant in all seriousness, I hold you as my liege lady.
1281–5 And all the time the lady behaved as if she loved him dearly; the knight was on his guard, but acted most courteously. 'Even though I were the fairest of women,' she thought, 'the less love would he bring with him on his journey'—because of the self-destruction he sought without respite.

Thenne ho gef hym god day, and wyth a glent laghed, *glance*
And as ho stod ho stonyed hym wyth ful *astonished*
stor wordes: *severe*
'Now he that spedes uche spech this disport yelde
yow!
Bot that ye be Gawan, hit gos not in mynde.'
'Querfore?' quoth the freke, and freschly he askes, *eagerly*
Ferde lest he hade fayled in fourme of his costes.
Bot the burde hym blessed, and bi this skyl sayde: *said as follows*
'So god as Gawayn gaynly is halden,
And cortaysye is closed so clene in hymselven,
Couth not lyghtly haf lenged so long wyth a lady,
Bot he had craved a cosse bi his courtaysye,
Bi sum towch of summe tryfle at sum tales ende.'
Then quoth Wowen: 'Iwysse, worthe as yow *indeed; let it be*
lykes;
I schal kysse at your comaundement, as a knyght falles, *befits*
And firre, lest he displese yow, so plede hit no
more.'
Ho comes nerre with that, and caches hym in armes, *nearer*
Loutes luflych adoun and the leude kysses.
Thay comly bykennen to Kryst ayther other;
Ho dos hir forth at the dore withouten dyn more;
And he ryches hym to ryse and rapes hym sone, *prepares; hurries*
Clepes to his chamberlayn, choses his wede, *calls; raiment*
Bowes forth, quen he was boun, blythely to masse. *goes; ready*
And thenne he meved to his mete that menskly hym keped,
And made myry al day til the mone rysed, *rose*
with game.

1292–3 May He who prospers every speech reward you for this entertainment! But I find it hard to believe that you are Gawain.

1295 Afraid lest he had failed in his manners.

1297–301 Gawain is rightly held to be so gracious, and courtesy is so completely contained in him, that he could not easily have stayed so long with a lady without being moved by his courtesy to ask for a kiss, if only by some small hint at the end of a speech.

1304 And (go even) further, lest he displease you.

1306–8 Bends down lovingly and kisses the knight. They graciously commend each other to Christ; she goes out through the door without another word.

1312 And then he went to the meal that awaited him in honourable fashion.

Was never freke fayrer fonge
Bitwene two so dyngne dame, *such worthy ladies*
The alder and the yonge; *older; younger*
Much solace set thay same.

And ay the lorde of the londe is lent on his gamnes, *has gone*
To hunt in holtes and hethe at hyndes barayne.
Such a sowme he ther slowe bi that the sunne heldet,
Of dos and of other dere, to deme were wonder.
Thenne fersly thay flokked in, folk at the laste, *eagerly*
And quykly of the quelled dere a querré thay maked. *slain; heap*
The best bowed therto with burnes innoghe,
Gedered the grattest of gres that ther were, *fattest*
And didden hem derely undo as the dede askes.
Serched hem at the asay summe that ther were,
Two fyngeres thay fonde of the fowlest of alle.
Sythen thay slyt the slot, sesed the erber,
Schaved wyth a scharp knyf, and the schyre knitten.
Sythen rytte thay the foure lymmes and rent of the hyde,
Then brek thay the balé, the boweles out token
Lystily, for laucyng and lere of the knot.

1315 Never was a man more graciously received.
1318 They greatly enjoyed themselves together.
1320–2 To hunt the barren hinds in wood and heath. By the time the sun had set he had slain so many does and other kinds of deer, that it is marvellous to relate.
1325 The highest in rank went up to it with all their attendants.
1327–52 And had them neatly cut up, as custom demands. They examined some of them, and found two finger-breadths of fat on the poorest of them all. Then they slit open the slot (i.e. the hollow running down the middle of the breast), took hold of the first stomach, cut it away from the flesh with a sharp knife, and tied it up. Next they lopped off the four legs, tore off the skin, then ripped open the belly and removed the bowels deftly, for fear of undoing and destroying the knot (i.e. the knot that tied up the *erber* mentioned in line 1330). They gripped the gullet, swiftly severed the weasand from the windpipe, and tossed out the guts. Then they cut out the shoulders with their sharp knives, and drew them through a small hole in such a way as to leave the sides intact. Next they slit open the breast and pulled it apart. Then they set to work on the gullet, promptly ripped it right up to the fork (of the legs), cleared out the numbles, and afterwards loosened all the membranes along the ribs. In the same way they correctly cleared the backbones straight down to the haunch which hangs from them, lifted up the whole haunch and hewed it off. And that is what they properly call the numbles, I believe. At the thigh-forks they loosened the folds behind; and they hurried to hew open the carcass and cut it in two along the backbone.

Thay gryped to the gargulun, and graythely departed
The wesaunt fro the wynt-hole and walt out the guttes.
Then scher thay out the schulderes with her scharp knyves,
Haled hem by a lyttel hole, to have hole sydes.
Sithen britned thay the brest and brayden hit in twynne.
And eft at the gargulun bigynes on thenne,
Ryves hit up radly ryght to the byght,
Voydes out the avanters, and verayly therafter
Alle the rymes by the rybbes radly thay lauce.
So ryde thay of by resoun bi the rygge bones
Evenden to the haunche, that henged alle samen,
And heven hit up al hole and hwen hit of there.
And that thay neme for the noumbles bi nome, as I trowe, bi kynde.
    Bi the byght al of the thyghes
    The lappes thay lauce bihynde;
    To hewe hit in two thay hyyes,
    Bi the bakbon to unbynde.

Bothe the hede and the hals thay hwen of thenne, *neck*
And sythen sunder thay the sydes swyft fro the chyne, *chine*
And the corbeles fee thay kest in a greve.
Thenn thurled thay ayther thik side thurgh bi the rybbe,
And henged thenne ayther bi hoghes of the fourches,
Uche freke for his fee as falles for to have.
Upon a felle of the fayre best fede thay thayr houndes *skin; noble beast*
Wyth the lyver and the lyghtes, the lether of the paunches, *lining; stomachs*
And bred bathed in blod blende ther-amonges. *steeped*
Baldely thay blw prys, bayed thayr rachches;
Sythen fonge thay her flesche folden to home,
Strakande ful stoutly mony stif motes.

1355 And they flung the raven's fee into a thicket. (The 'raven's fee' was a piece of gristle at the end of the breast bone which was thrown into the branches of a tree as a titbit for the crows and ravens.)

1356–8 Then they pierced through each thick flank near the ribs, and hung up each by the hocks of the haunches, every huntsman getting the portion due to him.

1362–4 Vigorously they blew the kill, and their hounds started baying; then they took home their meat closely packed, proudly sounding many bold notes on the horn.

Bi that the daylyght was done, the douthe was al wonen *company* *come*
Into the comly castel, ther the knyght bides ful stille, *stays* *quietly*
Wyth blys and bryght fyr bette.
The lorde is comen thertylle;
When Gawayn wyth hym mette,
Ther was bot wele at wylle. *joy; unbounded*

Thenne comaunded the lorde in that sale to samen alle the meny,
Bothe the ladyes on loghe to lyght with her burdes.
Bifore alle the folk on the flette, frekes he beddes
Verayly his venysoun to fech hym byforne;
And al godly in gomen Gawayn he called,
Teches hym to the tayles of ful tayt bestes,
Schewes hym the schyree grece schorne upon rybbes.
'How payes yow this play? Haf I prys wonnen?
Have I thryvandely thonk thurgh my craft served?'
'Ye, iwysse,' quoth that other wyye, 'here is wayth fayrest *spoils*
That I sey this seven yere in sesoun of wynter.' *saw*
'And al I gif yow, Gawayn,' quoth the gome thenne, *man*
'For by acorde of covenaunt ye crave hit as your awen.' *may claim* *own*
'This is soth,' quoth the segge, 'I say yow that ilke: *true* *the same*
That I haf worthyly wonnen this wones wythinne,
Iwysse with as god wylle hit worthes to youres.'
He hasppes his fayre hals his armes wythinne, *clasps; neck*
And kysses hym as comlyly as he couthe awyse: *graciously* *manage*
'Tas yow there my chevicaunce, I cheved no more;
I wowche hit saf fynly, thagh feler hit were.'

1368 Happily seated near a bright blazing fire.

1372–80 Then the lord commanded all the household to gather in the hall, and both the ladies to come downstairs with their maidens. In the presence of all the folk on the floor he orders his men to bring the venison in before him; and with due courtesy he gaily calls for Gawain, tells him the tally of the nimble beasts (he has slain), and shows him the fine flesh cut from the ribs. 'How does this sport please you? Have I won praise? Have I thoroughly deserved thanks for my skill?'

1386–7 What I have won with honour in this house shall as gladly be yours.

1390–1 There, take my winnings, for I got no more; but I would give them all, even if they were greater.

'Hit is god,' quoth the godmon, 'grant mercy therfore. *many thanks*
Hit may be such, hit is the better and ye me breve wolde
Where ye wan this ilk wele bi wytte of yorselven.'
'That was not forward,' quoth he, 'frayst me no more; *agreement; ask*
For ye haf tan that yow tydes, trawe ye non other
ye mowe.'
Thay laghed and made hem blythe *made merry*
Wyth lotes that were to lowe;
To soper thay yede asswythe, *straightway*
Wyth dayntés nwe innowe. *in plenty*

And sythen by the chymné in chamber thay seten, *fireplace*
Wyyes the walle wyn weghed to hem oft, *choice; brought*
And efte in her bourdyng thay baythen in the morn
To fylle the same forwardes that thay byfore maden:
That chaunce so bytydes, hor chevysaunce to chaunge,
What nwes so thay nome, at naght quen thay metten.
Thay acorded of the covenauntes byfore the court alle;
The beverage was broght forth in bourde at that tyme. *jest*
Thenne thay lovelych leghten leve at the last, *lovingly; took*
Uche burne to his bedde busked bylyve. *hastened*
Bi that the coke hade crowen and cakled bot thryse,
The lorde was lopen of his bedde, the leudes uch one,
So that the mete and the masse was metely delyvered,
The douthe dressed to the wod, er any day sprenged,
to chace.
Hegh with hunte and hornes *proudly; huntsman*
Thurgh playnes thay passe in space, *soon after*
Uncoupled among tho thornes *unleashed; thorns*
Raches that ran on race. *hounds; headlong*

[1393–4 They (i.e. Gawain's winnings) may be worth more, and so it is better if you tell me where you were clever enough to win this rich prize.
1396–7 For you have taken what is due to you, and you can rest assured you'll get nothing else.
1399 With words that were worthy of praise.
1404–7 And again they jestingly agreed to carry out next day the same covenant they had made before: come what may, they were to exchange their winnings when they met at night, whatever new things they obtained.
1413–16 The lord had leapt out of his bed, and all his men were up as well, so that mass and a meal were soon over, and before day dawned the company went off to hunt in the woods.

Sone thay calle of a quest in a ker syde,
The hunt rehayted the houndes that hit fyrst mynged,
Wylde wordes hym warp wyth a wrast noyce.
The howndes that hit herde hastid thider swythe, *swiftly*
And fellen as fast to the fuyt, fourty at ones. *trail*
Thenne such a glaver ande glam of gedered rachches
Ros that the rocheres rungen aboute.
Hunteres hem hardened with horne and wyth muthe; *encouraged*
Then al in a semblé sweyed togeder *pack; rushed*
Bitwene a flosche in that fryth and a foo cragge.
In a knot bi a clyffe, at the kerre syde, *on a rocky hill; marsh*
Ther as the rogh rocher unrydely was fallen, *rock; ruggedly*
Thay ferden to the fyndyng, and frekes hem after.
Thay umbekesten the knarre and the knot bothe,
Wyyes, whyl thay wysten wel wythinne hem hit were,
The best that ther breved was wyth three blodhoundes.
Thenne thay beten on the buskes and bede hym up ryse, *bushes; bade*
And he unsoundyly out soght segges overthwert—
On the sellokest swyn swenged out there,
Long sythen fro the sounder that synglere for olde,
For he was brothe, bor alther grattest,
Ful grymme quen he gronyed. Thenne greved mony,
For thre at the fyrst thrast he thryght to the erthe,
And sped hym forth good sped boute spyt more.

1421–3 Soon they called for a search to be made along the edge of a marsh, the huntsman urged on the hounds that first picked up the scent, and uttered wild cries with tremendous noise.

1426–7 Then such a babble and clamour rose from the assembled hounds that the rocks round about rang (with the din).

1430 Between a pool in the wood and a fearsome crag.

1433–6 They went on to dislodge their quarry, with the huntsmen after them. Men surrounded both the crag and the rocky hill, until they were sure they had inside their ring the beast that was announced by the bloodhounds.

1438–44 And with deadly ferocity he made for the men across his path—out rushed there the most marvellous boar, a solitary beast long since separated from the herd because of his age, but still a formidable creature, the greatest of all boars, who made a terrifying noise when he grunted. Then many men were dismayed, for at his first rush he hurled three of the hounds to the ground, and charged off unhurt.

Thise other halowed 'hyghe!' ful hyghe, and 'hay! hay!' cryed, *shouted; loudly*
Haden hornes to mouthe, heterly rechated.
Mony was the miyry mouthe of men and of houndes *merry cries*
That buskkes after this bor with bost and wyth noyse, *hurry; clamour*
to quelle. *kill*
Ful oft he bydes the baye *stands at bay*
And maymes the mute inn melle; *pack; on all sides*
He hurtes of the houndes, and thay *(some) of*
Ful yomerly yaule and yelle. *piteously; howl*

Schalkes to schote at hym schowen to thenne,
Haled to hym of her arewes, hitten hym oft; *loosed arrows at him*
Bot the poyntes payred at the pyth that pyght in his scheldes,
And the barbes of his browe bite non wolde,
Thagh the schaven schaft schyndered in peces,
The hede hypped ayayn were-so-ever hit hitte.
Bot quen the dyntes hym dered of her dryye strokes,
Then, braynwod for bate, on burnes he rases,
Hurtes hem ful heterly ther he forth hyyes,
And mony arwed therat and on lyte drowen.
Bot the lorde on a lyght horce launces hym after, *gallops*
As burne bolde upon bent his bugle he blowes,
He rechated and rode thurgh rones ful thyk,
Suande this wylde swyn til the sunne schafted. *pursuing; set*
This day wyth this ilk dede thay dryven on this wyse, *pass*
Whyle oure luflych lede lys in his bedde, *courteous knight*
Gawayn graythely at home, in geres ful ryche *pleasantly; bed clothes*
of hewe.

1446 Quickly sounded the rally (in order to call the huntsmen and hounds together).
1454 Then men pressed forward to shoot at him.
1456–63 But the points were turned by the roughness of his flanks, and the barbs would not pierce his (bristling) brow, for though the smooth-shaven shaft was shattered to pieces, the head rebounded wherever it hit. But, hurt by their unceasing blows and maddened by their baiting, he rushed at the men, wounding them savagely as he charged forward, and many of them were afraid and drew back.
1465–6 Like a bold knight on the battlefield he blows his bugle, sounded the rally and rode through the thick bushes.

The lady noght foryate, *did not forget*
Com to hym to salue; *greet*
Ful erly ho was hym ate *at him*
His mode for to remwe. *mood; change*

Ho commes to the cortyn and at the knyght totes. *peeps*
Sir Wawen her welcumed worthy on fyrst,
And ho hym yeldes ayayn ful yerne of hir wordes,
Settes hir sofly by his syde, and swythely ho laghes, *gently; very much*
And wyth a luflych loke ho layde hym thyse wordes: *loving; delivered*
'Sir, yif ye be Wawen, wonder me thynkkes,
Wyye that is so wel wrast alway to god,
And connes not of compaynye the costes undertake,
And if mon kennes yow hom to knowe, ye kest hom of your mynde. *teaches; put*
Thou has foryeten yederly that yisterday I taghtte *quickly*
Bi alder-truest token of talk that I cowthe.'
'What is that?' quoth the wyghe, 'iwysse I wot never.
If hit be sothe that ye breve, the blame is myn awen.'
'Yet I kende yow of kyssyng,' quoth the clere thenne, *taught; fair lady*
'Quere-so countenaunce is couthe, quikly to clayme;
That bicumes uche a knyght that cortaysy uses.' *every; practises*
'Do way,' quoth that derf mon, 'my dere, that speche,
For that durst I not do, lest I devayed were; *refused*
If I were werned, I were wrang, iwysse, yif I profered.'
'Ma fay,' quoth the mere wyf, 'ye may not be werned;

1477–8 Sir Gawain first greeted her courteously, and she answered him eagerly.

1481–3 Sir, if you are really Gawain, the knight who is so well disposed to noble behaviour, it seems strange to me that you cannot understand the manners of polite society.

1486 By the truest possible lesson that I could manage in words.

1487–8 'What is that?' said the knight, 'for indeed I don't know. If what you say is true, the blame is my own.'

1490 To stake your claim quickly where the lady's favour is plain to see.

1492 'Dear lady, don't say such things,' the brave man replied.

1494 If I were refused, I would be wrong to have offered.

1495 'By my faith,' said the noble lady, 'none could refuse you.'

Ye ar stif innoghe to constrayne wyth strenkthe, yif yow lykes, *strong*
Yif any were so vilanous that yow devaye wolde.' *ill-bred; refuse*
'Ye, be God,' quoth Gawayn, 'good is your speche,
Bot threte is unthryvande in thede ther I lende,
And uche gift that is geven not with goud wylle.
I am at your comaundement, to kysse quen yow lykes;
Ye may lach quen yow lyst, and leve quen yow thynkkes,
in space.' *in due course*
The lady loutes adoun *bends*
And comlyly kysses his face; *graciously*
Much speche thay ther expoun *they have much to say*
Of druryes greme and grace. *love's grief*

'I woled wyt at yow, wyye,' that worthy ther sayde,
'And yow wrathed not therwyth, what were the skylle
That so yong and so yepe as ye at this tyme,
So cortayse, so knyghtyly, as ye ar knowen oute—
And of alle chevalry to chose, the chef thyng alosed
Is the lel layk of luf, the lettrure of armes;
For to telle of this tevelyng of this trwe knyghtes,
Hit is the tytelet token and tyxt of her werkkes,
How ledes for her lele luf hor lyves han auntered,
Endured for her drury dulful stoundes,
And after wenged with her walour and voyded her care,
And broght blysse into boure with bountees hor awen—
And ye ar knyght comlokest kyd of your elde,
Your worde and your worchip walkes ayquere,

1499 But to use force is thought unworthy in the country where I live.
1502 You may take one when you like, and abstain when you like.
1508–11 I should like to learn from you, sir, if you won't be angry with me, why it is that one so young and active, so courteous, so chivalrous, as you are widely known to be. (Here the sentence breaks off and is resumed in line 1520.)
1512–19 Of all the chivalrous exploits, if one had to choose, the chief things to praise are the loyal sport of love and the lore of arms; for, in describing the deeds of true knights, the title and text of their works tell how men for true love have risked their lives, endured for love's sake grievous trials, and then have avenged themselves with valour, banished their sorrow, and brought happiness to a lady's bower by their excellence.
1520–4 And you are known as the noblest knight of your age, your fame and honour are spread everywhere, and yet I have sat by you on two different occasions and never heard you speak a single word that had anything to do with love.

And I haf seten by yourself here sere twyes,
Yet herde I never of your hed helde no wordes
That ever longed to luf, lasse ne more.
And ye, that ar so cortays and coynt of your hetes, *wise; vows*
Oghe to a yonke thynk yern to schewe
And teche sum tokenes of trweluf craftes. *true love's arts*
Why! ar ye lewed, that alle the los weldes,
Other elles ye demen me to dille your dalyaunce to herken?
For schame!
I com hider sengel and sitte *alone*
To lerne at yow sum game; *from*
Dos teches me of your wytte,
Whil my lorde is fro hame.' *home*

'In goud faythe,' quoth Gawayn, 'God yow foryelde! *reward*
Gret is the gode gle, and gomen to me huge, *gladness; pleasure*
That so worthy as ye wolde wynne hidere, *come*
And pyne yow with so pover a mon, as play wyth your knyght *trouble yourself; poor*
With anyskynnes countenaunce—hit keveres me ese.
Bot to take the torvayle to myself to trwluf expoun,
And towche the temes of tyxt and tales of armes
To yow that, I wot wel, weldes more slyght
Of that art, bi the half, or a hundreth of seche
As I am other ever schal, in erde ther I leve—
Hit were a folé felefolde, my fre, by my trawthe.
I wolde yowre wylnyng worche at my myght,
As I am hyghly bihalden, and evermore wylle *deeply*
Be servaunt to yourselven, so save me Dryghtyn!' *the Lord*
Thus hym frayned that fre and fondet hym ofte, *questioned; tempted*

1526 Ought to be eager to show a young woman.
1528–9 Why! can it be that you are ignorant, in spite of all the renown you enjoy, or do you think me too stupid to listen to your courtly conversation?
1533 Do teach me something of your wisdom.
1539 With any show of favour—it gives me comfort.
1540–5 But to take on myself the task of describing true love and of discoursing on the main themes and stories of arms to you who, I well know, have twice as much skill in that art as a hundred like me can ever have while I live on this earth—that would be a great folly, my noble lady, upon my word it would.
1546 I will do what you wish to the best of my ability.

For to haf wonnen hym to woghe, what-so scho thoght elles;
Bot he defended hym so fayr that no faut semed, *courteously* *was to be seen*
Ne non evel on nawther halve, nawther thay wysten bot blysse.
Thay laghed and layked longe; *amused themselves*
At the last scho con hym kysse,
Hir leve fayre con scho fonge,
And went hir waye, iwysse.

Then ruthes hym the renk and ryses to the masse, *bestirs; knight*
And sithen hor diner was dyght and derely served.
The lede with the ladyes layked alle day,
Bot the lorde over the londes launced ful ofte, *galloped*
Swes his uncely swyn, that swynges bi the bonkkes
And bote the best of his braches the bakkes in sunder *bit; hounds*
Ther he bode in his bay, tel bawemen hit breken,
And madee hym, mawgref his hed, for to mwe utter,
So felle flones ther flete when the folk gedered.
Bot yet the styffest to start bi stoundes he made,
Til at the last he was so mat he myght no more renne, *exhausted*
Bot in the hast that he myght he to a hole wynnes
Of a rasse, bi a rokk ther rennes the boerne.
He gete the bonk at his bak, bigynes to scrape, *got* *scrape (the ground)*

1550 In order to entice him to sin, whatever else she had in mind.

1552 And there was no evil on either side, nor did they know anything but happiness.

1556 She courteously took her leave.

1559–60 And afterwards their dinner was prepared and nobly served. The knight amused himself all day with the ladies.

1562 Pursues his ill-fated boar, that rushes over the slopes.

1564–7 Whenever he stood at bay, till bowmen got the better of him and made him move into the open, in spite of all he could do, so fiercely the arrows flew when the huntsmen came together. But yet at times he made the bravest men start aside.

1569–70 But as fast as he could he made for a hole in the bank, near a rock where the stream ran past.

The frothe femed at his mouth unfayre bi the wykes,
Whettes his whyte tusches. With hym then irked
Alle the burnes so bolde that hym by stoden
To nye hym on-ferum, bot neghe hym non durst
for wothe.
He hade hurt so mony byforne
That al thught thenne ful lothe *seemed; loath*
Be more wyth his tusches torne, *torn*
That breme was and braynwod bothe. *fierce; frenzied*

Til the knyght com hymself, kachande his blonk, *urging on horse*
Syy hym byde at the bay, his burnes bysyde. *saw*
He lyghtes luflych adoun, leves his corsour,
Braydes out a bryght bront and bigly forth strydes,
Foundes fast thurgh the forth ther the felle bydes.
The wylde was war of the wyye with weppen in honde, *wild beast; man*
Hef hyghly the here, so hetterly he fnast
That fele ferde for the freke, lest felle hym the worre.
The swyn settes hym out on the segge even,
That the burne and the bor were bothe upon hepes *in a heap*
In the wyghtest of the water. The worre hade that other, *swiftest; worst (of it)*
For the mon merkkes hym wel, as thay mette fyrst, *aims at*
Set sadly the scharp in the slot even,
Hit hym up to the hult, that the hert schyndered, *hilt burst asunder*
And he yarrande hym yelde, and yedoun the water
ful tyt.

1572–6 The froth foamed hideously at the corners of his mouth, and he whets his white tusks. By then the bold men who stood round him were tired of harassing him from a distance, but none dared run the risk of closing with him.

1583–5 He dismounts agilely, leaves his courser, draws out a bright sword and strides strongly forward, quickly crossing the stream to where the fierce beast is waiting.

1587–9 His bristles stood on end, and so fiercely he snorted that many were afraid for the knight, lest he should get the worst of it. The boar rushed straight at the man.

1593 Firmly planted his sharp blade in the hollow of his breast.

1595 And he snarlingly surrendered, and was quickly swept downstream.

A hundreth houndes hym hent, *seized*
That bremely con hym bite; *fiercely bit*
Burnes him broght to bent *bank*
And dogges to dethe endite. *do (him)*

There was blawyng of prys in mony breme horne,
Heghe halowing on highe with hatheles that myght;
Brachetes bayed that best, as bidden the maysteres, *hounds; bayed at*
Of that chargeaunt chace that were chef huntes. *hard; huntsmen*
Thenne a wyye that was wys upon wodcraftes
To unlace this bor lufly bigynnes:
Fyrst he hewes of his hed and on highe settes,
And sythen rendes him al roghe bi the rygge after,
Braydes out the boweles, brennes hom on glede, *pulls; burns red-hot coals*
With bred blent therwith his braches rewardes. *mixed*
Sythen he britnes out the brawen in bryght brode scheldes,
And has out the hastlettes, as hightly bisemes;
And yet hem halches al hole the halves togeder,
And sythen on a stif stange stoutly hem henges. *pole; hangs*
Now with this ilk swyn thay swengen to home; *set off quickly*
The bores hed was borne bifore the burnes selven,
That him forferde in the forthe thurgh forse of his honde so stronge.
Til he sey Sir Gawayne *saw*
In halle hym thoght ful longe; *it seemed to him*
He calde, and he com gayn *promptly*
His fees ther for to fonge. *dues; receive*

1601–2 The kill was blown on many a sturdy horn, and every man hallooed as loudly as he could.

1606 Began to cut up the boar with loving care.

1608 And then roughly rends him along the backbone.

1611–13 Then he slices up the flesh in broad white slabs, and takes out the entrails, as is proper and fitting; and also he fastens the two halves completely together.

1616–17 The boar's head was carried before the lord himself, who had destroyed him in the stream by the strength of his hand.

The lorde, ful lowde with lote, laghed myry
When he seye Sir Gawayn; with solace he spekes.
The goude ladyes were geten, and gedered the *brought*
meyny; *household*
He schewes hem the scheldes and schapes hem the tale
Of the largesse and the lenthe, the lithernes alse,
Of the were of the wylde swyn in wod ther he fled.
That other knyght ful comly comended his dedes,
And praysed hit as gret prys that he proved hade;
For suche a brawne of a best, the bolde burne sayde,
Ne such sydes of a swyn segh he never are.
Thenne hondeled thay the hoge hed, the hende mon *courteous*
hit praysed,
And let lodly therat the lorde for to here.
'Now, Gawayn,' quoth the godmon, 'this gomen is your *game*
awen
Bi fyn forwarde and faste, faythely ye knowe.'
'Hit is sothe,' quoth the segge, 'and as siker trwe *true; surely*
Alle my get I schal yow gif agayn, bi my trawthe.' *gains*
He hent the hathel aboute the halse and hendely hym kysses,
And eftersones of the same he served hym there.
'Now ar we even,' quoth the hathel, 'in this eventide, *quits*
Of alle the covenauntes that we knyt, *have drawn up*
sythen I com hider, *since*
bi lawe.' *in legal style*
The lorde sayde: 'Bi saynt Gile, *Giles*
Ye ar the best that I knawe;
Ye ben ryche in a whyle, *will be rich*
Such chaffer and ye drawe.'

1623–4 The lord, with a loud noise, laughed merrily when he saw Sir Gawain; he spoke joyfully.
1626–8 He shows them the slabs of boar's flesh, and gives them an account of the great size and length, the ferocity also, and the fighting display of the wild boar as he fled through the woods.
1630–2 And praised the great excellence he had given proof of; for a beast with such flesh on it, the bold knight said, or a boar with such flanks he had never seen before.
1634 And professed abhorrence of it in order to praise the lord.
1636 By an agreement final and binding, as you certainly know.
1639–40 He clasped the lord round the neck and kissed him courteously, and then he served him again in the same manner (i.e. kissed him a second time).
1647 If you carry on such a trade.

Thenne thay teldet tables trestes alofte, *set up; on trestles*
Kesten clothes upon. Clere lyght thenne
Wakned bi wowes, waxen torches
Segges sette, and served in sale al aboute.
Much glam and gle glent up therinne
Aboute the fyre upon flet, and on fele wyse
At the soper and after, mony athel songes,
As coundutes of Krystmasse and caroles newe,
With alle the manerly merthe that mon may of telle,
And ever oure luflych knyght the lady bisyde. *courteous*
Such semblaunt to that segge semly ho made,
Wyth stille stollen countenaunce, that stalworth to plese,
That al forwondered was the wyye, and wroth with hymselven; *astonished; man*
Bot he nolde not for his nurture nurne hir ayaynes,
Bot dalt with hir al in dayntė, how-se-ever the dede turned towrast.
Quen thay hade played in halle
As longe as hor wylle hom last, *lasted*
To chambre he con hym calle,
And to the chemné thay past. *fireplace*

Ande ther thay dronken and dalten, and demed eft nwe
To norne on the same note on Nwe Yeres even;
Bot the knyght craved leve to kayre on the morn, *depart*
For hit was negh at the terme that he to schulde.
The lorde hym letted of that, to lenge hym resteyed,
And sayde: 'As I am trwe segge, I siker my trawthe *give; word*

1649–56 A bright light then shone from the walls, as men set up wax torches, and served food all round the hall. A merry noise sprang up near the fire on the hearth, and at supper and afterwards they sang many splendid tunes, such as Christmas carols and the latest dance-songs, with all the seemly joy a man could describe.

1658–9 She looked at him so sweetly, with secret and stealthy glances, for the purpose of pleasing that stalwart knight.

1661–3 His good breeding prevented him from returning her advances, but he treated her with every courtesy, even though his behaviour might be misinterpreted.

1666 He (i.e. the lord of the castle) called him to his room.

1668–9 And there they drank and talked, and decided once more to propose the same terms for New Year's Eve.

1671–2 For it was near to the appointed time that he had to go. The lord dissuaded him from doing that, and prevailed on him to stay.

Thou schal cheve to the grene chapel, thy charres *get; business*
to make,
Leude, on Nw Yeres lyght, longe bifore pryme.
Forthy thow lye in thy loft and lach thyn ese,
And I schal hunt in this holt and halde the *forest*
towches, *covenant*
Chaunge wyth the chevisaunce, bi that I charre
hider;
For I haf fraysted the twys, and faythful I fynde the. *tested*
Now "thrid tyme, throwe best," thenk on the morne;
Make we mery quyl we may, and mynne upon joye, *think*
For the lur may mon lach when-so mon lykes.'
This was graythely graunted, and *readily*
Gawayn is lenged; *Gawain stayed*
Blithe broght was hym drynk, and thay to bedde *joyfully*
yeden *went*
with light.
Sir Gawayn lis and slepes
Ful stille and softe al night;
The lorde that his craftes kepes, *pursuits; attends to*
Ful erly he was dight. *prepared*

After messe a morsel he and his men token; *mass; took*
Miry was the mornyng, his mounture he askes. *mount*
Alle the hatheles that on horse schulde helden *men; follow*
hym after
Were boun busked on hor blonkkes *ready equipped; horses*
bifore the halle yates.
Ferly fayre was the folde, for the forst clenged,
In rede rudede upon rak rises the sunne,
And ful clere castes the clowdes of the welkyn.
Hunteres unhardeled bi a holt syde, *unleashed (the hounds); forest*

1675-6 Sir, in the dawn of the New Year, long before prime (i.e. 9 a.m.). And so lie in your room and take your ease.

1678 Exchange winnings with you, when I return here.

1680 'Third time pays for all,' remember this to-morrow.

1682 For a man can find sorrow whenever he likes.

1694–6 The earth was wondrously fair, for the frost clung to the ground, the sun rose fiery red on a rack of clouds, and with its radiance drove the clouds from the sky.

Rocheres roungen bi rys for rurde of her hornes.
Summe fel in the fute ther the fox bade,
Trayles ofte a traveres bi traunt of her wyles.
A kenet kryes therof, the hunt on hym calles;
His felawes fallen hym to, that fnasted ful thike,
Runnen forth in a rabel in his ryght fare.
And he fyskes hem byfore; thay founden hym sone,
And quen thay seghe hym with syght thay *saw*
sued hym fast, *pursued*
Wreyande hym ful weterly with a wroth noyse;
And he trantes and tornayees thurgh mony tene greve,
Haviloune s and herkenes bi hegges ful ofte. *doubles; listens*
At the last bi a littel dich he lepes over a spenné *quickset hedge*
Steles out ful stilly bi a strothe rande, *quietly; valley side*
Went haf wylt of the wode with wyles fro the houndes.
Thenne was he went, er he wyst, to a wale tryster,
Ther thre thro at a thrich thrat hym at ones,
al graye.
He blenched ayayn bilyve *drew back; quickly*
And stifly start onstray; *boldly started aside*
With alle the wo on lyve *woe on earth*
To the wod he went away.

Thenne was hit list upon lif to lythen the houndes,
When alle the mute hade hym met, menged togeder.
Suche a sorwe at that syght thay sette on his hede
As alle the clamberande clyffes hade clatered on hepes.

1698–1704 The rocks in the woods resounded with the noise of their horns. Some of the hounds hit on the trail of the fox where he was lurking, and kept weaving across it in their usual wily fashion. A small hound gave tongue at finding the scent, and the huntsman called to him; the other hounds joined him, panting hard, and rushed forward in a rabble on the right track. The fox ran before them; they soon found him.

1706–7 Denouncing him clearly with a furious noise; and he twists and turns through many a tangled thicket.

1711–14 Thinking to wander out of the wood and escape the hounds by his wiles. Then he came, before he was aware of it, to a fine hunting station, where three fierce hounds, all grey, threatened him at a narrow passage through the undergrowth.

1719–22 Then it was a lively pleasure to listen to the hounds, when all the pack, mingled together, had met him. At the sight of him they reviled him as loudly as if all the clustering cliffs were clattering down in ruins.

Here he was halawed when hatheles hym metten, *hallooed*
Loude he was yayned with yarande speche;
Ther he was threted and ofte thef called, *threatened; thief*
And ay the titleres at his tayl, that tary he ne myght. *hounds*
Ofte he was runnen at when he out rayked, *made for the open*
And ofte reled in ayayn, so Reniarde was wylé.
And ye he lad hem bi lag-mon, the lorde and his meyny,
On this maner bi the mountes quyle myd-over-under,
Whyle the hende knyght at home holsumly slepes *soundly*
Withinne the comly cortynes, on the colde morne.
Bot the lady for luf let not to slepe, *did not allow herself*
Ne the purpose to payre, that pyght in hir hert,
Bot ros hir up radly, rayked hir theder *quickly; went*
In a mery mantyle, mete to the erthe, *gay; reaching*
That was furred ful fyne with felles wel pured;
No hwe goud on hir hede, bot the hagher stones
Trased aboute hir tressour be twenty in clusteres;
Hir thryven face and hir throte throwen al naked, *fair; exposed*
Hir brest bare bifore, and bihinde eke.
Ho comes withinne the chambre dore and closes hit hir after,
Wayves up a wyndow and on the wyye calles, *throws; knight*
And radly thus rehayted hym with hir riche wordes, *rallied*
    with chere: *gaily*
  'A! mon, how may thou slepe?
  This morning is so clere.'
  He was in drowping depe, *slumber*
  Bot thenne he con hir here. *heard*

In drey droupying of dreme draveled that noble, *heavy; muttered*
As mon that was in mornyng of mony *troubled with*
  thro thoghtes, *eager*
How that destiné schulde that day dele hym his wyrde *fate*

1724 Loudly he was greeted with snarling words.
1728–30 And several times he suddenly turned back again, so wily was Reynard. And in this way indeed he led the lord and his company astray among the mountains till mid-morning.
1734 Nor (would she allow) the purpose, that was fixed in her heart, to weaken.
1737–9 Which was splendidly lined with well-trimmed furs; and there was no seemly coif on her head, but skilfully cut gems adorned her hair-net all round in clusters of twenty.
1741 Her breast was exposed, and her back also.

At the grene chapel, when he the gome metes, *man*
And bihoves his buffet abide withoute debate more.
Bot quen that comly he kevered his wyttes,
Swenges out of the swevenes and swares with hast.
The lady luflych com laghande swete, *laughing sweetly*
Felle over his fayre face and fetly hym kyssed. *bent; gracefully*
He welcumes hir worthily with a wale chere; *noble*
He sey hir so glorious and gayly atyred, *saw*
So fautles of hir fetures and of so fyne hewes, *complexion*
Wight wallande joye warmed his hert.
With smothe smylyng and smolt thay smeten into merthe,
That al was blis and bonchef that breke *happiness; burst forth*
hem bitwene,
and wynne. *joy*
Thay lauced wordes gode, *spoke*
Much wele then was therinne; *delight*
Gret perile bitwene hem stod,
Nif Maré of hir knyght con mynne.

For that prynces of pris depresed hym so thikke,
Nurned hym so neghe the thred, that nede hym bihoved
Other lach ther hir luf other lodly refuse.
He cared for his cortaysye, lest crathayn he were,
And more for his meschef, yif he schulde make synne
And be traytor to that tolke that that telde aght.
'God schylde,' quoth the schalk, 'that schal not *forbid; man*
befalle!'
With luf-laghyng a lyt he layd hym bysyde
Alle the speches of specialté that sprange of *special affection*
her mouthe.

1754–5 And must endure his blow without resistance. But when he had properly recovered consciousness, he started out of his dreams and answered hurriedly.

1762–3 Joy ardently welling up warmed his heart. With sweet and gentle smiles they slipped into joyful talk.

1768–9 They would both have stood in great danger, if Mary had not remembered her knight.

1770–5 For that noble princess pressed him so hard, and urged him so near to the limit, that he felt obliged either to accept her love or refuse it with loathing. He was concerned for his courtesy, lest he should behave churlishly, and even more for the evil plight he would be in if he committed a sin and was a traitor to the man who owned that dwelling.

1777 With a short but loving laugh he put aside.

Quoth that burde to the burne: 'Blame ye disserve, *lady; knight*
Yif ye luf not that lyf that ye lye nexte, *person*
Bifore alle the wyyes in the worlde wounded in hert,
Bot if ye haf a lemman, a lever, that yow lykes better,
And folden fayth to that fre, festned so harde
That yow lausen ne lyst—and that I leve nouthe.
And that ye telle me that now trwly, I pray yow;
For alle the lufes upon lyve, layne not the sothe
for gile.' *guile*
The knyght sayde: 'Be sayn Jon,' *St John*
And smethely con he smyle, *gently; smiled*
'In fayth I welde right non,
Ne non wil welde the quile.'

'That is a worde,' quoth that wyght, 'that worst is of alle; *person*
Bot I am swared for sothe, that sore me thinkkes.
Kysse me now comly, and I schal cach hethen; *go hence*
I may bot mourne upon molde, as may that much lovyes.'
Sykande ho sweye doun and semly hym kyssed, *sighing; stooped*
And sithen ho severes hym fro, and says as ho stondes: *departs*
'Now, dere, at this departyng, do me this ese, *comfort*
Gif me sumquat of thy gifte, thi glove if hit were,
That I may mynne on the, mon, my mournyng to lassen.' *think of* *lessen*
'Now iwysse,' quoth that wyye, 'I wolde I hade here
The levest thing for thy luf that I in londe welde,
For ye haf deserved, for sothe, sellyly ofte *exceedingly*
More rewarde bi resoun then I reche myght; *by rights; give*
Bot to dele yow for drurye, that dawed bot neked.

1781–4 (Who is) wounded in heart more than anyone else in the world, unless you have a loved one who is dearer to you and pleases you better, and have pledged your word to that noble lady, plighted it so firmly that you do not want to break it—and that is what I now believe.
1786 For all the loves on earth, do not hide the truth.
1790–1 Truly I have no loved one at all, nor do I want one at present.
1793 But I am answered truly, and it grieves me.
1795 As a woman who is much in love, I have nothing left in life but sorrow.
1799 Give me something as your gift, if it is only your glove.
1801–2 I wish, for your sake, I had here the dearest thing I possess on earth.
1805 But to give you a love-token would profit you little.

Hit is not your honour to haf at this tyme
A glove for a garysoun of Gawaynes giftes;
And I am here on an erande in erdes uncouthe, *regions unknown*
And have no men wyth no males with menskful thinges. *bags; precious*
That mislykes me, ladé, for thy luf at this tyme;
Iche tolke mon do as he is tan, tas to non ille
ne pine.'
'Nay, hende of hyghe honours,' *courteous knight*
Quoth that lufsum under lyne, *fair lady*
'Thagh I hade noght of youres,
Yet schulde ye have of myne.'

Ho raght hym a riche rynk of red golde werkes, *offered; ring*
Wyth a starande ston stondande alofte, *glittering*
That bere blusschande bemes as the bryght sunne; *cast; shining*
Wyt ye wel, hit was worth wele ful hoge.
Bot the renk hit renayed, and redyly he sayde: *knight; refused*
'I wil no giftes for Gode, my gay, at this tyme; *by God*
I haf none yow to norne, ne noght wyl I take.' *offer*
Ho bede hit hym ful bysily, and he hir bode wernes,
And swere swyftely his sothe that he hit sese nolde;
And ho sore that he forsoke, and sayde therafter: (*was*) *grieved; refused*
'If ye renay my rynk, to ryche for hit semes,
Ye wolde not so hyghly halden be to me,
I schal gif yow my girdel, that gaynes yow lasse.' *profits*
Ho laght a lace lyghtly that leke umbe hir sydes,
Knit upon hir kyrtel under the clere mantyle.
Gered hit was with grene sylke and with golde schaped,
Noght bot arounde brayden, beten with fyngres;

1807 A glove to treasure as Gawain's gift.
1810–12 I am sorry about this, my lady, for your sake; (but) every man must act as he is placed, (so please) don't take it amiss or be upset.
1820 It was worth a huge fortune, you can be sure.
1824–5 She offered it him eagerly, and he refused her offer, and swiftly swore an oath that he would not take it.
1828 (Because) you don't want to be so deeply obliged to me.
1830–3 She quickly took hold of a belt that was fastened round her waist and looped over her gown under her bright mantle. It was made of green silk and trimmed with gold, embroidered and decorated by hand at the edges only.

And that ho bede to the burne, and blythely bisoght, *offered* / *implored*
Thagh hit unworthi were, that he hit take wolde.
And he nay that he nolde neghe in no wyse
Nauther golde ne garysoun, er God hym grace sende *treasure*
To acheve to the chaunce that he hade chosen there.
'And therfore, I pray yow, displese yow noght,
And lettes be your bisinesse, for I baythe hit yow never to graunte.
I am derely to yow biholde *deeply*
Bicause of your sembelaunt, *(kind) behaviour*
And ever in hot and colde *through thick and thin*
To be your trwe servaunt.'

'Now forsake ye this silke,' sayde the burde thenne, *refuse*
'For hit is symple in hitself? And so hit wel semes.
Lo! so hit is littel, and lasse hit is worthy.
Bot who-so knew the costes that knit ar therinne, *properties; knit into lt*
He wolde hit prayse at more prys, paraventure;
For quat gome so is gorde with this grene lace, *man; girt*
While he hit hade hemely halched aboute, *closely; fastened round*
Ther is no hathel under heven tohewe hym that myght, *man; cut down*
For he myght not be slayn for slyght upon erthe.' *by any stratagem*
Then kest the knyght, and hit come to his hert, *pondered*
Hit were a juel for the jopardé that hym jugged were,
When he acheved to the chapel, his chek for to fech;
Myght he haf slypped to be unslayn, the sleght were noble.
Thenne he thulged with hir threpe and tholed hir to speke.
And ho bere on hym the belt and bede hit hym swythe;

1836 And he refused on any account to touch.
1838 To accomplish the adventure he had undertaken there.
1840–1 And stop importuning me, for I will never consent to it.
1848 See, it is so little, and even less in value.
1850 He would set a higher value on it, perhaps.
1856–60 It would be a treasure for the perilous deed assigned him, when he came to the chapel to receive his doom; if he managed to escape death, it would be a noble device. Then he was patient with her importunity and let her speak on. And she pressed the belt on him and offered it him eagerly.

And he granted, and ho hym gafe with a goud wylle, *consented*
And bisoght hym, for hir sake, discever hit never, *reveal*
Bot to lelly layne fro hir lorde. The leude hym acordes *loyally; conceal (it)*
That never wyye schulde hit wyt, iwysse, bot thay twayne,
for noghte.
He thonkked hir oft ful swythe, *very much*
Ful thro with hert and thoght. *earnestly*
Bi that on thrynne sythe
Ho has kyst the knyght so toght.

Thenne lachches ho hir leve and leves hym there, *takes*
For more myrthe of that mon moght ho not gete.
When ho was gon, Sir Gawayn geres hym sone, *attires*
Rises and riches hym in araye noble, *dresses*
Lays up the luf-lace the lady hym raght,
Hid hit ful holdely ther he hit eft fonde.
Sythen chevely to the chapel choses he the waye, *quickly; takes*
Prevely aproched to a prest, and prayed hym there *privately*
That he wolde lyfte his lyf and lern hym better *lift up*
How his sawle schulde be saved when he schuld seye hethen. *go; hence*
There he schrof hym schyrly and schewed his mysdedes *confessed; fully*
Of the more and the mynne, and merci beseches, *major; minor*
And of absolucioun he on the segge calles;
And he asoyled hym surely and sette hym so clene *absolved*
As domesday schulde haf ben dight on the morn.
And sythen he mace hym as mery among the fre ladyes,
With comlych caroles and alle kynnes joye,
As never he did bot that daye, to the derk nyght,
with blys.

1863–5 The knight agrees that none should ever know of it, apart from the two of them, for any reason at all.
1868–9 By then she had kissed the hardy knight three times.
1871 For she could get no more satisfaction out of him.
1874–5 Puts away the love-lace the lady had given him, and hid it very carefully where he could find it again.
1882 And begs the priest for absolution.
1884 As if the Judgment were appointed for the very next day.
1885–7 And then he enjoyed himself with the noble ladies more than he had ever done before that day, dancing and singing carols and taking part in every kind of joyful pastime, until the dark night came.

Uche mon hade daynté thare
Of hym, and sayde: 'Iwysse,
Thus myry he was never are,
Syn he com hider, er this.'

Now hym lenge in that lee, ther luf hym bityde!
Yet is the lorde on the launde, ledande his gomnes.
He has forfaren this fox that he folwed longe. *killed; followed*
As he sprent over a spenné to spye the schrewe,
Ther as he herd the howndes that hasted hym swythe,
Renaud com richchande thurgh a roghe greve,
And alle the rabel in a res, ryght at his heles.
The wyye was war of the wylde and warly abides,
And braydes out the bryght bronde and at the best castes.
And he schunt for the scharp and schulde haf arered;
A rach rapes hym to, ryght er he myght,
And ryght bifore the hors fete thay fel on hym alle
And woried me this wyly wyth a wroth noyse.
The lorde lyghtes bilyve and *dismounts quickly*
laches hym sone, *takes hold of*
Rased hym ful radly out of the rach mouthes, *snatched; quickly*
Haldes heghe over his hede, halowes faste, *high; halloos*
And ther bayen hym mony brath houndes. *bay at; fierce*
Huntes hyyed hem theder with hornes ful *huntsmen; hurried*
mony,
Ay rechatande aryght til thay the renk seyen.
Bi that was comen his compeyny noble, *when*
Alle that ever ber bugle blowed at ones, *carried; blew*
And alle thise other halowed, that hade no hornes.

1889–92 Everyone there had courteous treatment from him, and said: 'Indeed, never since he came here has he been as gay as this.'

1893–4 Now let him stay in that refuge, and love come his way! The lord of the castle was still out in the field, engaged in his sport.

1896–1905 As he jumped over a hedge to look for the rascal, at a place where he heard the hounds in hot pursuit, Reynard came running through a rough thicket, with all the pack hard on his heels. The lord, who had spotted the wild creature, waited cautiously, drew out his bright sword, and struck at him. The fox swerved from the sharp blade and would have retreated; a hound rushed at him before he could manage it, and right in front of the horse's feet they all fell on him, and worried the wily beast with a fierce noise.

1911 Sounding the rally in the proper manner till they caught sight of their lord.

Hit was the myriest mute that ever men herde, *cry*
The rich rurd that ther was raysed for Renaude saule *uproar*
with lote. *clamour*
Hor houndes thay ther rewarde,
Her hedes thay fawne and frote; *fondle; rub*
And sythen thay tan Reynarde *take*
And tyrven of his cote. *strip*

And thenne thay helden to home, for hit was *made for*
niegh nyght, *nearly*
Strakande ful stoutly in hor store hornes.
The lorde is lyght at the laste at hys lef home, *alighted; beloved*
Fyndes fire upon flet, the freke ther-byside, *hearth; knight*
Sir Gawayn the gode that glad was withalle—
Among the ladies for luf he ladde much joye.
He were a bleaunt of blwe that bradde to the erthe.
His surkot semed hym wel that softe was forred,
And his hode of that ilke henged on his schulder,
Blande al of blaunner were bothe al aboute.
He metes me this godmon inmyddes the flore, *in the middle of*
And al with gomen he hym gret, and goudly he sayde:
'I schal fylle upon fyrst oure forwardes nouthe,
That we spedly han spoken ther spared was no drynk.'
Then acoles he the knyght and kysses hym thryes, *embraces*
As saverly and sadly as he hem sette couthe.
'Bi Kryst,' quoth that other knyght, 'ye cach much sele
In chevisaunce of this chaffer, yif ye hade goud chepes.'
'Ye, of the chepe no charg,' quoth chefly that other,
'As is pertly payed the chepes that I aghte.'
'Mary,' quoth that other mon, 'myn is bihynde, *inferior*

1923 Proudly blowing their mighty horns.
1927–31 He greatly enjoyed the friendship of the ladies. He wore a blue tunic that reached to the ground, his softly furred surcoat suited him well, and a hood to match hung from his shoulder, both of them trimmed all round with ermine.
1933–5 And he (i.e. Gawain) greeted him joyfully, and courteously he said: 'I shall be the first this time to carry out our agreement, which we speedily rehearsed without sparing the wine.'
1937–41 With as much relish and vigour as he could muster. 'By Christ,' said the other knight, 'you're lucky to get this merchandise, providing you made a good bargain.' 'Don't worry about bargains,' said the other quickly, 'since I've openly paid over to you the goods I got.'

For I haf hunted al this day, and noght haf I geten
Bot this foule fox felle—the fende haf the godes!—
And that is ful pore for to pay for suche prys thinges *precious*
As ye haf thryght me here thro, suche thre cosses *given; earnestly*
so gode.'
'Inogh,' quoth Sir Gawayn, *enough*
'I thonk yow, bi the rode.' *cross*
And how the fox was slayn
He tolde hym as thay stode. *stood*

With merthe and mynstralsye, wyth metes at hor wylle,
Thay maden as mery as any men moghten, *could*
With laghyng of ladies, with *laughing*
lotes of bordes. *jesting words*
Gawayn and the godemon so glad were thay bothe,
Bot if the douthe had doted other dronken ben other.
Bothe the mon and the meyny maden mony *retinue*
japes, *jests*
Til the sesoun was seyen that thay sever moste; *come; part*
Burnes to hor bedde behoved at the laste. *men; had to go*
Thenne lowly his leve at the lorde fyrst *humbly*
Fochches this fre mon, and fayre he hym *takes; courteously*
thonkkes:
'Of such a selly sojorne as I haf hade here, *wonderful; stay*
Your honour at this hyghe fest, the hyghe kyng yow yelde!
I yef yow me for on of youres, if yowreself lykes;
For I mot nedes, as ye wot, meve to-morne,
And ye me take sum tolke to teche, as ye hyght,
The gate to the grene chapel, as God wyl me suffer
To dele on Nw Yeres day the dome of my wyrdes.'
'In god faythe,' quoth the godmon, 'wyth a goud wylle
Al that ever I yow hyght, halde schal I redé.' *promised; ready*

1944 But this miserable fox-skin—the devil take such goods!
1952 With all the foods they wanted.
1955–6 Gawain and the master of the house were both as happy as could be, unless indeed the whole company had been silly or else drunk.
1963–8 And for the honour you have done me at this noble festival, the High King reward you! I'll give you my services for those of one of your men, if you are willing; for I must, as you know, move on tomorrow morning, if you'll let me have someone, as you promised, to show me the way to the Green Chapel, so that I may receive on New Year's Day, as God wills, the sentence prepared for me by destiny.

Ther asyngnes he a servaunt to sett hym in the waye *assigns*
And coundue hym by the downes, that he no drechch
had,
For to ferk thurgh the fryth and fare at the gaynest
bi greve.
The lorde Gawayn con thonk, *thanked*
Such worchip he wolde hym weve. *honour; show*
Then at tho ladyes wlonk *of; noble*
The knyght has tan his leve. *taken*

With care and wyth kyssyng he carppes hem tille,
And fele thryvande thonkkes he thrat hom to have;
And thay yelden hym ayayn yeply that ilk.
Thay bikende hym to Kryst with ful colde sykynges.
Sythen fro the meyny he menskly *company; courteously*
departes;
Uche mon that he mette, he made hem a thonke *thanked*
For his servyse and his solace and his sere pyne
That thay wyth busynes had ben aboute hym to serve;
And uche segge as sore to sever with hym there
As thay hade wonde worthyly with that wlonk ever.
Then with ledes and lyght he was ladde to his *attendants*
chambre,
And blythely broght to his bedde to be at his rest. *joyfully*
Yif he ne slepe soundyly, say ne dar I,
For he hade muche on the morn to mynne, yif he wolde,
in thoght.
Let hym lyye there stille, *undisturbed*
He has nere that he soght; *nearly*
And ye wyl a whyle be stylle, *quiet*
I schal telle yow how thay wroght. *acted*

1972–4 And guide him over the hills, so that he would have no delay and could travel through wood and thicket by the shortest way.

1979–82 He spoke to them and kissed them sorrowfully, pressing on them many hearty thanks; and they returned the compliment, commending him to Christ with grievous sighs.

1985–8 For their kind service and for the trouble they had each taken to serve him diligently; and everyone was as sad to part company with him there as if they had always lived in honour with that noble knight.

1991–3 If he slept soundly, I dare not say, for there was much next day for him to think of.

IV

Now neghes the Nw Yere and the nyght passes, *draws near*
The day dryves to the derk, as Dryghtyn biddes.
Bot wylde wederes of the worlde wakned theroute,
Clowdes kesten kenly the colde to the erthe,
Wyth nyye innoghe of the northe, the naked to tene.
The snawe snitered ful snart, that snayped the wylde;
The werbelande wynde wapped fro the hyghe
And drof uche dale ful of dryftes ful grete.
The leude lystened ful wel, that ley in his bedde. *knight; lay*
Thagh he lowkes his liddes, ful lyttel he slepes; *shuts*
Bi uch kok that crue he knwe wel the steven.
Deliverly he dressed up er the day sprenged,
For there was lyght of a laumpe that lemed in his chambre. *shone*
He called to his chamberlayn, that cofly hym swared, *promptly answered*
And bede hym bryng hym his bruny and his blonk sadel;
That other ferkes hym up and feches hym his wedes, *gets up clothes*
And graythes me Sir Gawayn upon a grett wyse.
Fyrst he clad hym in his clothes, the colde for to were, *ward off*
And sythen his other harnays, that holdely was keped,
Bothe his paunce and his plates, piked ful clene,
The rynges rokked of the roust of his riche bruny;

1999–2005 The dawn followed on the darkness, as the Lord commands. But wild weather arose in the world outside, the clouds sent down bitter cold to the earth, with a troublesome wind from the north to torment the flesh. The snow sleeted down sharply and nipped the wild creatures; the whistling wind blew in gusts from the heights and filled every dale full of great drifts.

2008 Each cock that crowed told him the time. (An allusion to the belief that cocks crow three times during the night—at midnight, 3 a.m., and an hour before dawn.)

2009 Quickly he got up before day dawned.

2012 And asked him to bring his coat of mail and to saddle his horse.

2014 And dresses Sir Gawain in splendid style.

2016–18 And then in his armour, which had been carefully kept, both his belly-armour and his plate-armour, polished all clean, the rings of his rich mail-coat cleansed of rust.

And al was fresch as upon fyrst, and he was fayn thenne *at first; glad*
to thonk. *give thanks*
He hade upon uche pece, *put on*
Wypped ful wel and wlonk; *wiped; splendid*
The gayest into Grece,
The burne bede bryng his blonk *bade; horse*

Whyle the wlonkest wedes he warp on hymselven— *put*
His cote wyth the conysaunce of the clere werkes
Ennurned upon velvet, vertuus stones
Aboute beten and bounden, enbrauded semes,
And fayre furred withinne wyth fayre pelures—
Yet laft he not the lace, the ladies gifte; *left; belt*
That forgat not Gawayn, for gode of hymselven.
Bi he hade belted the bronde upon his balwe haunches, *when; smooth hips*
Thenn dressed he his drurye double hym aboute,
Swythe swethled umbe his swange swetely that knyght.
The gordel of the grene silke that gay wel bisemed,
Upon that ryol red clothe that ryche was to schewe.
Bot wered not this ilk wyye for wele this gordel,
For pryde of the pendauntes, thagh polyst thay were,
And thagh the glyterande golde glent upon endes,
Bot for to saven hymself when suffer hym byhoved,
To byde bale withoute dabate of bronde hym to were other knyffe.
Bi that the bolde mon boun *ready*
Wynnes theroute bilyve; *goes; quickly*
Alle the meyny of renoun *retainers*
He thonkkes ofte ful ryve. *very much*

2023 The fairest knight from here to Greece.

2026–9 His coat-armour with the badge (i.e. the pentangle) clearly worked on velvet, with potent gems set all round it, embroidered seams, and a marvellous lining of fine furs.

2033–42 Then he folded his love-token round himself twice, quickly and happily wound it round his waist. The girdle of green silk suited the gallant knight well, on top of a royal red cloth that was splendid to look at. But it was not for its richness that he wore the girdle, nor for pride in its pendants, though they were brightly polished and the gleaming gold glinted at the ends, but to save himself when he had to submit and suffer death without resisting or defending himself with sword or knife.

Thenne was Gryngolet graythe, that gret was and huge, *ready*
And hade ben sojourned saverly and in a siker wyse;
Hym lyst prik for poynt, that proude hors thenne.
The wyye wynnes hym to and wytes on his lyre,
And sayde soberly hymself and by his soth sweres:
'Here is a meyny in this mote that on menske thenkkes.
The mon hem maynteines, joy mot he have! *may*
The leve lady on lyve, luf hir bityde!
Yif thay for charyté cherysen a gest, *cherish*
And halden honour in her honde, the hathel hem yelde *Lord; reward*
That haldes the heven upon hyghe, and also yow alle!
And yif I myght lyf upon londe lede any quyle,
I schuld rech yow sum rewarde redyly, if I myght.' *give; willingly*
Thenn steppes he into stirop and strydes alofte.
His schalk schewed hym his schelde; on schulder he hit laght, *man; shield; slung*
Gordes to Gryngolet with his gilt heles, *spurs*
And he startes on the ston—stod he no lenger to praunce. *springs forward*
His hathel on hors was thenne, *man*
That bere his spere and launce. *carried*
'This kastel to Kryst I kenne: *commend*
He gef hit ay god chaunce!' *always*

The brygge was brayde doun, and the brode yates *drawbridge; lowered*
Unbarred and born open upon bothe halve. *laid; sides*
The burne blessed hym bilyve, and the bredes passed;
Prayses the porter bifore the prynce kneled,
Gef hym God and goud day, that Gawayn he save;

2048–54 And had been stabled snugly and securely; that proud steed was then fit and eager for a gallop. The knight went up to him and looked at his coat, and exclaimed earnestly to himself: 'Here in this castle is a company that is mindful of honour. Joy to the man who maintains them! And the dear lady, may love be hers all her life long!'

2058 And if I may live any length of time on this earth.

2071–3 The knight crossed himself quickly, and passed over the planks (of the drawbridge). He praised the porter, who kneeled before the prince and wished him good day, praying God to keep him safe.

And went on his way with his wyye one, *one attendant*
That schulde teche hym to tourne to that tene place
Ther the ruful race he schulde resayve.
Thay bowen bi bonkkes ther boghes ar bare, *passed; boughs*
Thay clomben bi clyffes ther clenges the colde. *climbed; clings*
The heven was up halt, bot ugly therunder;
Mist muged on the mor, malt on the mountes, *drizzled; melted*
Uch hille hade a hatte, a myst hakel huge. *cloak of mist*
Brokes byled and breke bi bonkkes aboute,
Schyre schaterande on schores ther thay doun schowved.
Wela wylle was the way ther thay bi wod schulden,
Til hit was sone sesoun that the sunne ryses
that tyde.
Thay were on a hille ful hyghe,
The quyte snaw lay bisyde;
The burne that rod hym by
Bede his mayster abide. *asked; to stop*

'For I haf wonnen yow hider, wyye, at this tyme, *brought; sir*
And now nar ye not fer fro that note place *noted*
That ye han spied and spuryed so specially after. *sought; asked*
Bot I schal say yow for sothe, sythen I yow knowe, *truly; since*
And ye ar a lede upon lyve that I wel lovy,
Wolde ye worch bi my wytte, ye worthed the better.
The place that ye prece to ful perelous is halden; *hasten; held*
Ther wones a wyye in that waste, the worst upon erthe, *lives; man*
For he is stiffe and sturne, and to strike lovies, *strong; loves*
And more he is then any mon upon myddelerde, *greater; earth*
And his body bigger then the best fowre

2075–6 Who was to show him how to get to that perilous place where he had to receive the grievous blow.

2079 The clouds were high up, but it was threatening below them.

2082–6 Streams boiled and foamed on the slopes round about, dashing brightly against their banks as they forced their way down. The path they had to take through the wood was very wild, but on they went till soon it was time for the sun to rise.

2095–6 And you are a man full of life whom I love well, if you would act on my advice you'd be the better for it.

That ar in Arthures hous, Hestor, other other.
He cheves that chaunce at the chapel grene,
Ther passes non bi that place so proude in his armes
That he ne dynges hym to dethe with dynt of his honde;
For he is a mon methles, and mercy non uses, *violent; shows*
For be hit chorle other chaplayn that bi the chapel rydes, *churl*
Monk other masseprest, other any mon elles,
Hym thynk as queme hym to quelle as quyk go hymselven.
Forthy I say the, as sothe as ye in sadel sitte, *sure*
Com ye there, ye be kylled, may the knyght rede,
Trawe ye me that trwely, thagh ye had twenty lyves to spende. *believe*
He has wonyd here ful yore, *lived; a long while*
On bent much baret bende.
Ayayn his dyntes sore *against; grievous*
Ye may not yow defende. *yourself*

'Forthy, goude Sir Gawayn, let the gome one, *therefore; alone*
And gos away sum other gate, upon Goddes halve!
Cayres bi sum other kyth, ther Kryst mot yow spede.
And I schal hyy me hom ayayn, and hete yow fyrre
That I schal swere bi God and alle his gode halwes—
As help me God and the halydam, and othes innoghe—
That I schal lelly yow layne, and lauce never tale
That ever ye fondet to fle for freke that I wyst.'
'Grant merci,' quoth Gawayn, and gruchyng he sayde: *reluctantly*

2102–5 Or Hector (of Troy), or anyone else. He brings it about at the Green Chapel that no one passes by that place, however proudly armed, whom he does not strike dead with a blow of his hand.

2109 He thinks it as pleasant to kill him as to be alive himself.

2111 If you come there you will be killed, if the knight has his way.

2115 And has led much fighting in the field.

2119–25 And go some other way, for God's sake! Ride through some other land, where Christ may help you. And I shall hurry home again, and I promise you besides to swear by God and all His saints—so help me God and the holy relics, and every other (sacred) oath—that I will keep your secret loyally, and never reveal that you fled away because of any man I have known.

'Wel worth the, wyye, that woldes my gode,
And that lelly me layne I leve wel thou woldes.
Bot helde thou hit never so holde, and I here passed,
Founded for ferde for to fle, in fourme that thou telles,
I were a knyght kowarde, I myght not be excused.
Bot I wyl to the chapel, for chaunce that may falle,
And talk wyth that ilk tulk the tale that me lyste,
Worthe hit wele other wo, as the wyrde lykes
hit hafe.
Thaghe he be a sturn knape
To stightel, and stad with stave,
Ful wel con Dryghtyn schape
His servauntes for to save.'

'Mary!' quoth that other mon, 'now thou so much spelles
That thou wylt thyn awen nye nyme to thyselven,
And the lyst lese thy lyf, the lette I ne kepe.
Haf here thi helme on thy hede, thi spere in thi honde, *helmet*
And ryde me doun this ilk rake bi yon rokke syde,
Til thou be broght to the bothem of the brem valay.
Thenne loke a littel on the launde, on thi lyfte honde,
And thou schal se in that slade the self chapel *valley; very*
And the borelych burne on bent that hit kepes.
Now fares wel, on Godes half, Gawayn the noble! *in God's name*
For alle the golde upon grounde I nolde *on earth; would not*
go wyth the,
Ne bere the felawschip thurgh this fryth on fote fyrre.'
Bi that the wyye in the wod wendes his brydel,

2127–39 Good luck to you, sir, who wish me well and who desire, I am sure, to keep my secret loyally. But however faithfully you kept it, if I passed by here and fled away in fear, in the manner you suggest, I would be a cowardly knight and there could be no excuse for me. But I will go to the chapel, whatever happens, and have what talk I please with that man, come weal or woe, as fate decides. Though he is a difficult fellow to manage, and armed with a club, the Lord is well able to protect his servants.

2140–2 Now you say so positively that you will take your own trouble on yourself, and it pleases you to lose your life, I've no wish to stop you.

2144–6 And ride down this path by the side of yonder rock, till you come to the bottom of the wild valley. Then look a little to your left across the glade.

2148 And the massive man who guards it there.

2151–2 Nor keep you company one foot further through this wood. Thereupon the man in the wood turns his bridle.

Hit the hors with the heles as harde as he myght,
Lepes hym over the launde, and leves the knyght there
al one.
'Bi Goddes self,' quoth Gawayn,
'I wyl nauther grete ne grone; *weep*
To Goddes wylle I am ful bayn, *obedient*
And to hym I haf me tone.' *committed myself*

Thenne gyrdes he to Gryngolet and gederes the rake,
Schowves in bi a schore at a schawe syde,
Rides thurgh the roghe bonk ryght to the dale.
And thenne he wayted hym aboute, and *looked*
wylde hit hym thoght, *it seemed to him*
And seye no syngne of resette bisydes nowhere,
Bot hyghe bonkkes and brent upon bothe halve, *steep; sides*
And rughe knokled knarres with knorned stones;
The skwes of the scowtes skayned hym thoght.
Thenne he hoved and wythhylde his hors at *halted; held back*
that tyde,
And ofte chaunged his cher the chapel to seche.
He sey non suche in no syde, and selly hym thoght.
Save a lyttel on a launde, a lawe as hit were,
A balw berw bi a bonke the brymme bysyde,
Bi a fors of a flode that ferked thare;
The borne blubred therinne as hit boyled hade.
The knyght kaches his caple and com to the lawe,
Lightes doun luflyly, and at a lynde taches
The rayne and his riche with a roghe braunche.
Thenne he bowes to the berwe, aboute hit he *goes; mound*
walkes,

2160–2 Then he spurs Gryngolet on and picks up the path, pushes his way along a bank by the side of a wood, and rides down the rough slope right into the dale.

2164 And saw no sign of a shelter anywhere near.

2166–7 And rough rugged crags with gnarled stones; the very skies seemed to him to be grazed by the jutting rocks.

2169–77 And he kept looking in all directions in search of the chapel. He saw no such thing anywhere, which seemed to him strange, except what looked like a mound a little way off in a field, a smooth-surfaced barrow on a slope by the water's edge, near a waterfall in a stream that ran down there; the water bubbled in it as if it were boiling. The knight urged on his horse and came to the mound, dismounted agilely, and fastened the reins of his noble horse to the rough branch of a tree.

Debatande with hymself quat hit be myght.
Hit hade a hole on the ende and on ayther syde, *each*
And overgrowen with gresse in glodes aywhere;
And al was holw inwith, nobot an olde cave, *hollow; nothing but*
Or a crevisse of an olde cragge—he couthe hit noght deme
with spelle.
'We! Lorde,' quoth the gentyle knyght,
'Whether this be the grene chapelle?
Here myght aboute mydnyght
The dele his matynnes telle! *devil; matins*

'Now iwysse,' quoth Wowayn, 'wysty is here; *desolate*
This oritore is ugly, with erbes overgrowen; *chapel; weeds*
Wel bisemes the wyye wruxled in grene
Dele here his devocioun on the develes wyse.
Now I fele hit is the fende, in my fyve wyttes, *senses*
That has stoken me this steven to strye me here.
This is a chapel of meschaunce—that chekke hit bytyde!
Hit is the corsedest kyrk that ever I com inne.' *most accursed*
With heghe helme on his hede, his launce in his honde,
He romes up to the roffe of tho rogh wones.
Thene herde he of that hyghe hil, in a harde roche
Biyonde the broke, in a bonk, a wonder breme noyse.
Quat! hit clatered in the clyff as hit cleve schulde,
As one upon a gryndelston hade grounden a sythe.
What! hit wharred and whette, as water at a mulne.
What! hit rusched and ronge, rawthe to here.

2181 And was overgrown everywhere with patches of grass.
2183–4 He could not tell which.
2191–2 It is very fitting for the man clad in green to perform his devotions here in devilish fashion.
2194–5 Who has thrust this appointment on me to destroy me here. This is an evil chapel—bad luck to it!
2198–2211 He made his way up to the roof of that rough dwelling. Then from that high hill he heard a wonderfully loud noise coming from a hard rock on the slope beyond the brook. What on earth! It clattered inside the rock as though it would split it in two, or as though someone were sharpening a scythe on a grindstone. Listen! It made a whirring, grinding noise, like water at a mill. It rushed and rang in a way horrible to hear. 'By God,' said Gawain, 'this contrivance, I believe, is prepared in my honour, to greet a knight with due ceremony. Let God do as He will! (To say) "Alas" will not help me at all. Though I lose my life, no noise shall make me afraid.'

Thenne 'Bi Godde,' quoth Gawayn, 'that gere, as I trowe,
Is ryched at the reverence me, renk to mete
bi rote.
Let God worche! "We loo"—
Hit helppes me not a mote.
My lif thagh I forgoo,
Drede dos me no lote.'

Thenne the knyght con calle ful hyghe: *called; loudly*
'Who stightles in this sted, me steven to holde?
For now is gode Gawayn goande ryght here. *walking*
If any wyye oght wyl, wynne hider fast,
Other now other never, his nedes to spede.'
'Abyde,' quoth on on the bonke aboven over his hede, *someone*
'And thou schal haf al in hast that I the hyght ones.' *promised* *once*
Yet he rusched on that rurde rapely a throwe,
And wyth quettyng awharf, er he wolde lyght.
And sythen he keveres bi a cragge and comes of a hole, *makes his way* *(out) of*
Whyrlande out of a wro wyth a felle weppen, *nook; fierce*
A denes ax nwe dyght, the dynt with to yelde,
With a borelych bytte bende by the halme,
Fyled in a fylor, fowre fote large—
Hit was no lasse, bi that lace that lemed ful bryght.
And the gome in the grene gered as fyrst, *arrayed; at first*
Bothe the lyre and the legges, lokkes and berde, *face*
Save that fayre on his fote he foundes on the erthe,
Sette the stele to the stone and stalked bysyde.

2213 Who is master here, to keep his appointment with me?

2215–16 If any man wants anything, let him come here quickly, now or never, to get his business done.

2219–20 Yet he rapidly went on with his whirring noise for a while, and turned aside to his grinding, before he would come down.

2223–6 A Danish axe newly sharpened to return the blow, with a massive blade curved towards the handle, sharpened on a grindstone, and four feet broad—it was no less, measured by the brightly shining thong. (See line 217.)

2229–30 Except that he now firmly goes on foot, setting the handle to the ground and stalking along beside it.

When he wan to the watter, ther he *came*
wade nolde, *would not*
He hypped over on hys ax and orpedly strydes, *vaulted; boldly*
Bremly brothe, on a bent that brode was aboute,
on snawe.
Sir Gawayn the knyght con mete, *greeted*
He ne lutte hym nothyng lowe;
That other sayde: 'Now, sir swete,
Of steven mon may the trowe.

'Gawayn,' quoth that grene gome, 'God the mot loke! *may; guard*
Iwysse thou art welcom, wyye, to my place, *certainly; sir*
And thou has tymed thi travayl as truee mon schulde. *journey; true*
And thou knowes the covenauntes kest uus bytwene: *arranged*
At this tyme twelmonyth thou toke that the *what fell to your lot*
falled,
And I schulde at this Nwe Yere yeply the quyte. *promptly; repay*
And we ar in this valay verayly oure one; *by ourselves*
Here ar no renkes us to rydde, rele as uus likes.
Haf thy helme of thy hede, and haf here thy pay. *take*
Busk no more debate then I the bede thenne
When thou wypped of my hede at a wap one.' *single blow*
'Nay, bi God,' quoth Gawayn, 'that me gost lante,
I schal gruch the no grwe for grem that falles.
Bot styghtel the upon on strok, and I schal stonde stylle
And warp the no wernyng to worch as the lykes,
nowhare.'
He lened with the nek, and lutte,
And schewed that schyre al bare,
And lette as he noght dutte;
For drede he wolde not dare.

2233–4 Fiercely angry, across a broad field covered with snow.
2236 He did not bow at all low to him.
2238 You can be trusted to keep an appointment.
2246 Here are no men to part us, and we can be as violent as we like.
2248 Don't offer any more resistance than I did.
2250–4 'No,' said Gawain, 'by God who gave me a soul, I shan't bear you the least grudge for any harm that happens to me. But limit yourself to one stroke, and I shall stand still and offer no resistance at all to anything you care to do.'
2255–8 He leaned his neck forward, and bent down, exposing his white flesh, and behaving as if he feared nothing; he was resolved not to shrink with fear.

Then the gome in the grene graythed hym *got ready*
swythe, *quickly*
Gederes up hys grymme tole, Gawayn to smyte; *lifts*
With alle the bur in his body he ber hit on lofte,
Munt as maghtyly as marre hym he wolde.
Hade hit dryven adoun as drey as he atled,
Ther hade ben ded of his dynt that doghty was ever.
Bot Gawayn on that giserne glyfte hym bysyde,
As hit com glydande adoun on glode hym to schende,
And schranke a lytel with the schulderes for the scharp yrne.
That other schalk wyth a schunt the schene wythhaldes,
And thenne repreved he the prynce with mony prowde *rebuked*
wordes:
'Thou art not Gawayn,' quoth the gome, 'that is so goud halden,
That never arwed for no here by hylle ne be vale,
And now thou fles for ferde er thou fele harmes. *flinch; fear*
Such cowardise of that knyght cowthe I never here.
Nawther fyked I ne flaghe, freke, quen thou myntest,
Ne kest no kavelacion in kynges hous Arthor.
My hede flaw to my fote, and yet flagh I never;
And thou, er any harme hent, arwes in hert. *received; are afraid*
Wherfore the better burne me burde be called *man; I ought to*
therfore.'
Quoth Gawayn: 'I schunt ones, *flinched*
And so wyl I no more;
Bot thagh my hede falle on the stones, *though*
I con not hit restore.

'Bot busk, burne, bi thi fayth, and bryng me to the poynt.
Dele to me my destiné and do hit out of honde,

2261–8 With all the strength in his body he swung it aloft, and aimed a blow mighty enough to kill him. If it had come hurtling down as hard as he seemed to intend, the ever valiant knight would have died from his blow. Gawain glanced sideways at the battle-axe, as it came flashing down to destroy him, and his shoulders shrank a little from the sharp weapon. With a sudden movement the other man checked the bright blade.

2271 Who was never afraid of any army by hill or dale.

2273–6 I never heard of such cowardice on the part of that knight. I neither flinched nor fled when you aimed a blow at me, sir, nor raised any objection in King Arthur's house. My head flew to my feet, and yet I did not flinch.

2284 But hurry up, man, if you value your honour, and come to the point with me.

For I schal stonde the a strok, and start no more *stand up to your stroke*
Til thyn ax have me hitte—haf here my trawthe.' *word*
'Haf at the thenne,' quoth that other, and heves hit alofte,
And waytes as wrothely as he wode were.
He myntes at hym maghtyly, bot not the mon rynes,
Withhelde heterly his honde er hit hurt myght.
Gawayn graythely hit bydes and glent with no membre,
Bot stode stylle as the ston other a stubbe auther *stump (of a tree)*
That ratheled is in roché grounde with rotes a hundreth. *entwined; rocky*
Then muryly efte con he mele, the mon in the grene: *again; spoke*
'So now thou has thi hert holle, hitte me bihoves.
Halde the now the hyghe hode that Arthur the raght,
And kepe thy kanel at this kest, yif hit kever may!'
Gawayn ful gryndelly with greme thenne sayde: *fiercely; anger*
'Wy, thresch on, thou thro mon, thou thretes to longe; *strike; fierce*
I hope that thi hert arwe wyth thyn awen selven.'
'For sothe,' quoth that other freke, 'so felly thou spekes, *fiercely*
I wyl no lenger on lyte lette thin ernde
right nowe.'
Thenne tas he hym strythe to stryke *takes; stance*
And frounses bothe lyppe and browe; *puckers*
No mervayle thagh hym myslyke
That hoped of no rescowe.

He lyftes lyghtly his lome and let hit doun fayre,
With the barbe of the bitte bi the bare nek.

2289–92 And glared as fiercely as though he were mad. He aimed a mighty blow at him, but did not touch him, checking his hand before it could do any harm. Gawain duly waited for the blow and did not flinch in any limb.
2296–8 Now you've regained your courage, I really must hit you. May the high order (of knighthood) that Arthur gave you preserve you now, and save your neck from this blow if it can!
2301 I do believe your own heart is terrified of you.
2303–4 I'll no longer hinder or delay your mission from now on.
2307–8 No wonder that Gawain, who had no hope of rescue, felt annoyed.
2309–13 He lifted the weapon lightly and let it fall straight down, with the edge of the blade close to the bare neck. Though he struck fiercely, he hurt him none the more for that, but nicked him on one side, severing the skin. The sharp blade sank into the flesh through the fair fat.

Thagh he homered heterly, hurt hym no more,
Bot snyrt hym on that on syde, that severed the hyde.
The scharp schrank to the flesche thurgh the schyre grece,
That the schene blod over his schulderes schot to the erthe. *bright; spurted*
And quen the burne sey the blode blenk on the snawe, *saw; gleam*
He sprit forth spenne-fote more then a spere lenthe,
Hent heterly his helme and on his hed cast, *seized; quickly*
Schot with his schulderes his fayre schelde under,
Braydes out a bryght sworde, and bremely he spekes— *draws; fiercely*
Never syn that he was burne borne of his moder
Was he never in this worlde wyye half so blythe—
'Blynne, burne, of thy bur, bede me no mo!
I haf a stroke in this sted withoute stryf hent, *place; received*
And if thow reches me any mo, I redyly schal quyte *give; repay*
And yelde yederly ayayn—and therto ye tryst—
and foo.
Bot on stroke here me falles; *only one*
The covenaunt schop ryght so, *directed*
Festned in Arthures halles, *arranged*
And therfore, hende, now hoo!' *good sir; stop*

The hathel heldet hym fro and on his ax rested, *turned from him*
Sette the schaft upon schore and to the scharp lened,
And loked to the leude that on the launde yede,
How that doghty, dredles, dervely ther stondes
Armed, ful awles; in hert hit hym lykes.
Thenn he meles muryly wyth a much steven, *speaks; great voice*
And wyth a rynkande rurde he to the renk sayde: *ringing voice*

2316 He leapt forward, feet together, more than a spear-length.
2318 With a shrug of his shoulders he tossed his good shield in front of him.
2320–2 Never since his mother bore him had he been half so happy—'Cease your blows, sir, and offer me no more!'
2325 And return (them) promptly—be sure of that—and fiercely.
2332–5 Set the handle on the ground and leaned on the sharp blade, and gazed at the knight in the field, observing how that brave man, without fear, boldly stood there in his armour, quite undaunted; and it did his heart good.

'Bolde burne, on this bent be not so gryndel. *field; fierce*
No mon here unmanerly the mysboden habbes,
Ne kyd bot as covenaunde at kynges kort schaped.
I hyght the a strok and thou hit has, *promised*
halde the wel payed; *consider yourself*
I relece the of the remnaunt of ryghtes alle other.
Iif I deliver had bene, a boffet paraunter
I couthe wrotheloker haf waret, to the haf wroght anger.
Fyrst I mansed the muryly with a mynt one,
And rove the wyth no rof sore, with ryght I the profered
For the forwarde that we fest in the fyrst nyght;
And thou trystyly the trawthe and trwly me haldes,
Al the gayne thow me gef, as god mon schulde.
That other munt for the morne, mon, I the profered;
Thou kyssedes my clere wyf, the cosses me raghtes.
For bothe two here I the bede bot two bare myntes
boute scathe.
Trwe mon trwe restore,
Thenne thar mon drede no wathe.
At the thrid thou fayled thore, *there*
And therfor that tappe ta the. *blow; take*

For hit is my wede that thou weres, that ilke *article of clothing*
woven girdel;
Myn owen wyf hit the weved, I wot wel for sothe. *gave; know*
Now know I wel thy cosses and thy costes als,
And the wowyng of my wyf; I wroght hit myselven.
I sende hir to asay the, and sothly me thynkkes *test; truly*

2339–40 No one has treated you in an unmannerly way, or behaved otherwise than according to the agreement made at the King's court.

2342–55 I release you from the rest of all your other obligations. If I had been nimble, I could perhaps have dealt you a harsher blow, and done you harm. First I threatened you playfully with a single feint—not ripping you open with a terrible wound—and this I rightly did to you because of the agreement we made on the first night; for then you faithfully kept your word and gave me all your winnings, as a good man should. The second feint, sir, I offered you for the following day, when you kissed my fair wife and passed the kisses on to me. For both these days I offered you two mere feints, without doing you any harm. An honest man makes honest reparation, and then need fear no danger.

2360–1 Now I know all about your kisses and your behaviour too, and about the wooing by my wife; I contrived it myself.

On the fautlest freke that ever on fote yede.
As perle bi the quite pese is of prys more,
So is Gawayn, in god fayth, bi other gay knyghtes.
Bot here yow lakked a lyttel, sir, and lewté yow wonted;
Bot that was for no wylyde werke, ne wowyng nauther,
Bot for ye lufed your lyf—the lasse I yow blame.'
That other stif mon in study stod a gret whyle, *strong*
So agreved for greme he gryed withinne.
Alle the blode of his brest blende in his face,
That al he schrank for schome that the schalk talked.
The forme worde upon folde that the freke meled:
'Corsed worth cowarddyse and covetyse bothe!
In yow is vylany and vyse that vertue disstryes.' *destroys*
Thenne he kaght to the knot and the kest lawses,
Brayde brothely the belt to the burne selven:
'Lo! ther the falssyng, foule mot hit falle!
For care of thy knokke cowardyse me taght
To acorde me with covetyse, my kynde to forsake,
That is larges and lewté that longes to knyghtes.
Now am I fawty and falce, and ferde haf ben ever; *faulty; afraid*
Of trecherye and untrawthe bothe bityde sorwe and care! *perfidy; befall*
I biknowe yow, knyght, here stylle, *confess; privately*
Al fawty is my fare; *conduct*
Letes me overtake your wylle,
And efte I schal be ware.' *henceforth; careful*

2363–8 (That you are) the most faultless man who ever walked (on this earth). As a pearl is more precious than a white pea, no less is Gawain than other fair knights. In this one point you were a little at fault, sir, and your loyalty fell short; yet it was not for any intrigue, nor for love-making either, but because you loved your life—and I blame you the less.

2370–4 So overcome with grief that he shuddered inwardly. All his heart's blood rushed to his face, so that he shrank with shame at what the man had said. The first words he spoke were: 'A curse upon cowardice and covetousness too.'

2376–81 Then he caught hold of the knot and loosened the fastening, and angrily flung the belt at the man: 'Look, there's the false thing, bad luck to it! Because I was anxious about your blow, cowardice taught me to come to terms with covetousness and forsake my true nature, the generosity and loyalty that belong to knights.'

2387 Let me understand your will, i.e. let me know what you want me to do.

Thenn loghe that other leude and luflyly sayde: *laughed; amiably*
'I halde hit hardily hole, the harme that I hade;
Thou art confessed so clene, beknowen of thy *cleared*
mysses, *faults*
And has the penaunce apert of the poynt of myn egge.
I halde the polysed of that plyght and pured as clene
As thou hades never forfeted sythen thou was fyrst borne.
And I gif the, sir, the gurdel that is golde-hemmed.
For hit is grene as my goune, Sir Gawayn, ye maye
Thenk upon this ilke threpe ther thou forth thrynges
Among prynces of prys, and this a pure token
Of the chaunce of the grene chapel at chevalrous knyghtes.
And ye schal in this Nwe Yer ayayn to my *(come) back*
wones, *dwelling*
And we schyn revel the remnaunt of this ryche fest *shall*
ful bene.' *pleasantly*
Ther lathed hym fast the lorde, *invited; pressingly*
And sayde: 'With my wyf, I wene, *think*
We schal yow wel acorde, *reconcile*
That was your enmy kene.' *keen*

'Nay, for sothe,' quoth the segge, and sesed hys helme
And has hit of hendely, and the hathel *takes; courteously*
thonkkes:
'I haf sojorned sadly. Sele yow bytyde,
And he yelde hit yow yare that yarkkes al menskes!

2390 I consider that any injury I received is now wholly atoned for.

2392–4 And have openly done penance at the point of my weapon. I consider you absolved of that offence and made as clean as though you had never sinned since first you were born.

2396–9 Because it is as green as my gown, Sir Gawain, you may remember this contest when you ride out among noble princes, and it will be a perfect token to chivalrous knights of the adventure of the Green Chapel.

2409–24 I have stayed long enough. Good luck to you, and may He who bestows all honours fully reward you! And commend me to that courteous lady, your fair wife, and to both those honoured ladies, who have so skilfully deceived their knight with their stratagem. But it is not to be wondered at if a fool behaves madly and comes to grief through women's wiles. For here on earth was Adam beguiled by one, and Solomon by many different (women), and Samson too—Delilah dealt him his doom—and later on David was deceived by Bathsheba and suffered great misery. Now since these were brought to grief by the wiles of women, it would be a great gain to love them well and never believe them, if a man could do it. For these were the noblest men of ancient times, who were favoured by fortune above all others who lived (lit. 'thought') beneath the heavens.

And comaundes me to that cortays, your comlych fere,
Bothe that on and that other, myn honoured ladyes,
That thus hor knyght wyth hor kest han koyntly bigyled.
Bot hit is no ferly thagh a fole madde
And thurgh wyles of wymmen be wonen to sorwe.
For so was Adam in erde with one bygyled,
And Salamon with fele sere, and Samson eftsones—
Dalyda dalt hym hys wyrde—and Davyth therafter
Was blended with Barsabe, that much bale tholed.
Now these were wrathed wyth her wyles, hit were a wynne huge
To luf hom wel and leve hem not, a leude that couthe.
For thes wer forne the freest, that folwed alle the sele
Exellently of alle thyse other under hevenryche
        that mused;
    And alle thay were biwyled *beguiled*
    With wymmen that thay used. *by; had dealings with*
    Thagh I be now bigyled,
    Me think me burde be excused. *I ought to*

'Bot your gordel,' quoth Gawayn, 'God yow foryelde! *reward*
That wyl I welde wyth guod wylle, not for the *wear*
  wynne golde, *splendid*
Ne the saynt, ne the sylk, ne the syde pendaundes,
For wele ne for worchyp, ne for the wlonk werkkes;
Bot in syngne of my surfet I schal se hit ofte *as a sign; fault*
When I ride in renoun, remorde to *remember with remorse*
  myselven
The faut and the fayntyse of the flesche *frailty*
  crabbed, *perverse*
How tender hit is to entyse teches of fylthe.
And thus quen pryde schal me pryk for prowes of armes, *stir*
The loke to this luf-lace schal lethe my hert. *humble*
Bot on I wolde yow pray, displeses yow never:
Syn ye be lorde of the yonde londe ther I haf *since*
  lent inne *stayed*
Wyth yow wyth worschyp—the wyye hit *the One*
  yow yelde *reward*

2431–2 Nor for the material, the silk, or the long pendants, nor for its costliness, worth, or rich workmanship.
2436 How liable it is to catch the plague spots of sin.
2439 Just one thing I would ask of you, and don't be offended by it.

That uphaldes the heven and on hygh sittes— *dwells*
How norne ye yowre ryght nome, and thenne no more?' *say*
'That schal I telle the trwly,' quoth that other thenne,
'Bertilak de Hautdesert I hat in this londe. *am called*
Thurgh myght of Morgne la Faye, that in my hous lenges,
And koyntyse of clergye, bi craftes wel lerned.
The maystrés of Merlyn, mony ho has taken,
For ho has dalt drwry ful dere sumtyme
With that conable klerk, that knowes alle your knyghtes
at hame.
Morgne the goddes
Therfore hit is hir name;
Weldes non so hyghe hawtesse *possesses; pride*
That ho ne con make ful tame.

Ho wayned me upon this wyse to your wynne halle
For to assay the surquidré, yif hit soth were
That rennes of the grete renoun of the Rounde Table.
Ho wayned me this wonder your wyttes to reve,
For to haf greved Gaynour and gart hir to dyye
With glopnyng of that ilke gome that gostlych speked
With his hede in his honde bifore the hyghe table.
That is ho that is at home, the auncian lady; *aged*
Ho is even thyn aunt, Arthures half-suster,
The duches doghter of Tyntagelle, that dere Vter after
Hade Arthur upon, that athel is nowthe.
Therfore I ethe the, hathel, to com to thy naunt, *entreat*
Make myry in my hous. My meny the lovies, *household; loves*
And I wol the as wel, wyye, bi my faythe, *wish*
As any gome under God, for thy grete trauthe.' *faithfulness*

2446–51 (I am what I am) through the might of Morgan le Fay, who lives in my house, and through her skill in magic and her well-learned arts. She has acquired many of Merlin's powers, for she once had a love-affair with that excellent sage, as all your knights at home will know.

2456–62 She sent me in this guise to your splendid hall to put your pride to the test, and to find out what truth there is in the current renown of the Round Table. She sent this marvel to deprive you of your senses, to distress Guinevere and make her die with terror at the sight of the man ghoulishly speaking with his head in his hand before the high table.

2465–6 Daughter of the Duchess of Tintagel, on whom the noble Uther begat Arthur, who is now king.

And he nikked hym naye, he nolde bi no wayes.
Thay acolen and kyssen, bykennen aythe other *embrace; commend each*
To the prynce of paradise, and parten ryght there
  on coolde. *the cold ground*
  Gawayn on blonk ful bene *steed; fine*
  To the kynges burgh buskes bolde, *hastens*
  And the knyght in the enker grene *bright*
  Whiderwarde-so-ever he wolde. *to wherever*

Wylde wayes in the worlde Wowen now rydes
On Gryngolet, that the grace hade geten of his lyve.
Ofte he herbered in house and ofte al theroute, *lodged; in the open*
And mony aventure in vale, and venquyst ofte,
That I ne tyght at this tyme in tale to remene.
The hurt was hole that he hade hent in his nek, *healed; received*
And the blykkande belt he bere theraboute, *shining*
Abelef as a bauderyk, bounden bi his syde,
Loken under his lyfte arme, the lace, with a knot,
In tokenyng he was tane in tech of a faute.
And thus he commes to the court, knyght al in sounde. *quite safely*
Ther wakned wele in that wone when wyst the grete
That gode Gawayn was commen; gayn hit hym thoght.
The kyng kysses the knyght, and the whene alce, *queen; also*
And sythen mony syker knyght that soght hym to haylce, *trusty; greet*
Of his fare that hym frayned; and ferlyly he telles,
Biknowes alle the costes of care that he hade—

2471 And he (i.e. Gawain) said no to him, and that he would not on any account (accept Bertilak's invitation to stay with him).
2480 Whose life had been spared by God's grace.
2482–3 And (had) many an adventure in the dales, and often won victories which at this time I do not intend to recall.
2485–8 He wore the shining belt round it (i.e. his neck), cross-wise like a baldric, secured to his side and fastened with a knot under his left arm, as a sign that he had been found guilty of a fault.
2490–1 There was joy in the castle when the great king heard that good Sir Gawain had come; it seemed a fortunate thing to him.
2494–5 Who asked him about his journey; and he told them the marvellous story, and confessed all the tribulations he had suffered.

The chaunce of the chapel, the chere of the knyght, *adventure; behaviour*
The luf of the ladi, the lace at the last. *belt*
The nirt in the nek he naked hem schewed, *nick*
That he laght for his unleuté at the leudes hondes *received; disloyalty*
for blame.
He tened quen he schulde telle, *was grieved*
He groned for gref and grame; *shame*
The blod in his face con melle, *rushed*
When he hit schulde schewe, for schame.

'Lo! lorde,' quoth the leude, and the lace hondeled,
'This is the bende of this blame I bere on my nek,
This is the lathe and the losse that I laght have
Of couardise and covetyse that I haf caght thare.
This is the token of untrawthe that I am tan inne, *perfidy; taken*
And I mot nedes hit were wyle I may last. *wear; live*
For non may hyden his harme bot unhap ne may hit,
For ther hit ones is tachched twynne wil hit never.'
The kyng comfortes the knyght, and alle the court als, *also*
Laghen loude therat, and luflyly acorden *laugh; amiably agree*
That lordes and ladis that longed to the Table, *belonged*
Uche burne of the brotherhede, a bauderyk schulde have, *baldric*
A bende abelef hym aboute, of a bryght grene,
And that, for sake of that segge, in swete to were.
For that was acorded the renoun of the Rounde Table,
And he honoured that hit hade, evermore after,
As hit is breved in the best boke of romaunce. *told*
Thus in Arthurus day this aunter bitidde, *adventure; took place*
The Brutus bokes therof beres wyttenesse.
Sythen Brutus, the bolde burne, bowed hider fyrst, *since; came*

2506–8 This that I wear on my neck is the sign of my fault, of the injury and loss I have suffered because of the cowardice and covetousness I fell prey to there.

2511–12 For no man can hide his (spiritual) harm without misfortune befalling him, for once it has become fixed it will never leave him.

2517–19 A band cross-wise around him, of a bright green, wearing one like Sir Gawain's, for his sake. For it was agreed to be good for the renown of the Round Table.

After the segge and the asaute was sesed at *siege; ceased*
Troye,
iwysse,
Mony aunteres here-biforne
Haf fallen suche er this.
Now that bere the croun of thorne, *(He) that wore*
He bryng uus to his blysse! AMEN.

HONY SOYT QUI MAL PENCE.

2527–8 Many adventures like it have happened in times past.

APPENDICES

I. Note on Spelling and Grammar

The following brief note includes some of the spellings and grammatical forms in the poems which may cause difficulty to a modern reader.

1. *Spellings.*

(i) *i* and *y* are used indifferently to represent short [i] or long [i:]: *prince, prynce, ride, ryde.*

(ii) Etymological final *i* and *ie* are sometimes written *e* (printed here as *é*): *worthé*, 'worthy'; *balé*, 'belly'; *Maré*, 'Mary'; *cortaysé*, 'courtesy'.

(iii) *ou* and *ow* usually represent the sound *oo* in Mod. Eng. *moon: broun, roun, soun, now.*

(iv) *u* represents the sound of French *u* in such words as *bur*, *burde*, *burne*, but the sound of *u* in Mod. Eng. *put* in *much*, *such* and *uch*, 'each'.

(v) Final *b, d, g* are unvoiced to [p], [t], [k] and are sometimes represented by the spellings *p, t, k*: *lomp*, 'lamb'; *justyfyet*, 'justified'; *nothynk*, 'nothing'. Conversely, *d* is sometimes written for final *t*: *marked*, 'market'.

(vi) *3* (Old Eng. *g*) has been replaced in this edition by *y*, except in medial and final positions where *gh* or *w* is the spelling in use today, as in *negh(e)*, 'near, nigh'; *oghte*, 'ought'; *bowed*, 'turned, went'; *folwed*, 'followed'. Medially between front vowels (*e, i, y*) the spelling *y* or *gh* represents a glide: *lyye*, 'to lie'; *seye*, 'saw'; *yye*, 'eye'; *hyghe*, 'high'. Before *t* and finally the spelling *gh* represents: (a) after *e, i, y* the sound of *ch* in German *ich*, as in *feght*, *dight*, *myght*, *welnegh*; (b) after *a, o* the sound of *ch* in German *noch*, as in *naght*, *noght* and *flagh*, 'fled, flinched'.

(vii) *qu* is used, beside *wh* and *w*, to represent the sound [w] in such words as *quo*, *who*, 'who'; *quat*, *what*, 'what'; *quyt*, *whyt*, 'white'; *quyle*, *while*, *wyle*, 'while'. Conversely, *w(h)* is used to represent *qu* in *whene*, 'queen' and *swyeres*, 'squires'.

(viii) *w* is sometimes written for *v*, and *v* for *w*: *merwayle*, 'marvel'; *awenture*, 'adventure'; *vyf*, 'wife'.

(ix) *w* can be used to represent a diphthong [iu]: *hwe*, 'hue'; *nw(e)*, 'new'; *swe*, 'to follow'; *trw(e)*, 'true'.

(x) The Anglo-Norman sound and spelling *w* is found, beside *g*, in *Wawan*, *Gawan*, 'Gawain'.

2. *Nouns.*

(i) Some nouns have no ending in the genitive singular: *womman lore*, 'woman's (womanly) fashion'; *segge fotes*, 'man's feet'.

(ii) A few nouns have no ending in the plural: *halve*, 'sides'; *honde*, 'hands'; *thyng*, 'things'.

(iii) There is one plural in *-en* and one in *-er*: *yyen*, 'eyes'; *chylder*, 'children'.

3. *Adjectives.*

(i) The singular of the weak form of adjectives (used after demonstratives and in the vocative) often ends in *-e*: *the hyghe gate*, 'the highway'; *thou hyghe kyng*. But this ending is sometimes dropped: *the fyrst gemme*.

(ii) The plural often ends in *-e*: *Both his wombe and his wast were worthily smale* (*Gawain* 144). But this ending is sometimes dropped within the line: *So smal, so smothe her sydes were* (*Pearl* 6).

(iii) The plural of *that* is *tho*, 'those'.

4. *Pronouns.*

(i) *Second Person.* The singular pronouns *thou* (*thow*), *the* are used in familiar talk between equals, in addressing an inferior, or in a prayer to God; the plural pronouns *ye*, *yow* are used in addressing a superior.

(ii) *Third Person.*

(a) The nominative singular feminine is *ho*, *scho*, 'she'.
(b) The possessive singular feminine is *her*, *hir*, *hyr*, 'her'.
(c) The possessive singular neuter is *hit*, 'its' (nominative *hit*, *hyt*).
(d) The plural forms are: *thay*; *her*, *hor*, 'their'; *hem*, *hom*, 'them'.

5. *Relative.*

(i) *That* is the normal form used for both persons and things.

(ii) Oblique forms of the relative include: *wham*, *quom*, 'whom'; *that . . . him*, 'whom'; *that . . . his*, 'whose' (*Gawain* 912–13, 2105).

6. *Verbs.*

(i) The present indicative first person singular ending is usually *-e*, but *-es* is also found where the verb is separated from its pronoun subject (*Pearl* 568).

(ii) The present indicative second and third person singular ending is *-(e)s*.

(iii) The present indicative plural ending is *-e(n)*, occasionally *-es*.

(iv) The imperative plural ending is *-(e)s*.

(v) The present participle ending is *-ande*, but *-yng* occurs three or four times.

(vi) The past participle ending is *-en*, occasionally *-e*. There is one example of the old prefix retained: *ichose* (*Pearl* 904).

(vii) *con* is often used as an auxiliary with a following infinitive to form the present or past tense: *con fle*, 'flees' (*Pearl* 294); *con roun*, 'whispered' (*Gawain* 362).

II. Note on Metre

Pearl

The *Pearl* stanza consists of twelve four-stress lines rhyming *ababababbcbc*, with a variable number of unstressed syllables in each line. There is usually a light caesura after the second stress:

To a pérle of prýs // hit is pút in préf. (272)

In some of the shorter lines, however, there is little or no medial pause:

Thou art no kynde jueler. (276)

Two or more of the stressed syllables may alliterate, but often there is no alliteration at all. In general, the alliteration is heaviest in the descriptive passages and lightest in exposition and debate.

Sometimes the rhythm approximates to that of the iambic-octosyllabic line:

Wy bórde ye mén? // So mádde ye bé! (290)

Nevertheless considerable freedom is allowed in the arrangement of stressed and unstressed syllables, as well as in the number of unstressed syllables. In order to recapture the rhythms of *Pearl* the line should be read as a development of the native four-stress alliterative line, and not as a clumsy attempt to put together four iambs or anapaests.

Cleanness and *Patience*

These poems are written in long unrhymed alliterative lines like those of *Sir Gawain*. Marginal marks in the manuscript indicate that the lines are arranged in groups of four.

Sir Gawain and the Green Knight

The *Gawain* stanza consists of a group of long unrhymed alliterative lines followed by five short lines rhyming *ababa*.

The long lines usually have two stressed syllables and a variable number of unstressed syllables on each side of the medial pause:

Ther tóurnayed túlkes // by týmes ful móny. (41)

Sometimes, however, the first half-line has three stresses instead of two:

Máke we méry quyl we máy, // and mýnne upon jóye. (1681)

The first short rhyming line (the 'bob') has one stress, and each of the following four (the 'wheel') has three stresses.

In the long unrhymed lines the alliteration often falls on two of the stressed syllables in the first half-line, and on the first stressed syllable only in the second half-line. But alliteration on five stressed syllables is not uncommon:

Brókes býled and bréke // bi bónkkes abóute. (2082)

The alliteration is more strictly functional in *Sir Gawain* than in *Pearl*: it not only reinforces the stressed words but serves as a link between the two half-lines.